W9-DGI-040

A Psychologist of Sorts

STANLEY D. PORTEUS

A Psychologist of Sorts

THE AUTOBIOGRAPHY AND PUBLICATIONS OF THE INVENTOR OF THE PORTEUS MAZE TESTS

Pacific Books, Publishers, Palo Alto, California

Library of Congress catalog card No. 68–31287.

Printed and bound in the United States of America.

Pacific Books, Publishers
P. O. Box 558
Palo Alto, California 94302

Preface

Any autobiographical effort which passes a lengthy period in general review, inevitably results in focussing attention on what would, in an ordinary book, be considered defects. Some of these are particularly apparent in the present volume.

It covers too much ground. Its geographical reference may jump from New Jersey to South Africa, to Europe, Australia, Southeast Asia, and Oceania in between. Inevitably the reader with psychological background will complain that much of the text reads like a travelogue, and psychologists as a class are sedentary. One of the reasons for this preface is to set forth the inescapability of such kaleidoscopic changes.

In this respect, let it be remembered that this is in part the life story of an individual who passed the first thirty-five years of his existence in a continent very remote from America; who changed his citizenship in 1932 when he was fifty years of age; who possessed a background of preparation very different from that of his professional colleagues; and, finally, spent over half a century in university life, albeit in a small and undistinguished collegiate institution, not as a teacher, but in practise and research.

However, this research gave him exceptional opportunities to concern himself with one main problem—the effect of environment on mental and cultural evolution—a problem that could be resolved best in study, on the spot, of some primitive ethnic groups, almost unreachable because of their peculiar habitats in earth's wildest regions, such as the desert wastes of the Kalahari or interior Australia. Even those who made exploration their special business found it most difficult to make contact with their elusive inhabitants.

Next, the inclusion of results of the writer's excursion into nonprofessional territory seemed necessary for the simple reason that six years is a considerable segment of time and should be accounted for. I regret that no more modest type of presentation than reviews, some of which are overlaudatory, has occurred to me.

Finally, the mere fact of longevity may determine degree of interest. When this is combined with variety of experience, it means that neither author nor reader quite knows what to expect next. Octogenarians, too, have some shadow of right to be discursive, though not repetitious.

Contents

Illustrations

PART I

Autobiography

CHAPTER 1

Growing Up in Australia

On April 24, 1883, in the very modest Methodist parsonage at Box Hill, Victoria, Australia, there was born to David and Katharine Porteus their first and only son. I was duly christened Stanley David after Stanley, the American explorer whose search for David Livingstone was probably the most dramatic story of the century. Less than fifty years before, Melbourne, of which Box Hill was an outer suburb, had been a city of gold-diggers' tents. In 1850 my father and his two brothers, newly arrived from Northern Ireland, were the first to beat a footpath from the river Yarra, across the paddocks of Richmond, where the Melbourne Cricket Club's grounds are still situated.

As a pioneer in a vast and almost empty human landscape, pressed upon by a wilderness of broken ranges, my father undoubtedly felt a kinship with the heroic explorers of Africa, and as a minister wished to identify himself to some degree with the long-sought missionary. He was always a dreamer of dreams, and it is quite possible that calling his son after two such famous adventurers might be a fortunate augury for the infant's future.

This last is merely conjecture, but the previous arrival on the scene of three girls, the eldest of whom died of scarlet fever, must have been disquieting. My own appearance promised relief from the prospect of petticoat government, for resistance to which he was inadequately equipped. In early 1883 he was fifty-three years of age and the chances of male issue were getting dim. Eight years later another girl was born, so that I represented the last throw of the reproductive dice in the effort to perpetuate the name.

As far as inclusion in an urban population was concerned, my birthplace represented a random splash, rather than a rising tide of settlement. Along with Canterbury, Mitcham, and Ringwood, these eastern suburbs were then mere villages, or as Australians called them, townships. Their very names suggested homesickness, for people still spoke and thought of the British Isles as "home." Each of these "suburbs" was enclosed within its own private hinterland of bush. Snakes, possums, bell-birds, normally shy animals that found it difficult to come to terms with civilization, withdrew slowly; magpies, willie-wagtails, kookaburras, that tolerated humans more readily, settled comfortably in our Old World gardens, while English skylarks rose and sang from nearby meadows. As a boy, I grew up in an atmosphere of compromise between the new and the old. Possibly my personality was divided, belonging in neither of the two worlds. Nurtured and nourished in the atmosphere of the old, at one with its history and cognizant of its goals, I yet preferred to hew my own trail through the wilderness of facts or appearances. That striving, I believe, has been the history of art, and to a lesser degree, of science in Australia; in the beginning a rather slavish acceptance and adoption of older standards, followed by a bold striking out for other shores, only to find that without the traditional compass the perils increased. But these adjustments were to come much later; in the meantime there was the business of physically growing up.

There are two schools of thought with regard to the most critical period of life, critical, that is, from the standpoint of the development of personality, or of what Gordon Allport calls "life-style." If this needs elaboration, we can define it as ways of thinking and acting that become characteristic of any individual.

One kind of psychologist believes that the foundations of character are established in the individual during very early childhood, and while later influences may modify, they can never basically alter these acquired traits. To this Allport adds: "Even Adler, who agrees with Freud on little else, dates the adoption of a lasting style of life around the age of four or five." On the basis of my own development I do not accept that chronology.

As to susceptibility to external pressures, some individuals like myself are extremely resistant, so much so that any appearance of cajolery or coercion sets them flying off in the opposite direction. Childhood, on the other hand, is for many individuals a period of vulnerability to suggestion, but only if they are naturally suggestible. Trends towards nonconformity appear just as early as those of conformity. Unfortunately, psychologists have as yet no measure of suggestibility. My long-time friend, Dr. Thomas Jaggar, eminent vulcanologist, devised an instrument akin to a dentist's drill that would measure the degree of pressure necessary to scratch the surface of a given substance. By this means he could allot its place on a scale of hardness, or resistance to pressure. I wish we had something analogous to apply to temperament. My index of scratchability would be, I believe, extremely high.

We should remember that psychoanalysts deal with a population of patients who tend to be mentally disturbed, morbidly curious, overanxious, and easily suggestible. I think that analysts are unduly prone to project conclusions derived from such patients to the general population. For example, some children undoubtedly pass through a phase of infantile sexuality, followed by a period of latency, ending in normal heterosexual interest and activity. The difficulty in deciding what is normal seems to depend on what we call "sexual." For the ordinary individual, I believe that sexual development must bide its time; that infancy is not as overtly sexual nor the middle childhood period as sexually latent as they appear to be.

With regard to the ordinary course of "growing up," the idea that the mind of a child should be regarded as a *tabula rasa,* a blank page upon which environment writes what it pleases, had little meaning for me. I am sure that I exercised considerable choice as to what should be inscribed thereon. For this reason I should be a most unsatisfactory patient for a psychiatrist, especially if he were of the psychoanalytic persuasion. Neither of us would be inclined to believe the other, and that would mean an almost hopeless therapeutic situation.

There is a family tradition that I was an extremely difficult child to rear. My tastes were abnormal in that I preferred what we called "dripping" (the fat from roast meat) to good butter, but was not very interested in either. I could not be persuaded to eat at all unless my mother sang one of Moody and Sankey's hymns to me during breakfast. If conditioning is so easily effective, then the strains of "When Mothers of Salem" should set my mouth watering for toast and dripping, just as the sound of the feeding bell set Pavlov's dogs furiously salivating. Something must have happened to "extinguish" my response. Perhaps I learned to like hymns less or butter better.

As is common among parsons' sons, I did not take kindly to Sunday School. After I had learned to read, a process the intermediate stages of which I lack all recollection, I spent considerable time in searching the Scriptures to dig out apparent contradictions in the Old Testament record with which to confound my teacher, as for example the creation of light before the sun. When he complained to my mother, I was accused of being a bad example and warned that my attitude, if continued, would bring me to a bad end. The rebuke lost some of its force when my sister overheard my mother relaying a report to my father with the added remark that Mr. Jones (the teacher) was not, she was afraid, very bright. With this judgment I agreed.

However, along with her uncompromising attitude toward religious beliefs, my mother was the business head of the family. Methodist ministers in Australia were gravely voted an annual salary of one hundred and fifty pounds sterling whether the money was available or not. The stipend came from gifts and collections, and if there were a deficit, no one offered to make it up. Hence, to keep up a required appearance of genteel poverty took the utmost economy and foresight, which my mother duly supplied. My father wisely left all financial decisions to her. In battling with the world he supplied the inner strength, she the cutting edge.

She was the daughter of a rather highly placed civil servant who settled in the colony of Tasmania, and was responsible for the engraving of the state's paper currency. As a child I never quite understood why, when he actually made the money, he could not keep a few of the ten-pound notes for his own purposes. Perhaps bankers' children are similarly confused.

The steps a man had to take to graduate from gold-digging to the pulpit are still unclear to me, except that I knew they involved long study, a period of strict probation, an oral examination, and finally a trial sermon before the already established ministers, followed by a formal ordination. Meanwhile, the Porteus family were scattered far and wide from their original home in Enniskillen, Northern Ireland; one sister and brother went to America, another sister married rather well and lived in Plymouth, England, while three boys, Tom, Dick, and David, reached Australia.

I believe that it was my Aunt Kate in England who supported my father's early efforts to acquire an education. This included the building up of a library of a thousand volumes, a circumstance most important to me since his reading tastes were indeed catholic, with Carlyle and Emerson in the background. Many of his books belonged in the class of "Christian apologetics," which did not impress me as did the battles in the history of Protestantism.

The eldest brother, William, obtained a D.D. degree in America and was for years minister at the First Presbyterian Church in St. Louis, Missouri. Tom and Dick eked out a precarious living as gold prospectors, the former in Hokitika, New Zealand, the latter at Warrandyte on the river Yarra. Of these relatives, I saw only one, but I've concluded they made up a remarkable if undistinguished family.

Uncle Tom used to send us articles he had contributed to the New Zealand papers; Uncle Dick was in demand for Shakespearean recitations at social occasions in rural Warrandyte, while my father was noted for his natural eloquence and a retentive memory. He kept all his sermons in little handbooks, would read over on Saturday afternoon a discourse written perhaps two years previously, and deliver it word-perfect the next morning. Though he was largely self-taught, no one seemed aware of his deficiencies in formal education. My own education was, to say the least, unconventional, but the gaps were not so apparent as to prevent the bestowal of some of the accepted badges of scholarship, such as an honorary Phi Beta Kappa, Sigma Xi, and sundry fellowships in learned societies. In any case, my grandfather's rather doubtful acceptance of a man twenty years his daughter's senior as a suitor for her hand was undoubtedly assisted materially by the possession of a brass plate inscribed Rev. David Porteus.

Along with her rather rigid standards of belief and conduct, my mother developed a business sense that kept the family solvent. On the other hand, my father was distinguished by a somewhat naïve faith in his fellow man, which was not always justified. She was much more cautious in her social approvals, and this reserved approval extended also to her son. Thus I had one parent with an exaggerated belief in my abilities, and another with a similarly inflated opinion of my luck. Without any serious offense to modesty, my own self-appraisal would fall somewhere in between.

It would not be reasonable in any self-portrait to omit all reference to religious attitudes and the circumstances of their emergence. It was one of the few disappointments of my father's life that I could not accept his faith. We observed the same facts but drew absolutely different conclusions.

He would point to the panoply of heaven—and Australian stars are the brightest I have ever seen—and wonder how I could fail to see this evidence of their Creator's omnipotence and our debt to His omniscience. I would acknowledge the immensity of space and the complexities of nature and enquire as to how our fire-fly existence could possibly be of any importance to a supreme creator if there were such a being. Because I could not account

The author's father, the Rev. David Porteus, about 1883.

for this overwhelming mystery seemed no reason why I should accept the Biblical explanation.

Undoubtedly my feeling toward the Church and its teachings was affected by a touch of resentment as regards the sources of our family support. The passing of the collection plate seemed to me to savor of charity. These were the early days of Methodism, when not only did a man's left hand know what his right hand was doing, but all the people in the neighboring pews knew also. A thrippenny bit (three pence) made a very tiny tinkle as it was dropped in the plate, but a florin (two shillings) or an occasional half crown when dropped from a carefully estimated altitude was a very ringing assurance of religious support. But in rural community churches such gifts were inordinately rare.

By the time I was eleven or twelve years of age, I was old enough to harness the horse and act as my father's driver on his parochial weekend visits. It was soon apparent that a well-timed Saturday evening call at a more or less prosperous farm house invariably resulted in an invitation to stay the night and conduct the next morning's church service. To the sensitive mind of a boy this bid for hospitality seemed scarcely dignified, even though for good measure the farmer's wife had unobtrusively stowed away a leg of lamb or a jar of preserves in the back of the parson's buggy. No matter how unostentatious the giving, it was soon apparent that though the Lord loved a cheerful giver, my father was undoubtedly a glad receiver.

Looking back, this disquietude was probably no more than a boyish priggishness, for my father was a good talker and an avid reader, and to these isolated pioneers any intellectual stimulation was like manna from heaven. It was often after midnight when my father came to bed, and men whose overnight welcome had seemed to me perfunctory shook his hand warmly on our departure, with a sincere reminder not to leave the family off the next pastoral visitation list. My mother, I noticed, never accompanied him on these visits. Possibly the fact that for all his clerical garb, he had battled for a living in "the early days," with blisters on his hands and sweat on his brow formed a bond of common interest and experience with these country dwellers. My mother was a lady, respected and admired but hardly to be accepted on such easy or familiar terms.

The democratic plan of rotating ministers in rural parishes or circuits was fortunate for me, since it meant that I grew up on exceptionally good terms with the Australian out-of-doors. I have always believed that everyone with a satisfaction-filled youth should have a little river in his life. A small stream near Shepparton, called the Seven Creeks (probably so named for the conjunction of its earliest sources), was just such a stream. Seventy years ago, the Australian bush was only partly explored and almost wholly unexploited, and offered all the hunting, fishing, swimming, trapping that a growing boy could desire, except for the spice of danger. The only lethal perils that the bush contained were venomous reptiles, numerous enough, but so rarely aggressive that cases of snakebite were rare. Yet drop for drop, the venom of our tiger snake was the most deadly in the world.

Strange though it may seem, this lack of dangerous wild life created by way of contrast a strong trend of interest in everything American. Our largest animal was the kangaroo, though in ancient times Australia had its monsters. Cave deposits have yielded the bones of diprotodons the size of a small hippopotamus, 25-foot lizards, and a giant form of kangaroo, but no bears, wolves, buffalo, cougars, antelope—not even a buzzard or vulture. Our scenery, too, was monotonous, with our highest mountain hardly reaching 7,300 feet. We had one large riverine system, the Murray, and our lakes of any size were salt. True, our wide horizons beckoned, but there was little of interest beyond them or between. We had our heroic explorers who travelled thousands of lonely miles, and in some cases gave their lives, to discover—nothing.

Our parents, who came hither from the British Isles in search of adventure, must have felt themselves cheated. They made no long treks in covered wagons—the cover wasn't necessary. Our history was a happy vacancy, our only battle the storming of a stockade built by gold-diggers in protest against payment for mining licences. Coming so far to seek their fortunes, these men felt they had the right to seek it where they wished, unimpeded by government control. Our outlaws too were of the Robin Hood rather than the Jesse James variety and therefore seemed more like storybook heroes. The aborigines posed no such threat as did the Red Indians of the American plains. We did not even fight among ourselves. Our early novelists found little exciting to write about, except for convicts. In short, our country, for all its vastness and natural vicissitudes, was tame.

Small wonder was it, therefore, that Australian youth turned avidly to America for stories of romance and adventure. School prizes were such books as *From Log Cabin to White House, The Adventures of Tom Sawyer,* and the Leatherstocking series written by Fenimore Cooper. Out of all Rudyard Kipling's imaginative Jungle Books, Australia was represented by one nature tale—the story of Red Dog Dingo. Our fiction was as arid as our continent. Thus in the long winter evenings family reading was mainly Scott or Dickens, and as we grew older we turned to the American Winston Churchill, to Mary Johnston for Civil War history, and later still to a flood of Wild West thrillers. It was not at all strange that we felt an affinity with American writers. There was much that we could not understand about U.S. politics and attitudes, but it was not difficult to discover a strong bond of common interest in that both our peoples were pioneers. This fact did not weaken our ties with Britain. England was our defensive shield and there lay our loyalties, but as regards our way of life we looked toward America. Our friends across the Pacific might be surprised to learn that George Washington was to our minds a national hero and that the revolution he led solved many problems for us in our political relations with Britain.

But to return to my own personal development, I know that many of my reactions could be glibly summed up as what the psychiatrists call "compensatory." As a minister's son I was handicapped by my sense of dependence upon others. I was also slightly built and somewhat of a weakling. Exercises, morning and night, seemed powerless to add an inch of diameter to a stringy biceps, and no amount of deep breathing could add a cubit to my chest capacity.

But what I lacked in strength I found could be attained by quickness and agility. I do not believe I was *driven* to compete with my fellows—I simply loved games. I did not think that I had any special urge to excel my companions, but merely to prove myself, to myself, and thus build up my self-esteem. So by fifteen years of age I was holding my own in men's teams of cricket and Australian football. In the latter sport there is room for speedy or alert lightweights to a degree no longer possible in the American game.

As to cricket, there fell into my hands on a recent visit to Australia a score book of the 1905–1906 season and found to my surprise that I obtained top score (runs batted in) in six matches played in a cricket-mad district. In football my name appeared often in a "most successful" player category, and I still possess trophies in rifle-shooting and tennis. After coming to America I shared the

West Jersey doubles championship, and though I did not take up golf until after my 47th birthday, I managed for years to play in the low eighties. It seemed as if I had the facility to become a better than average performer in every sport, but I could not become a really good player in any.

I offer this record merely to show that though competitive, I was not fiercely so. I felt no urgent desire to reach the top of the list in anything. In my early years I was so devoted to games that my mother used to say that I thought cricket was the main business of life. At that time she was probably right.

A couple of years earlier my father's rotation of circuits brought our family to a little rural place called Toolleen, just about the center of the state of Victoria. There was only a part-time post office and one store, with the church and parsonage and a one-room school about a mile and a half distant. The farmers raised more cattle and sheep for a living than crops, but more rabbits than anything else. Fences were piled-up logs, in the hollows of which rabbits and an occasional snake found refuge. Our nearest neighbors were the Pascoes, a family of six stalwart young men, built like the sons of Anak. A couple of them were splendid riders and won all the prizes in the backjumping contests in the district. They had located a gold-bearing reef on their land and several of them spent much of their time "puddling" the alluvial dirt.

This process entailed the building of a huge wooden vat surrounded by a towpath around which an old horse dragged a set of iron harrows, converting into liquid sludge the mass of gold-bearing dirt dug from the mine-shaft. The water was drained off and the residue run over tables, the interstices containing quicksilver with which the gold amalgamated. In the evenings after school I was allowed to drive the horse around the towpath and soon found that it responded best to volleys of stones and lurid language. My deficiencies in the latter respect were soon made up, for these young men attended to my education in matters other than gold mining. I'm afraid I spent more time at the mine than in conventional boyish pursuits, and enjoyed to the full my reputation as a most unusual parson's son.

At other times, when I was not engaged in trapping and shooting rabbits—skins were worth one shilling and threepence a pound —I attended a school presided over by a red-headed Irishman named McMahon, who had some original ideas in teaching methods. Fifty years later I enjoyed a reunion of the class of 1900 in

Honolulu and boasted to my University colleagues that there was 100 per cent attendance. This was not as remarkable as it sounded since there were only two of us in the sixth or highest class. By 1950 my classmate had become parliamentary clerk to the governing political party and was on his way through Honolulu to London to attend a British Commonwealth conference. We felt that the occasion warranted celebration and drank a toast to ourselves and exchanged congratulations.

But McMahon had one extremely original idea of utmost future important to me. He persuaded my parents to allow him to nominate me to sit in competitive examination with the rest of the boys in the state for a government scholarship that would pay my tuition fees for three years. To diminish the odds against me, he put my application in for the Melbourne Educational Institute. That school offered ten scholarships, whereas the other Melbourne preparatory colleges of higher class offered usually two or four scholarships.

I was extremely surprised at McMahon's action, for he had never indicated any belief that I had any more than ordinary ability. Nor for that matter had my mother and sisters. My father, however, who was an incurable optimist where my reputed cleverness was concerned, thought I had a reasonably good chance. To my notion, sitting for the examination was McMahon's wild idea, rather like taking a shot at the moon, and Irishmen, I knew, would shoot at anything.

However, one hot December morning my father and I hitched up the horse to the buggy for the thirty-mile drive to the town of Bendigo. My only recollections of the trip are of dust and heat, the crossing of the Campaspe, the third river I had ever seen, and the habit of the presiding inspector of schools, Mr. Gates, of wrinkling up his nose in a strange fashion. It was a facial expression with which I was to become very familiar in later years during a long personal relationship with the then chief inspector.

My surprise was complete when, about a month later, our biweekly mail contained a postcard from McMahon, who was away on vacation, bearing the single word "Congratulations." Possibly he was too flabbergasted to write more. Not until a week later did I learn what I was to be congratulated upon, when the Melbourne papers showed my name as number 10 on the list of Melbourne Educational Institute awards. Probably out of the thirty scholarship winners in the state I was the only successful candidate from a one-room school. Fortunately all this happened just before my father was appointed minister to the Ringwood church, just fifteen miles and an hour's journey from Melbourne.

Of my secondary education there is little worth recording, except that Livingstone, the principal, took a very dim view of my abilities. My best friend was a boy named Wilkie Simmons, and when his mother enquired about his progress, Livingstone informed her that her son might have brains, but had no application. Possibly with the idea of sharing the bad tidings, she asked about me.

"Oh, Porteus," he replied, "he has neither brains nor application."

At that time one measure of a school's achievement was the number of pupils who passed the University matriculation examination, and so at the end of my second year, I duly entered the tests with the unhappy feeling that I was wasting as entrance fees a couple of guineas of my parents' money. Also on the principle that I might as well be hung for a sheep as a lamb, I registered in eight subjects, two more than were necessary for matriculation. In due course, along with a thousand or more others, I wrote busily for five full days in Wilson Hall at the University.

The Melbourne papers published first the names of matriculants and later the results by individual subjects. The initial P comes rather far down on the alphabetical list of names. It was a hot summer and I have sometimes wondered whether the examiners were getting weary of reading papers in a heat wave and so passed over a bunch of papers with only casual scrutiny. Whether or not this was the case did not affect my pleasure when I found the name Porteus, Stanley D. shining, yes, literally shining in the list of matriculants.

I do not remember the mile and a half walk from the post office, but do recollect throwing myself and the paper in mock despair on the couch at home.

"How did you do?" enquired my elder sister rather acidulously.

"Just as I expected," I replied, dispiritedly.

"That's too bad, I'm so sorry," my mother said quite gently, while the rest of the family adjusted their features to the right degree of sympathy.

"Too bad," I roared, bouncing up from the couch. "I PASSED!"

Later, detailed publication of results showed that my one failure was Euclid—now called plane geometry. To pass in seven subjects with an apparent minimum of effort changed Livingstone's classification of my abilities from dullard to near-genius, and from that time onward I studied or otherwise just as I pleased. Next year I sat for honors in English and history and succeeded in one of them, but which it was is now beyond my remembrance.

Of the rest of my growing-up process there is little to write. Through playing football I was able to realize one fact that was to be an illumination to me in my subsequent studies of Australian aborigines.

A couple of miles from the mountain-rimmed town of Healesville there was an aboriginal settlement known as Corranderrk. There, under joint mission and police control, were gathered together the remnants of the Yarra River tribes. On various occasions the blacks (as we called them) lent interest to certain social gatherings by exhibitions of skill in boomerang and spear-throwing, fire-making by friction, etc. In between times, the abos smoked, drank (when they had the chance), fought, fornicated, hunted, tracked game, and did all the things idle aborigines could think of. In addition, they played cricket and football. The former called for more sporting equipment than a blackfellow could be bothered taking care of, but Australian football needed only a couple of goal posts, a football and a level space on which to play. Occasionally they challenged neighboring teams and once played a match against the Ringwood Club, of which I was a team member.

All the blacks played barefoot, and some were excellent players. But the most interesting feature was that among the twenty players there were at least six captains. These were graybeards, who had lost their agility but not their authority. They were all over the field, kicking the ball whenever they got the chance, but ceaselessly shouting orders and generally getting in the young men's way.

This was my first experience of "old man domination" among the natives which governs every aspect of tribal life—social observances, marriage restrictions, food distribution, and plans for survival. Even in football no one questioned the tribal elders' authority. The powers of the tribal council, composed mainly of the old men, was later to become one of the central themes of my book *The Psychology of a Primitive People.* Except for the hindrances imposed on the younger players, the aboriginals would have undoubtedly won the match. Some of the former were excellent individual players, and their running, kicking, and handling of the ball were remarkably good. Foot-racing was one of their favorite sports, and provided they could be prevented from selling their chances, they won most of the local competitions.

Two miles from the Ringwood railway station lay several thousand acres of virgin bush, an area that had quite an influence in my process of growing up. Australia today is noted for its profuse bird life with many indigenous species, probably outnumbering those of any other continent. There were no Gould leagues or Audubon societies in those days and our egg-collecting led to a strange paradox. Our destructive efforts were limited to a single egg from each nest and our bird-watching, in the interests of search and discovery of nests, increased our knowledge and skill far above the level of more restrained modern youngsters. To avoid getting lost required close attention to the lay of the land and photographic memory of rocks, hills, and gullies that distinguished the terrain. The utmost distinction we could anticipate was recognition as "a good bushman." Though I did not know it, I was undergoing experiences that would be helpful in my wanderings in Northwest Australia and South-Central Africa. This I consider an invaluable part of education. The result was that I cannot remember being lost more than twice in the Australian bush or in Africa, and even then, though benighted, I found my way back to camp entirely by my own efforts.

Autobiographies give writers an opportunity to make acknowledgments, usually belated, to those who have exerted a deep influence in the molding of their personalities. I think I learned one most valuable lesson in resiliency, resistance to fatigue, and aversion to quitting, even after every bone and sinew have signalled that by all human standards they have made their maximum effort.

When I was nineteen years of age, I spent much time in the bush with a young man, Stanley Burchett, who was ten years my senior. He had risen to the top of a peculiar business, that of tea-taster to the well-known Melbourne firm of Griffiths and Co. Australians, as is well known, are great tea-drinkers. Nothing in every-day life, be it death, wedding, family reunion, or any other critical event occurs but is signalized by brewing and ingesting quantities of tea. One old lady attributed her century of living to one simple formula—she met every crisis in life by going to bed with a "cuppa." What non-Australians do not understand is how careful the tea-drinker is about the excellence of his special blend. Tea was commonly sold in 25- or 50-pound containers, and when ordered in such quantities, the customer required just the right proportions of Indian, Ceylon, and Chinese teas. One blend, for example, Panyong Soochong, is made up of tea grown in a certain province and picked at a certain season. To ensure just the right flavor, the tea-taster may need to sample and classify 40 or 50 blends on a single morning. This was a most unusual occupation, one that necessitated extraordinary dietary restrictions. Potatoes in any form, for example, ruined my friend's palate. He found, however, that simple meals eaten out-of-doors were most innocuous, and so twenty-mile walks at a weekend were not uncommon. This issued finally in a challenge to walk sixty miles to the beautiful farming location of Poowong in South[1] Gippsland. At twenty-five miles from home my feet were already blistered but we continued on, finally arriving at the Burchett family home at 12 midnight after leaving Ringwood at 5:30 A.M. As I had already walked a mile and a half to reach our starting point, I had covered 61½ miles in about 18 hours. That would have been enough for me, but my companion insisted on getting up at eight o'clock next morning and beginning our walk home. We were able to be driven 20 miles, but the rest of the journey was inexpressively painful and difficult.

Two things I learned. The first was that after the human body has given what it deems its utmost, there are still reserves of strength and endurance that can be drawn upon from heaven knows where. I almost crawled the last long mile that brought me home at 3:30 A.M. on Monday morning. I had walked over 100 miles in something less than 48 hours.

The second thing I became aware of was the degree to which one's spirit leans on another's for courage and persistence. Alone I would have dropped by the wayside, but the consciousness of my companion moving steadily a half-pace ahead of me drove me on. The most important stimulus to a man is not fear, danger, or fatigue, but the presence of another human being whose purpose is at one with his own.

Whether this supreme effort contributed to a tragic ending, I do not know, but a year after, my friend, apparently recovering from an attack of ordinary influenza, suddenly collapsed and died. It was more likely that excessive tea-drinking had weakened his heart.

[1] Gippsland includes all the country east of Melbourne. Its two political divisions are South and East Gippsland.

CHAPTER 2

Cycling into Psychology

My first teaching assignment, a couple of years after the turn of the century, was in the state's second largest town, the gold-mining center of Ballarat, well known as the site of Australia's only armed revolt, the Eureka Riots. This occurred in the very early days of the gold rush when the miners erected a stockade in defiance of the government's efforts to collect fees for mining licences. Much later it became well known throughout Australia as the home of the South Street Debating Society, which conducted annual literary and artistic competitions.

In my mind my stay in this small city was memorable only by reason of the fact that it was in the *Ballarat Courier* that my first writing efforts, a series of imaginative nature studies and essays, appeared. I have not seen nor read them for sixty years and therefore cannot say whether they were good or bad. Since I used a pseudonym (Odel), no one else can make any judgment upon them. The editor, however, was encouraging, though he did warn me that if I ever dipped my fingers in printer's ink the stain would be ineradicable. He was right.

Promotion in the Victorian Education Department was dependent entirely on experience gained in conducting tiny rural schools, usually in localities far removed from railways. One of those advertised in the *Victorian Teachers' Gazette* attracted my attention because of its name, Glenaladale. It was 12 miles from Fernbank, a railway station on the line from Melbourne to Bairnsdale, the leading town in East Gippsland. I knew the South Gippsland area well, and the name of the school conjured up visions of great forests of trees, nearly 300 feet in height, cool shadowed gullies where thirty-foot tree ferns grew in profusion among gently swelling hills that some enthusiastic nature writer had compared to women's breasts. About these I had no experience and little interest, so I was content with this rather fulsome comparison. But as any Australian knows, contiguous areas in that continent vary enormously in character. South Gippsland was in the belt of frequent rainfall and rich soil that quickly recovered from the infrequent brush fires that ravaged the forest.

There were ferns at Fernbank but only of the common brown bracken variety, while the banks were merely sandy rises covered with monotonous eucalyptus scrub, broken only by an occasional banksia tree with flowers like bottle brushes, one of the first trees to be named by Sir Joseph Banks, the botanist who accompanied Captain Cook on his voyage of discovery. At the railway siding were three or four houses, huddled beside a dispirited road whose only purpose seemed to be to get lost as quickly as it could in the bush.

Glenaladale, as I discovered when I walked out there next morning, had a little better claim to its mellifluous name. Before me lay the inevitably named Stony Creek—there must be twenty thus named in Australia—flowing from some hills, broken by rocky gorges, alongside some clearings which might be considered by some homesick Scotsman "dales," but they were sparsely populated. Seven miles from Fernbank the road divided and one signpost read "Lindenow 12 miles, Bairnsdale 30 miles." The other fork was labelled "Dargo, 60 miles," with no mention of Glenaladale in between. The reason for the omission I soon discovered; there was no such place except a schoolhouse surrounded by virgin forest, with only one other dwelling in sight.

At the back of the schoolroom was a brick fireplace which warmed it and the small lean-to rooms that were the teacher's quarters. This provided space for what was called a "colonial oven." On top of this oven a fire could be lit for occasional frying-pan cooking. For more ambitious culinary efforts hot coals could be shovelled in underneath the oven. In the two and a half years I "batched" at Glenaladale, I rarely attempted anything but the simplest cooking.

The pupils averaged a three-mile walk to and from school, a

fact which indicates the sparsity of population. The building stood in an 80-acre uncleared forest. Dargo, once a gold-mining town, had lost any reason for being, other than the presence of less than half a dozen men who ranged their cattle over leased land of a few hundred thousand acres, for which they paid the government a nominal fee. Another exit road led away from Dargo to Briagolong, a more settled region, so that a couple of travellers a year used the road that ran past the school. The place could, I expect, be called lonely, for on occasion you could count more kangaroos than kids on the school ground. But I don't think I worried too much about loneliness. After all, that was what could be expected in pioneer territory. Perhaps that last designation also needs some elaboration. If any one of the parents of the pupils, even though he saw only three or four strangers in a year, had been called a pioneer to his face, he would have looked amazed. "Pioneer" was a term invented and used only by city folk in Australia. It is in common American usage but is comparatively recent. "I'm no pioneer," a settler in Glenaladale would have told you, "I just live here."

As for my one neighbor, I saw little of him, though his children and stepchildren attended school regularly. My friend Jim Campbell summed up his character briefly but adequately.

"Pat Reeves," he told me, "is a better neighbor when he's in jail than out. His present wife is quite a decent woman—she'll do your laundry for you—but how she came to take up with Pat, God only knows!"

"What does he get into jail for?" I asked.

"Nothing serious," said Jim. "A little cattle duffing [rustling], some kangaroo shooting out of season, drunk and disorderly once a month when he goes to Bairnsdale, and now and then assault and battery on his wife. Nothing worth talking about."

"Cattle duffing?" I enquired.

"Oh yes," replied Jim. "Pat claims his eyesight is poor. He can see all of a nice fat heifer except his neighbor's brand!"

But lonely or not, I think that my two years at Glenaladale had considerable effect on my personality. The bottom layer of the trunk my mother packed for me was filled with books—Carlyle, Emerson, Marcus Aurelius, Epictetus, Omar Khayyam, Montaigne's essays, Ruskin, Lowell, Shakespeare, and last but not least, Palgrave's Golden Treasury. These made up my library and I read them well. Someone has said that the key to a man's character is revealed by his book shelves. I do not think I can agree. I should have been a very serious character. It is not what a man reads that counts, but what he thinks about, and his book shelf is at best a patchy guide to his thinking.

At school the children and I got along famously. There were no apples to put on the teacher's desk, but two of the girls who lived four miles away in the mountains evidently made weekly bush excursions and came back laden with bright flowers, while the boys, knowing my interest in aboriginals, regularly combed the site of a native stone-implement factory and brought to me stone axes, adzes, quartzite spearheads, and all kinds of flint scrapers. Much of the worked stone material had been transported to the factory site, since that was where the natives found the heavier grinding stones. Incidentally, the spot selected was admirably suited for defence or escape. It occupied a bare saddle between two hills with a fairly precipitous gorge at its back, so that as soon as an alarm sounded the aborigines could step over the rim and melt away up the gorge in a matter of moments. This was an excellent instance of native foresight. With the aid of a thin screen of scouts, they could never be cut off or surrounded, and could leave their grinding stones *in situ*.

One circumstance about my teaching experience occupies an uncomfortable niche in my memory. After the bi-weekly arrival of the Melbourne papers at Fernbank, I made it my business to read and discuss with the older children the cable news. The time was just after the Boer War. The struggle between England and Germany for African colonies was coming to a head, and the atmosphere in Australia was decidely jingoistic. I hope I did not add fuel to the flames, but seven out of the eleven boys at Glenaladale school enlisted some years later in World War I; out of this group two were killed and two wounded.

In 1959, fifty-five years later, I revisited the school, then empty of scholars, but on the wall hung what was called "The Roll of Honour," bearing the names of the seven volunteers. As far as glowing patriotism went, it was a magnificent record, but I could not keep back some insistent questions.

Why did these lads, born twelve thousand miles away, who had never heard a shot fired in anger, shed their blood or cough their lives away in Gallipoli trenches or on the fields of Flanders? Their national flower was not the lethal poppy, but the golden wattle; their national anthem, the bird songs of the dawn, their daily challenge to pit their strength against jungle and forest that threatened their survival, their weapons the ploughshare, the saw, axe, and shovel. It was their own choice, but I wondered whether any words of mine had kindled their resolution, and sent them forth to struggle and die. I hope not, even though a blind pacifism has never been one of my obsessions.

With a sense of deep humility and the feeling more of a grey ghost than a grey eminence, I inserted my card into the frame of the pictured roll, thinking that no one would ever see it; but I was mistaken. Two weeks later an invitation arrived asking me to

In 1959, fifty-five years later, the author revisited Glenaladale, the first rural school at which he taught.

attend a reunion at the school on the following Sunday to meet some of my pupils and their grandchildren. It seemed that, now while there were not enough children to maintain a school at "the Glen," the grounds were used as a tennis and other recreational center for people who came from miles around. Someone had found my card and promptly organized a gathering in my honor, just fifty-five years later. Rarely, I thought, has anyone roamed so far and yet lived to come home to obtain even such a brief glance at his beginnings.

The old eucalypt tree with its hollows, still serving as a nesting place for birds and opossums, stood a few yards from the school door, and no doubt remained a rallying point to repel the assaults of the five-foot goannas—huge tree-climbing lace lizards that inhabit the bush. No matter what the subject of instruction, any unusual bird outcry always brought teacher and pupils piling out to repel the invader with a volley of stones. Occasionally the intruder was a snake, but fortunately it was only rarely that a poisonous reptile showed any desire to attend school, though one or two were killed in the playground.

Among my most pleasant recollections were the nature excursions the kids and I made to the nearby gorges, particularly the narrow gash through which Iguana Creek made its way to the Mitchell River. Eons before, possibly a million years, Devonian sandstone had been laid down in flat beds across the face of the country. The stream cut its way down, leaving precipitous walls, broken down in places, so that all manner of unusual vegetation found a lodgment, thus providing a verdurous contrast to the red and grey sandstone cliffs. Beneath the monotonous grey-green of the ordinary bush "upstairs," a river of darkest green offered not a sea, but a land change. Gone were the gum trees and wattles, and taking their place was a riot of vegetation only to be found several hundreds of miles further north—currajongs, lilli-pillis (kanookas), pittosporums, all bound together with lianas of creepers, twisting around and grasping rocks and tree trunks with living ropes as thick as a man's arm.

It would be ungracious to omit reference to the bird chorus, especially when so much of the Australian bush is silent. Fifty years ago lyre birds were common until imported English foxes made war on the ground-ranging bird population. The lyre bird is surely the best mimic in the world, for every other bird call, with the exception of that of the kookaburra, is faithfully echoed. In the shady depths the bell birds provided a tinkling accompaniment to the piercing cry of the currawong. These birds, twice the size of a pigeon, seem to place their calls above the rocky canyons where the sound will be magnified by the waiting echoes. Only when the lyre bird was broadcasting to the whole bush did the currawongs fall silent, for the former provided not a single performer but a whole orchestra. Anyone who would like to realize the great variety of bird sounds that Australia offers will save himself hundreds of miles of travel if he will just sit quietly for a quarter of an hour and listen to the lyre bird. Unfortunately, the odds on survival run greatly against the birds. To one who knew its haunts fifty years ago, the bush is now strangely empty.

Anyone who elects to write his life history is under obligation not to omit those experiences which had a share in making him the kind of man he became. One does not live alone in the bush for two years without some impress, more or less deep, on his unfolding personality. So at the risk of delaying a little the recital of events that made me a psychologist—of sorts—I must devote a couple more paragraphs to the spell that Glenaladale laid upon me.

In one of those rather rare flashes of insight that poets have, Walt Whitman wrote:

> There was a child went forth every day,
> And the first object he looked upon that object he became,
> And that object became part of him for the day,
> or a certain part of the day,
> Or for many years, or stretching cycles of years.

If I were to try to name the things that I absorbed, and which remain part of me to this day, the list would include sunlit slopes flowing into shadowed gullies; those sudden breaks in the terrain where the blanket of eucalypts ended and the life of the gorge began; sandstone ledges where the wombats used to wander from burrow to burrow, attending, no doubt, to the business of wombathood; smooth reaches of the Mitchell River, broken here and there by sudden rapids of inflow and discharge, the whole fringed with waterside thickets, playgrounds for satin birds, noted for building bowers, not for nests but merely for display. Here they collected sticks and decorated each mound with any bright objects available—bits of glass, china, feathers, flowers, shells, and if nothing else served, with pieces of colored paper torn from the wrappings of school children's lunches. Here I spent over two years as a bachelor, and at Lindenow, 20 miles distant, met my future wife.

Later on, when I was swamped with psychological work in an industrial suburb of a large city, stifled by heat, racket, and human fetidity, I gained refreshment and peace of mind from the consciousness that somewhere these green sanctuaries existed, awaiting my return. I pity those who, in the bustle of living, have no such place of retreat.

When after marriage I had to seek promotion by leaving Glenaladale with its singing name, my wife and I still chose places

The gorge of Dead Cock Creek near Glenaladale School about 1906.

whose names fell gently on the ear, the first, Leneva, and the second, Benambra. The latter, to which I was transferred in 1911, was situated on the edge of a lake bed, and was rimmed about by high mountains. In very wet seasons the drainage from these partially filled the lake. Perhaps because of its lacustrine history no trees grew by the lake bed except where a sandy rise bisected the plain. Benambra had long been settled, with the earliest arrivals picking out and owning the choice locations. There they ran sheep, cattle, and horses, products that could travel to market on their own hooves. This was a vital consideration, since the nearest railhead was a hundred miles distant and the access road was a dusty, pock-marked highway through the mountains, allowing of only one

Stanley D. Porteus and his wife, Frances, in photographs taken about 1906.

detour, rarely if ever used. The well-to-do ranchers sent their offspring to college preparatory schools in Melbourne, 270 miles distant. The one-room school over which I presided took care of the rest. I had two assistants, the one much too young, the other much too old, to be of much use. Thus, unless I was to take a great deal of my time teaching little children, I was forced to use what psychology I knew in devising new approaches to the learning process.

It may be strange to say so, but the two spurs to my inventiveness were my own laziness and that of my scholars. I soon decided that my goals would be accomplished if instead of teaching the children myself, I could devise the means by which the children would, with a minimum of supervision, manage to teach themselves. Considering the lengthy partnership between psychology and education, a matter surely of a hundred years, it had always seemed to me that psychologists, who were so mightily concerned with theories of learning and the principles of education, had managed to escape being involved in learning *practices*. How does it come about that a man, who has gained a Ph.D. (and a good job) for his studies of how the mind works, has so little to offer? When the teacher possessing only a diploma of education and inferior status appealed to his colleague for hints as to how he should go about his job of persuading infants to learn, his instructors seemed to know nothing about teaching.

It appeared to me at the outset that little children who had learned without too much trouble to feed themselves with fork and spoon or to manipulate their fingers in tying knots or dressing and undressing themselves should be able to acquire the manipulative skill of writing without any special difficulty. They were presented with pencils, crayons, and paper but no one bothered to make sure that they put these utensils to the right use. Some kind of easily progressive steps had to be supplied. In other words, teaching the child to feed or dress himself or even to learn to walk required some study of the process so that it could be broken down into easy stages. Surely no one expected the supine infant to rise up suddenly and make his way into his mother's arms. Two things were necessary: first, the child's desire to become mobile had to be utilized, and second, he had to be shown by practise that locomotion could be made safe and easy. No one has to teach a child to walk by catching its legs and painfully putting one foot in front of the other.

Muscular coordination is normally a maturational process. In addition, it seemed to me important for the little learner to have his goal clearly in mind. In simplest terms, he had to see or know where he wanted to go. If he did not want to go to his mother's arms, it was useless to try and get him to practise the operation.

Applying these principles to the teaching of my pupils to write took relatively a very short part of my stay in Benambra. I tried first to establish a memory image of the writing form, the goal to be attained. I found that all the elements of cursive script could be reduced to eight—or ten, if one included some small details such as the little loop in the letter *f*, which only differed in size from the larger loop in *l*. I then had these letter elements grooved out of wooden forms larger than writing size. The first exercise was to have the child practise running his finger within the groove enough times to develop visuo-motor images, as for example the writing element *c* . After a few tracings with his finger along the groove, the wooden form was placed face down. If then with fair success the learner could indicate with his finger the shape of the hidden element, he was on his way toward writing. When presented with crayon or chalk, he could reproduce the form that he was to depict. Thus he was already writing. The next procedure was to continue the practise with the other elements, such as *7* , *v* , *l* , etc., and combine them into letters.

A couple of years later, after my experimental work had been transferred to Melbourne, this system was described in an article, published in the October 1914 *Education Gazette and Teachers' Aid,* which thus ranks first in my bibliography. Not for another fifty years did I return to the educational field with a monograph entitled "Streamlined Elementary Education," and a paper on "Educational Wastage," which appeared in *Perceptual and Motor Skills* (Vol. 20, 1965).

These two publications set forth in detail the system of teaching the facts or skills necessary for elementary arithmetic, reading, and spelling. Little needs to be discussed here except the fact that the child could teach himself with a minimum of instruction and supervision on the part of the teacher.

Briefly stated, all that was required for learning arithmetical addition and subtraction was a balance, usually a gold-buyer's scales, and a double set of cardboard boxes graduated in weight by filling them with shot and cotton wool. Thus, for example, the child learned that a 10 box in one scale would exactly balance two 5s, a 9 and a 1, an 8 and a 2, a 7 and a 3, and a 6 and a 4. It is obvious that with the numbers plainly printed on the boxes the child could teach himself the correct combinations. Being naturally lazy, he could then avoid the trouble of using the boxes and the scales.

For learning multiplication and division factors, all that was necessary was to provide what amounted to a new color notation for the four prime factors. These were blue (2), red (3), yellow (5), green (7) and their combined products or color symbols which the children had to memorize. For example, if a green bar stood for 7, then 7 by 7 would be two green bars, the symbol for 49. If the factor

2 was represented by a blue bar and 3 by a red bar, then 24 was denoted by three blue bars and one red. With this color combination before his eyes (or memorized), the pupil could regroup the combinations and read off mentally the facts that 8 by 3, 6 by 4, and 2 by 12 also made the product 24. With a color chart no larger than 12 by 10 inches displayed on the wall, the child could read all the factors up to 100 and therefore did not need the arithmetical tables. But after a time the pupil found it easier to memorize the color combinations than to constantly refer to the chart, just as he found it easier to memorize the facts in addition without bothering to use the weighted blocks and the gold-buyer's scales. By eight years of age every youngster had clearly in mind all the data he needed for simple arithmetic. Two years ago I had a letter from a 68-year-old woman in Australia telling me that arithmetic learned in this manner gave her no trouble during all her further schooling. I also well remember that the eight-year-olds were quicker than I was in elementary multiplication and division. However, reading and spelling had to wait for sixty years before we succeeded in making learning so easy as to become almost automatic. At least we were able to demonstrate that three-year-old Japanese children could learn to read and spell 15 words in less than 40 minutes cumulative instruction, and that Australian aboriginals could learn almost as quickly words presented in their own Arunta language.

By means of cards inserted in the machine with slots of different length cut out at their bases, pupils soon learned to press the letters in correct sequence as they appeared in little windows on the reading-spelling machine. Thus, for example, the letters c a t, when pressed in that order, appeared in succession alongside the picture of the animal. Moreover, the child could not make a visible mistake. If he pressed the wrong letters or pressed them in the incorrect order, the cards did not fall into their allotted positions, and nothing happened. Thus a great obstacle in primitive learning was eliminated—frustration due to unsuccessful efforts.

This invention, however, had to wait many years before Dr. A. L. Diamond and I worked on the device. It also would have worked well with the mentally retarded, but not until Dr. Diamond hit on the idea of slotted cards falling into sequential position by gravity was the device entirely feasible. My writing and arithmetical devices had already been in teaching practice sixty years before, and this fact had really accounted for my initial projection into psychology. As was the case with so many young men at that time, I found that the teaching profession provided the first rungs of the ladder that led to a more highly regarded occupation.

In 1912, while I was still carrying on my experimental teaching at Benambra, one of those minor events that changed the whole course of my future occurred. One of the school children fell sick with some suspicious red spots on his chest. The nearest doctor was fourteen miles away, and when I telephoned him and described the symptoms, he concluded that it was a case of measles and promptly closed the school. No other children were affected, and it may have been a mistake in diagnosis, but in any case the health officer was the sole arbiter. Just before this happened, my wife with our infant son had been offered a drive down to her parents' home so that she could escape the hundred-mile coach journey. She gratefully accepted.

About this time a notice appeared in the *Teachers' Gazette*, inviting applications for the position of superintendent of special schools in Melbourne. This development had been inspired by glowing reports from Italy of Madame Montessori's success in teaching mentally defective children by using sense training. The only things wrong with her system—and this is true today—were that she was training the wrong sense and directing the training toward the wrong objects.

Part of the Montessori system involves feeling around the edges of various shapes, such as squares, triangles, and the like, and even fishing them out of bags by feel. But the child never comes in touch with squares and triangles in cursive writing. Why not direct the training toward the recognition of forms he must use in writing, and second, why put such emphasis on touch, which is one of our earliest and most limited sense receptors, essential to snails but much less important to humans? On the other hand, vision, which has displaced the more primitive sensory perceptors is our most direct pathway to learning. Of course, if the child is blind, then he must depend for survival on the tactile sense. The trouble with the Montessori system is that it is based on faulty psychology, in disregard of the history of brain evolution.

But in the meantime if I believed I had a better psychological approach, it was my business to demonstrate it in the right quarters, and the training of defectives seemed to me to provide the best proving ground. I decided that I must, in popular terms, sell myself and my ideas to the heads of the Education Department, which had a new position of organizing mental defectives in their gift.

But I was 116 miles by coach from the railroad station and another 170 miles from Melbourne. Hence I could reckon on a three-day journey before I could present myself at the central department and demonstrate my new ideas in elementary education, in the hope that they would be applied to the mentally retarded.

If instead of catching the Cobb & Company coach, the ordinary mode of transportation, I could ride a bicycle, branch off the coach road on a track through the mountains leading to a mine at a place called Sheep Station Creek, I could save fifty miles and a whole day in transit. With a great deal of luck, I could, by leaving Benambra on Friday afternoon, present myself and my credentials at the Melbourne offices early Monday morning, just before the deadline for applications.

The only drawbacks to the scheme were first that I had no bicycle, second, rumors that the mine had closed were current, and finally the knowledge that the road which had been built to carry the ore to the crushing mills at Bulumwaal had never functioned regularly and had not been travelled, so it was reported, for two years. The track ran for sixty uninhabited miles through the mountains and no one knew its condition. Nevertheless, I decided that only a personal appearance at the central department would help me to gain the job. In addition, this plan would save me coach fare for 116 miles, no inconsiderable item. Then someone offered to loan me a bicycle, and with a small suitcase lashed to the handle bars, I set off.

But the first downward slope revealed the fact that the bicycle had no brakes, so that I was reduced to back-pedalling until the declivity became too steep for safety, when my only recourse was to hold the saddle with one hand, throw myself off backwards, and trust to luck to land on my feet uninjured. Unfortunately, the road had to traverse what was called the Tongio Gap, through which the road descended a couple of thousand feet in several miles. However, I solved this problem by cutting a large eucalyptus branch and tying it to the bike saddle to serve as a brake-drag. All went well until I met the evening coach and its passengers on a sharp turn on the way up. The four horses stood on their hind legs, the women passengers shrieked in fright, the driver cracked his whip and cursed me loudly, while I swept by in a cloud of dust on my way down the mountain road. Needless to say, I did not wait to see the outcome, but concluded that the coach escaped careening off the road down the mountain side. At least I heard of no such accident.

At the bottom of the gap I found the signpost "To Sheep Station Creek" and began a six-mile hike, wheeling my bicycle uphill only to find that the mine was deserted and the hotel closed. The owners were departing the scene on the following morning, with a two-horse wagon carrying them and all they owned, including a milking cow tied on behind. But the former landlady was kind, made up a couch for me, and in the morning found two fresh laid eggs for my breakfast—probably the hens' last contribution before being devoured by foxes. Her husband was very doubtful whether I would find the road passable on account of washouts and fallen trees, but the hired man, a born optimist, told me that a bike only needed six inches' width of good road at a time and that after the road passed Mount Baldhead it was downhill for thirty miles to the little mining town of Bulumwaal. From there it was only twenty miles through the mountains to Lindenow, where my wife's people had their "ranch" on the Mitchell River. All I had to do, he told me, was to watch for what lay at the bottom of hidden curves, and if trees had fallen across the road, to lift my bike over them and proceed. He forgot to mention that the road was quite steep in places, with the descent interrupted by many short rises that I must surmount on foot. The last words I heard from the former hotelkeeper were an earnest injunction to ride carefully, for if I sprained an ankle or broke a leg, it would be at least a month before the alarm went out and a search party could be organized. Hoping to surprise my wife, I had not informed her by letter of my intended arrival, and the last twenty miles after I reached Bulumwaal was directly through the mountains, untravelled except by an occasional logger, locally called a timber-getter. There were no settlers living in between. But at nine o'clock on Saturday evening I staggered into the farm house, having travelled continuously by foot and bicycle since six o'clock in the morning. If I convinced the Chief Inspector and gained the post, I had the distinction of being the first man who had literally cycled his way into psychology.

After all these difficulties, nine A.M. on the Monday morning found me in the Chief Inspector's office in Melbourne, armed with various exhibits that put into practice the psychological principles underlying the teaching approach to slow learners. Here I renewed acquaintance with Mr. Gates, who had supervised my scholarship examination some 17 years earlier. He still had the habit of wrinkling his nose in perplexity or other emotional states, and my description of my unconventional teaching aids creased his nose with more wrinkles than ever. Teaching multiplication by colors surprised him to the extent that he called in a colleague, Inspector Bothroyd, well known for his critical attitude. Bothroyd's comment on the novelty of this approach did me no harm.

"That is no handicap," he remarked, "elementary school teachers have not entertained a new idea for a hundred years."

Had I known it, my application was very opportune. Mr. Gates had, a year previously, picked out a man for the job, and the Education Department had given him a travelling scholarship which enabled him to visit training centers in America, England, and continental Europe, and thus to become familiar with the latest ideas in educational psychology. But when the position was advertised, the individual concerned decided that the salary of 1500 dollars a year was inadequate and failed to apply.

It so happened that the whole state educational system was directed by Mr. Frank Tate, who as the civil service head, had the habit of standing his ground against criticism by politicians, reporters, editors, and the like. Also he objected strenuously to being "held up" by any kind of threat or pressure. His instructions to Mr. Gates were explicit—get another man!

I was a rather unimpressive answer to prayer, but I believe the fact that less than three days before I had been situated in Benambra, about 300 difficult miles from Melbourne, argued well for my determination and faith in my own ideas. Gates promptly appointed me and then was stricken with freezing doubts. The situation called for psychological experience with defectives, and since no one in sight had any, he decided he might just as well take the long chance with me.

"This experiment," Gates warned me, "will be watched very carefully by the press, medical men, and other professional people. Do you think you would have the courage to tackle it?" "Yes, sir," I assured him.

"You certainly have plenty of assurance, young man," he told me, "but perhaps that is what is wanted for this job. That was a lucky epidemic of measles in Benambra—one solitary case, I believe. But that gives us time. You had better return to Benambra, close the school until your successor arrives, and report to me here. A city school at Bell Street, Fitzroy, is being remodelled for your use, and in the meantime you can learn all you can about the feeble-minded. You should arrange to work closely with the school medical officers."

Actually, Mr. Gates was so worried about his decision that for three months he avoided presenting me for inspection to the Director, Mr. Tate. He was very much afraid I looked far too young for the job. Meanwhile, reporters were getting curious, and the time came when the Chief Inspector could delay no longer his announcement of my appointment. He escorted me to the great man's room, made the excuse of having urgent business elsewhere, and left me to my fate. His urgent business was biting his nails in trepidation in his own office, waiting for the expected storm.

Mr. Tate's first questions revealed that he knew quite a lot about mentally defective children and their training problems. He was interested in my teaching devices and the psychological theories that lay behind them. The five-minute interview stretched to twenty minutes. Then I returned to Mr. Gates' office, where it was my turn to do the nail-biting, for which my teeth were ill-equipped, while he answered the summons to the Director's room. In a little while he returned with a broad smile displacing the nose wrinkles.

"Congratulations!" he cried, "Mr. Tate is highly pleased and has told me that anything you need—books, teaching material, staff, etc.—are to be put at your disposal, regardless of expense."

My friends, Dr. Harvey Sutton, Australia's first Rhodes scholar, and Drs. Jane Greig and Eileen Fitzgerald, school medical officers, were delighted with this support. Dr. Sutton sat down with me and we ordered from America enough equipment to stock a small psychological laboratory. Then we worked through all the material from sphymographs to letter cancellation tests, using each other as subjects. Then I began the task of assembling what might prove to be diagnostic tests applicable to defectives.

Not until years later did I learn that Mr. Tate had a very special reason for his deep personal interest in the plight of the mentally retarded. Whether it was true or not, information came to me that one of his near relatives was subnormal. Tate was, in my opinion, the best director of education the State of Victoria ever had, and in the years to come he was my staunchest backer. I do not believe either he or Mr. Gates realized what a long chance they took in selecting me, but when visiting me later after my establishment in the clinic at the University of Hawaii, Mr. Tate took great pleasure in assuring me that he thought his department had made a not inconsiderable contribution to psychology in Australia through my appointment.

CHAPTER 3

Filling up Leaky Vessels

In a very short time I realized that my job in Melbourne was to be psychological even more than educational. Here had been instituted an attempt to help the mentally retarded, a project rather enthusiastically backed by officialdom, the press, and the public. But to begin with, it posed one overriding question—who are the feebleminded? Last August, 53 years later, I wrote an article on the same subject, so the matter has not yet been completely settled.

The Department circularized all its urban school principals, asking them to make out lists of all children whom they thought needed special education. The response was overwhelming. Every slow reader, every rebellious or delinquent pupil, the halt and the lame, the partially deaf or blind, even those with adenoids and those who preferred truancy to the confines of the classrooms found a place on the list. Apparently, to the teachers, no child who gave any trouble was normal. The Special School at Bell Street, Fitzroy, an industrial suburb of below-average social and residential grade, promised ordinary teachers a pedagogical millennium—relief from all the woes that the subnormal or maladjusted occasioned. With all this confusion regarding mental standards, our greatest need was to establish some system of discriminatory diagnosis.

Naturally we turned to psychology for help—and received little. This was just the beginning of what is now known as clinical psychology. Among the testing material that we had imported was a booklet which gave in detail outlines of the Binet-Simon tests, then becoming popular in America. This manual of instructions was by Dr. Edmund Huey of Baltimore, and it introduced to us the Goddard Revision of the Binet Scale. Just about this time, Dr. Harvey Sutton and his colleagues found that the duties involving medical inspection of schools were increasing beyond their capacity to keep up with the work. They made available to me their medical library, including all the journals and books that dealt in any way with the problems of mental deficiency. They gave me their farewell blessing, and even offered their collective shoulders for me to weep on when frustrations thickened beyond all bearing. But they informed me that, with the exception of physical examinations of Bell Street pupils brought to me to Fitzroy, I was on my own. It was my baby and a very fractious, neglected infant at that.

So before the contractors had finished rebuilding the two-story school, the Education Department authorized the erection of a wooden structure in the school yard to serve me as an office and an examination center. Dr. Sutton and I had previously enlisted the help of a technician in the Physics Department at Melbourne University, and he put together various pieces of equipment that I thought I needed. Thus began the operation of a mental clinic, the first of its kind in Australia and one of very few in the world. This was an entirely unofficial affair, but soon parents and private medical practitioners began bringing or sending children for psychological study. Not only was I using the Binet, but other testing scales, such as the Treves-Saffioti, and a number of individual sub-tests as well. The high-ranking Collins Street pediatricians in Melbourne were soon referring all cases of suspected mental deficiency to me. When the parents happened to be well-to-do, the doctors collected fees; I did the work, but was quite satisfied with the arrangement. It was of reciprocal advantage. When poor parents brought their children to me with physical handicaps which I did not understand, I could refer these youngsters for thorough medical examinations without charge. Besides, I learned much about the physical aspects of mental defect.

Since I had no brass plate and kept strictly to my own field, and charged no fees, the doctors began accepting me as a psychological colleague. Since psychology at the University was lumped with Logic and Ethics and had no concern whatsoever with the feebleminded, I had no competitors.

Because the only residential care that was provided for this class of unfortunates was the "insane asylum," I began my first experience with psychotic patients. Dr. Gamble, medical superintendent at the Kew Asylum, had under his supervision what were called the "Idiot Cottages" at that institution. In view of this responsibility, he gave me all the help and information at his disposal. I have never forgotten his bitter comment as we stood before the cot of a hydrocephalic imbecile, whose head was so distended that he could not lift it from the pillow. Though it was infantile in appearance, it was twenty years old.

"Porteus," said Dr. Gamble, "wouldn't you think that God Almighty would be ashamed of creating something like that?"

I could not help replying: "What about the doctors who have kept this poor creature alive for all these years. Would it not be better to devote their skill and attention to individuals with some prospect of improvement?"

"That," he said, "will be your job, and I certainly wish you joy of it."

One other lesson I soon learned; physical appearance may provide an unreliable index of mentality. Occasionally, though rarely, a child may bear none of the "stigmata" of defect. It may be well formed, apparently active and alert, but still lacking in the potentialities for normal development. It is the parents of such cases who so resist the idea that there is anything radically wrong with their child, or at least nothing that it will not "grow out of."

On the other hand, many children who have suffered birth trauma or are polio victims may be far brighter than they look. Spastic cases with little muscular control and coordination may slaver, slobber, and shake in the obvious effort to communicate something to the observer; in short, they show some purposive initiative, whereas a doll-like placidity may conceal a profound mental vacancy.

By the middle of 1913 I had begun the weeding-out process and had tested probably 300 children. Then just about this time I had concluded that, useful as it was, the Goddard Revision of the Binet failed to tell me all I wished to know about individual personality. It appeared to me that there should be some measure of initiative and purpose, but where it was to be found I did not know. A little later the Fernald-Healy tests came under my notice and for a time I was buoyed up with the hope that one of their devices might give me the approach I wanted.

This was what they called a "puzzle-box," and consisted of a small case with a glass lid, through which the contents could be viewed. These consisted of hooks and loops of string fastened in such a way that if they were released in proper order, the box could be opened. The person tested had to determine the relationship of each part and thus decide the sequence of his actions. Two openings cut in the sides of the box, through which a button-hook could be inserted, made it possible to release various springs by taking the loops off their hooks. The time taken to open the contrivance was the examinee's score, but I soon found that I was measuring his manual dexterity as well as his planning ability. Both the puzzle box and the button-hook are now museum pieces, of no present use or value. The important thing is that the search for a measure of planfulness was ready to be begun.

Fortunately, no one in authority attempted any control over my activities. I think the attitude of my superior officers was that I had tackled an almost insuperable problem and that, sink or swim, I should be left alone to work out my own failure or salvation. Perhaps I was trading on their sympathies.

There was, however, one misinterpretation of my motives, namely, that I must be actuated by whole-hearted devotion to a task demanding exceptional patience, and that I must have a deep-seated sympathy for the mentally handicapped. In short, I found myself being put on a pinnacle of admiration where I certainly did not belong.

My response was not to a humanitarian challenge but to a psychological or scientific problem. Ill-equipped and inexperienced as I then was, I conceived it to be my duty to learn all I could about the essential features of mental deficiency. What was there about these children that made them different; in short, what was subnormality? Empathy rather than sympathy was needed. I had to try to put myself in their places, think as they thought, follow their fumbling attempts to come to terms with an environment that was indifferent if not hostile to them. First of all was the problem of their recognition, their diagnosis.

Obviously their learning ability was inferior, but that was merely a blanket observation which called for easy analysis. There were many degrees of defect. Possibly there was more hope for those with some glimmerings of reason and purpose, just as among psychotics the patient who has not given up the fight and is still struggling has the best chances of recovery. Of course, the two problems differed, one a matter of defective development, the other of mental breakdown. In spite of all Montessori's claims, mental defect was the more permanent, the incurable condition. Psychiatrists could perhaps correct or change behavior, but it was impossible to put into the child's make-up what wasn't there. Meanwhile, there was the problem of delimiting the bounds of normal and abnormal behavior. Gradually the purpose to acquire what understanding I could hardened in me. In short, I was becoming a psychologist—of sorts.

One temperamental change in myself was apparent. Contact with a great human problem of deep complexity served to ameliorate my tendency to brashness. I was suddenly faced with the realization of how little any of us knew of the mind and its workings. Facility with words that my reading and writing had engendered was of no use to me. I could neither talk nor bluff my way out of this situation. Nor could I find any great help in whatever textbooks of psychology I studied. It seemed to me that psychologists at that time concerned themselves with perplexities of their own devising, such as the body-mind relationship. Whether it be psychophysical parallelism, or associationism, or what not, did not seem to me to matter. Mind and physical organization were all in the same body anyhow. On the other hand, the differences between human individuals increasingly thrust themselves on my notice. Here were the misfits, the delinquents, the feebleminded, and the intellectually limited. What was to be done about them? How did they differ from the great mass of the underprivileged? Our knowledge of the causes of all these conditions was spread so thin as to be practically invisible. Before we could even suggest remedies, we had to define our problems.

At that time I had the hope that though we could not expect to "cure" mental deficiency, perhaps we could by education advance individuals through lower to higher grades of mental dullness. Even the feebleminded could be taught something of value. It might be impossible to make a silk purse out of a sow's ear—which was most people's excuse for neglecting the problem—but there were many other purses besides the silken variety, and one of leather might be less showy but just as serviceable.

In the meantime, my own problem was to assemble the children who might be expected to profit by special education. For a measure of educability I found the Goddard-Binet quite useful, but was soon in the position to realize that it was far from being "the perfect instrument of research" that Goddard himself had declared it to be.

I remember being worried over the application of the mental age concept. It seemed to me foolish to wrap together in the one parcel or index dissimilar abilities. For example, rote memory is examined by asking children to repeat digit numbers after one dictation. On the other hand, vocabulary was examined by finding out whether the subject could supply meanings of selected words. Levels of specific achievement were, of course, widely different since rote memory has little relation to language facility. These important differences then were merely concealed under a blanket index of mental age. This appeared to be like putting educational blinders on the teacher. If an eight-year-old child happened to have the vocabulary of a twelve-year-old, that fact was surely worth keeping in view. The concept of test validity, especially with regard to the individual tests included in a scale, had not been recognized nor has the question yet been satisfactorily resolved. In terms of another badly misused index, the IQ, two individuals may have the same IQ but be entirely different intellectually, with different potentialities of industrial adjustment.

Meanwhile, the screening process went on so that by the time the Special School—promptly dubbed the "silly school"—was completely rebuilt, we began operations with 150 children and a carefully selected staff of teachers. Any hope that I had entertained on the basis of Binet results that this group would prove to be, in any educable sense, homogeneous was doomed to disappointment. The Goddard Revision did not reflect temperamental or behavioral oddities, and the teachers, with the best will in the world, could not cope with the emotional and other crises that occurred. All the children could be included under the same category of "mentally retarded," but the differences between them were even more marked than among "normal" children.

In this regard I had aggravated my own problems. Parents were so eager to have their children trained or taught that I agreed that those who were able and willing to bring and call for their children, could enroll them for a couple of hours each day. This provision became an opportunity cherished by some parents and I found myself much more troubled in mind on behalf of parents than of children who could not realize their inadequacies. This permissive enrollment constituted the greatest handicap to our work. I had not the heart to dash the hopes of parents by excluding their children from attendance. Until we did exclude them, epileptic cases, for example, would occasionally disrupt a whole class.

One boy of very normal appearance had to be watched most closely. If the gate was left unlocked for a moment, he would be off like a shot and be lost to sight in traffic. His mother, when informed that her child had disappeared, was much less disturbed than I.

"The police always find him," she told me. "I have his name and address stitched on the waist band of his trousers. He'll be back before nightfall."

Finally, some sort of order, I discovered, could be established even in Bedlam. The staff soon learned that a sense of humor helped and that they could not afford to be shocked at anything that occurred.

We had installed all usable types of manual or practical training, and were no doubt well ahead of our times. In the tasks provided by simple toy-making and painting, shoe-mending, basketry and wire work for boys, simple cooking and housework for girls, we found the most surprising differences among the children. The idea that the retarded were naturally better with their hands than with their heads was soon dispelled. In most cases the pupils were feeble-handed as well as feebleminded. A boy could be taught to saw wood or hammer a nail, but marking off the right length to be sawn or putting the nail where it was wanted was another matter. The girl could learn to make regular needlework stitches, but there was no guarantee that they would go in the right place or direction. They had very poor ideas of planning a job or following a plan even if it were set up for them.

This long and tiresome description of the job of teaching defectives has been inserted to reach a point that was most important to me. I discovered that the Binet tests failed to pick out for us the children with the rudiments of practical common sense. Worst of all, we could not use it to help us to segregate those who could develop some ability to foresee what was needful, in short, to plan a simple job unaided.

Perhaps the reader having persevered so far will bear with a little more discussion of the evidence that planfulness is the most conspicuous lack in the mentally inferior person, and that this is mainly due to his inability to hold his goal clearly in view. Just as the artist or sculptor must have clear prevision of what he is trying to achieve with chisel or brush, so the mental defective must have a clean-cut idea of what a square must look like before he attempts to draw one.

Briefly, here is a simple illustrative experiment which I worked out. Part of the testing apparatus commonly used was the Seguin or Goddard form board, with the original inventor named first, the developer second. A thick wooden board has a number of forms cut and sunken into its surface, such as a square, circle, triangle, and the like. The corresponding blocks, called insets, match these forms and fit easily into the board. The child is supposed to insert these insets into their proper places, and the time he requires to do this is the basis of his score. If defective, he will do so clumsily, by trial and error, paying more attention to the size of the inset than to its shape. Thus he will frequently waste time trying to fit the square into the circle. He will need considerable practice, but will learn finally to do it correctly.

After the child had done this several times without error, I put the insets at the other end of the room. I then indicated which one of the forms I wanted, and then sent the child to bring it. Unable to keep the shape in mind, he would frequently become confused and bring back the wrong inset. Even after this maneuver had been successfully practised, any extra distraction, such as having to pass through a group of other children was sufficient to blur or confuse his intentions. In short, he forgot what he came for. If I could devise a test that would examine purposeful action and the ability to keep a purpose in mind, it seemed to me that I would be helping to demonstrate the most outstanding deficiency that a feebleminded subject displays, namely, ineffective planning. It would have to be a sufficiently interesting task to cause him to disregard any distracting features. The main problem was to find the right kind of testing material.

In our shoe-mending class was a boy named Claude, who had so much practical intelligence and ability to concentrate on what he was doing that he stood head and shoulders over his fellows. In practical tasks he seemed to know what the job should look like when it was finished. Hence, he was the only boy the instructor could trust to cut out of the "side" of leather the shape which when trimmed would fit the sole of the shoe he was mending. All he needed was some help when the leather was very tough. In spite of the fact that Claude's Binet score was very low, this boy was not in my opinion mentally defective. He had far too much practical intelligence to be so classified. Especially in rural districts I had met many of Claude's type. They were the minor handymen of their communities.

At our suggestion parents brought their children's shoes to be repaired. If they lived a couple of blocks away, Claude was able, if a simple plan was drawn for him, to deliver the mended footwear. If he failed to find the place, he had sense enough to return and re-examine the map and try again. If the situation were too complicated, I would send the instructor with him to correct any obvious misdirection. Incidentally, I once sent a woman teacher with Claude and both of them got lost in a maze of side streets.

A flash of insight hit me. That was what we needed—a printed maze of streets which could be graded in difficulty by multiplying the blind alleys and introducing false openings. These traps would require the subject to look before he leaped; in other words, trace with his eye the course before he committed himself to it. Actually the idea of a maze of the Hampton Court variety was not fundamental to my thinking. In that type of maze the individual could not survey and plot his course in advance and thus eliminate chances of error, but he could do this with a pencil-and-paper labyrinth.

I have taken this much time to tell in detail the events that led up to the devising of a test, the use of which has spread throughout the world.[1] It has been responsible for keeping many hundreds of reputed mental defectives out of institutions. The demonstration of their possession of normal planning capacity has raised hopes that though scholastically they might be out of the bottom drawer, they have intelligence enough to make themselves self-supporting and self-managing in their communities. These experiments constituted applications of the principles of planning in the educational field. For example, the mental etching of "memory images" of spatial forms so that the child knew what to write before he tried to write it, formed the basis of a teaching system that was at least five times faster and more effective than ordinary methods of instruction, including the Montessori system. This mental trial-and-error process introduced a new word into

[1] According to the latest (1966) review of a book on the Porteus Maze by Dr. Laurence Shaffer, a former president of the American Psychological Association, the value of the test has by no means been exhausted. In spite of its more than fifty years of psychological use he calls it "a vigorous youngster."

our psychological vocabulary—*prehearsal.* This was set up in contradistinction to *rehearsal,* which was better applied to the repetition of something already learned. Prehearsal was the initial step in learning something new. This pointed up one of the lessons that pedagogues had missed, namely, that it was wasting time to spend the effort on teaching the child *how* to write before he knew *what* to write. In more sophisticated terms, any goal will be more easily achieved if it can be clearly defined.

Obviously the threading of a printed maze offered what I needed—a measure of those abilities that were not adequately tested by the Binet. The next step was to devise a series graduated in difficulty; in short, a scale. I needed normal subjects, and nightly I had my wife working through test designs so that next day I could apply them to my Bell Street cases. Once a scoring system had been evolved, I could apply it widely. I was much heartened to find that those children who came out very well in my test were those who demonstrated the best social and industrial adjustments of behavior.

One problem was the extension of the scale to the lower ages. For this purpose ordinary maze designs were too difficult. But fortunately I found that the same basic principle, that of inability to anticipate changes in direction, could be applied. In tracing a diamond shape or double Maltese Cross, the child became so engrossed in drawing between the guide lines that when the direction suddenly changed (as in a right-angled turn in a Maltese Cross) the child was ill-prepared and ran over the guide lines. By five years of age children normally could deal with the simplest mazes, but at three and four years fidelity in following guide lines was a good measure of adjustability.

Meanwhile, the pediatricians who were referring cases to me were finding that I could give them more than a flat verdict of "feebleminded," or otherwise. There was some attention to be given to the children's strong points as well as to their deficiencies. Somehow the word spread, appointments became numerous, mainly through doctors, and soon I was testing cases from the other States of the Commonwealth.

In early 1914 I had a very important and interested visitor—Dr. John Smyth, professor of education at the University of Melbourne and the principal of Teachers' College. The only applied psychology that was available to students came from Professor Smyth and his staff, who were stirred by reports from abroad of developments in clinical psychology. Suddenly Smyth realized that some noteworthy experiments were being carried on right under his nose. Soon observation visits and lectures at Bell Street became an important part of the Teachers' College curriculum.

It was not at all difficult to maintain Professor Smyth's interest in what I was beginning to call my "motor-intellectual tests." The name had been adopted from J. E. W. Wallin, the American psychologist and authority on subnormal children. Later, I dropped this as a descriptive title after publishing one article describing the new measure under that name.

My chief problem in connection with the tests was to obtain sufficient data on normal performance for standardization purposes. I had tested for a time in a Melbourne kindergarten and had been greatly encouraged to find that the teachers agreed that those who dealt most adequately with the three-, four-, and five-year designs seemed to be those who were well adapted socially and who absorbed most readily pre-school instruction. But this work applied only to a small group of very young children. With my defective subjects the tests worked satisfactorily, but I still did not know how well or ill the new measure actually differentiated them from normals.

My friend, J. Hounslow Burchett, had taken up what was to be a lifelong interest in teaching the deaf, and he told me that at the Institution School for the Deaf where he was employed it was a long and costly process to weed out those children who were not only deaf and dumb but feebleminded also. Out of 140 children in residence, the teachers agreed that a little over ten per cent (16) of the cases were unteachable because of a basically feebleminded condition. It would be a crucial experiment if, without knowing the children and with no means of oral communication with them, I could test the deaf school population and pick out the sixteen cases who, on the basis of experience, the teachers thought to be defective. Dr. Smyth agreed that this would indeed be the severest trial we could possibly devise of the diagnostic value of the new psychological measure. He offered to supervise the whole experiment and duly attended the opening test session. Then he threw up his hands.

"If you can pick out the 'unteachables' under these circumstances," he told me, "then your test is one of the most remarkable I've ever heard of. But don't build your hopes too high. It looks like an impossible task to me."

I'm afraid it looked the same to me also, but it was my own proposal. To shorten the job, the school authorities mixed the "suspects" at random in among a group of 100 other deaf children. At the end of the testing I made out a list of 14 children who fell so much below the rest in Maze performance that it seemed probable that they were truly mentally deficient. On the teachers' list, to which I had no previous access, these fourteen with two others appeared. One of these latter had been marked "doubtful" by a couple of teachers. In short, the test had correctly differentiated 87½ per cent.

"This," said Dr. Smyth, "is marvellous. The British Association for the Advancement of Science is to hold its overseas meeting in Melbourne in August, and I am on the program for a half-hour paper. I shall cut this in half and allot you ten or fifteen minutes of my time. I'm sure that nothing I can say will be as important as what you have to offer." This was indeed a generous endorsement.

Had he been living now, I am sure that he would have decided that his act of sacrifice has borne fruit. I still have a letter he sent me in September 1921, seven years later.

"It is also very gratifying to me," he wrote, "to see you are embracing all your opportunities, how your power for work grows with the opportunity, and what a mastery of your subject your writings reveal."

Actually it was Smyth himself who was responsible for that opportunity and I am most grateful to him. In 1923, I spoke to the Teachers' College assembly and the professor introduced me as "a man whose career reads like a fairy tale." If so, it was Dr. Smyth who waved the magic wand.

Meanwhile, the B.A.A.S. meeting was only five weeks away. Fortunately my experience with overseas visitors made me aware of the fact that their attitude to "colonial" ideas, particularly educational, was usually one of good-humored tolerance, and I expected my paper to get short shrift. So I had my text mimeographed, complete with copies of all the test designs, plus tables comparing Binet and Maze results. This material I intended to distribute to the audience beforehand, so that if my paper was cut short in the middle, those interested would have some information to carry away.

My worst forebodings promised to be realized. Our British visitors were deeply interested in their own contributions to the proceedings but paid little attention to local offerings. Perhaps this attitude was understandable in delegates from Oxford, Cambridge, and London, visiting an undistinguished university in the antipodes, but it seemed to me to be very rude. Though Dr. Smyth was nominally chairman of the section, his paper was about half-read when the acting presiding officer banged his gavel on the table and informed the essayist that his time was up. He even refused Smyth's request to be allowed to finish the page, with the reminder that the session had already been long and the lunch hour was approaching. While the professor gathered up his unread pages, my name was called.

Taken entirely aback by such arrant discourtesy, I passed around my mimeographed material, scrabbled my papers together, stuffed them into my pocket and began to speak with the intention of saying all I could before the guillotine fell. As to my paper, I knew I could talk faster than I could read, and if I was going to make a mess of my opportunity, it might as well be complete.

However, with my first mention of Binet inadequacy, my audience stiffened to attention, pencils appeared and papers fluttered. Had I known it, I had touched the right spot. It will be remembered by some of the older psychologists that the new test scale had arrived in England via America and at that time the British attitude was: Can any good come out of Nazareth? Justifiably, there was considerable distrust of any instrument that promised an adequate appraisal of mentality, temperament, and personality on the basis of an hour's interview with a psychologist.

Meanwhile, the presiding officer forgot to sound his bell and at the end of half an hour, having said all I wanted to, I sat down to a buzz of conversation and a small barrage of questions. A little later the session was adjourned, but I was immediately surrounded with a group of people eager to make further queries. Among them Professor Green of Sheffield University in England asked for my paper to be sent him for publication in the *Journal of Experimental Pedagogy,* of which he was editor. My head was swimming; I was so elated. I really did not know what had happened to me. Then the bombshell fell. Dr. J. A. Leach, an inspector of schools and a first-class ornithologist but an indifferent educator, bustled up to the group surrounding me, a bundle of mazes in his hand.

"Porteus," he said, "did you say that these tests examine planning, foresight, and mental alertness?"

"Yes," I cheerfully admitted, "I did."

"Well, I've just given them to the Vice-Chancellor of this University and he could barely pass at a twelve-year-level!"

From my temporary throne in the clouds I wished for a hole in the ground to open up where I could hide from view. Never was anyone deflated so thoroughly. The faces in the group about me looked blank, but none offered me concealment or sympathy. Then a lady at my elbow spoke up.

"Did you say twelve years?" she asked.

"Yes," said Leach triumphantly, "only twelve years."

"Well, I am surprised," she remarked. "Personally, I would have put his potential score at about ten years."

"You see," she explained to the group, "I happen to be the Vice-Chancellor's wife. No doubt he can run the University very well, but in all practical home matters I must do all the planning. If I didn't, we could arrive at the railway station to set off for our vacation without the money for our tickets, no hotel reservations, and the like."

"Dr. Porteus," she added, "I think your test is wonderful. My husband would, I believe, agree."

I had no chance to disclaim the doctoral title, for suddenly my parachute had opened and I floated gently down to earth.

Professor Smyth was so delighted that I believe he forgot the brush-off he had suffered, and the neglect with which his carefully prepared description of pioneer educational policies in a new country had been so discourteously received.

At a downtown restaurant, where I knew I could certainly not afford to eat, Frank Tate as Director of Education was entertaining a bunch of bigwigs, but he left his table to shake my hand in congratulation, assuring me at the same time that any support I needed for further research was mine for the asking. I have no idea what I ate for lunch nor what it cost, but I then and there declared a half-holiday, caught the train home and spent the rest of the day and half the night boasting to my wife. Her one regret was that she had missed the lunch but accepted the idea that next month, after our check came in, we would do our celebrating all over again.

As previously mentioned, I had been rather dubious about the standardization and interpretation of the tests arranged for young children, and in 1917 I was greatly encouraged by a published evaluation of their usefulness. This was written by E. R. Shaw in an American journal, *The Kindergarten and First Grade*, and stated:

> A surprisingly correct view of individual differences can be gained through such a test. The slow child who habitually leaves his work half-done, the child who is prone to misunderstand spoken directions, the child who makes careless mistakes but quickly corrects them himself, the child who improves with practice, the child who tires or loses interest and hence does worse instead of better in a second trial —all these and many more types that we all know, reveal their everyday traits in this five-minute test as clearly as in a year's work.

CHAPTER 4

Brains and Education

ANOTHER visitor at Bell Street was Dr. R. J. A. Berry, Professor of Anatomy at Melbourne University, who had become greatly interested—perhaps overinterested—in the possible relation between the size of the brain and intelligence. Berry was an excellent teacher, though lacking the brilliance of my later friend and collaborator, Professor Frederic Wood Jones. Incidentally, Berry was a small man with iron-grey hair—and a large head.

Some of his medical confreres must have told Berry about the occurrence of small-headed or microcephalic imbeciles and advised him to consult me as the most likely source of information on such cases. Several visits to my clinic ensued, at which he acted as observer while I carried out mental examinations. Then he made a surprising proposal. It seemed that he had at his disposal a position designated as "Government Scholar in Anatomy." It had not been filled because no funds were on hand to support the scholarship. He suggested that, if I would shift my headquarters to the University, he would set aside a room for my exclusive use in his Anatomy Department and would offer me every facility, including the right to attend all his lectures and do all dissections just as if I were a medical student, with the important difference that I would be, to use his phrase, "in on the ground floor."

Berry had established an excellent anatomical museum noted for the illustrative material he used in teaching. The museum also had an anthropological extension filled with skulls, most of them of aborigines. What was more important, he had a fine library, and what was called a "Millionaire calculating machine." The Melbourne *Herald,* an evening newspaper, had given him a small grant to set up what he called a Laboratory of Educational Anthropology, and since titles were easy, I would be Co-director. He explained that there would be no salary but also no set duties, only unlimited opportunities for research.

"Porteus," he told me earnestly, "you don't belong down here. You are wasting your time and talents on the feebleminded. Come in with me and we'll do something worth while. That test of yours looks fine, but what it needs is a solid backing of research."

I was naturally, as an impressionable young man, greatly flattered—but I had a living to earn.

"What about my position at Bell Street under the Education Department?" I enquired.

"No trouble at all," he assured me. "I'll go down tomorrow and see Frank Tate. He's on the University Control Board and I think I can persuade him to have you seconded in your Bell Street position and set you free for research."

Next day he rang, asking me to call at the University. He met me, all smiles.

"I had to use no persuasion at all," he told me. "For some reason you appear to be Tate's white-haired boy. He agreed without objection to my idea that some one else can deal with the feebleminded provided that you can give general supervision. He seemed to be quite pleased with the idea of the two of us working together. Perhaps you didn't know that his son is doing medicine, and he was careful to mention the fact, of course very, very casually. In any case, you seem to stand very well with him. I think he regards you as his personal discovery, and would promise you the moon. A lot of us at the University doubt that he has it in his gift, but Frank wouldn't admit it."

So in a little while I was embarked on a full program of research. With medical students as assistants, I was kept busy measuring heads by the hundred, for Berry's plan was to map the course of brain development from infancy to maturity. I was somewhat doubtful as to how this information, when gathered, could be applied, but human growth of any kind was worth investigating. Problems of spurts and plateaus in development were especially interesting to me. British scientists such as Karl Pearson, and American workers like Whipple, Doll, and Boas were at work in this field.

Meanwhile, Mr. Tate was even better than his word. Not only was a man appointed to carry on at Bell Street under my supervision, but two assistants were allotted to me for research purposes. I at once proceeded with their training and set them to work gathering data on normal performance in the Binet and the Porteus Maze, my goal being the tabulation of results on one thousand school children. About a year later, Professor Smyth, influenced no doubt by the fact that the work at Bell Street was already closely related to courses being given at Teachers' College, offered me a position on the University staff as lecturer in Experimental Education. Since this would automatically give me not only M.A. status, but the free use of the general library and other privileges, I at once accepted. This brought me into close contact with a group of mature students, among them K. S. Cunningham, who after the war obtained his doctor's degree from Columbia and returned to Australia to organize the Australian Committee on Educational Research. Coincidentally, Dr. Cunningham along with Professors Norman Munn, Roger Russell, Dr. Phillips, and myself were elected in 1966 as the first five honorary members of the Psychological Association of Australia, now independent of its parent organization, the British Association.

So it came to pass that I was soon running my own three-ring circus. I was either lecturing or listening, protesting or dissecting, and in between, directing my own research and self-selected education. Berry's assistant, old Preston as he was affectionately called, was photographer, handy man, distributor of parts (for dissection), formalin injector (of cadavers), and confidant of a rising generation of doctors. He took me under his wing and loaded me with advice. Unfortunately, he had become so involved in his circumlocutions, so used to wrapping up the facts with hints, winks, and innuendoes that half the time I did not know what he was trying to impart. I cannot say whether his advice was good or bad. Meanwhile, I can evade the question as to how adequate that self-elected education was. In Australia, 55 years ago, it was all that was available for my own special purposes. The citation for the fellowship previously mentioned stated the fact that I was "probably the first practising psychologist in Australia." Certainly there was no one to whom I could go for instruction.

Had I been interested, I could have gained inside knowledge of the private lives and peccadilloes of half the University staff, and, willy-nilly, I found myself privy to all the professorial feuds on the campus. Also I learned the peculiar lecturing and working habits of professors in general, and also what the students thought of them. Sometimes animosities spilled over into the classrooms. The professor of anatomy had been known to allude to the professor of physiology as "that ethereal bugger," who effectively countered with "my *learned* colleague the great anatomist."

As I believe is the case in all medical schools, there was keen competition for human parts to dissect. In spite of the fact that there were no two-headed cadavers and that complete brains were in short supply, I had all the cerebra I had time to dissect. Whatever Berry's faults, his anatomy lectures were so clearly presented that if anybody failed to learn it was entirely his own fault. After I had got used to the drastic change from the atmosphere of the classroom to that of the dissecting theater, I learned quite readily. Fortunately, being by definition an outsider, I was able to keep a foot in both the physiology and anatomy camps. One other thing I learned was the impersonal attitude to the human body that familiarity with the naked dead engenders.

The reader may note that I bracketed together dissecting and protesting. Anatomy was so obviously a descriptive rather than an interpretative science that as soon as anatomists stepped over into the field of anthropology, where free-floating generalizations were common, they were on uncertain territory. That was the day when cranial indices were considered crucial in a number of problems—racial relationships, achievement (scientific and otherwise), and even fighting ability. Wars had, so it seemed, pitted narrow-headed (dolichocephalic) against broad-headed (brachycephalic) peoples, yet this division seemed to be more geographical than anatomical in basis. This equating of achievement with physical characters was a most attractive game for thinkers who lacked the disciplinary control of sufficient facts. Psychologists were just swinging toward quantitative approaches, and were beginning to talk of measures of reliability as applied to those figures. Conclusions re the Esquimaux, based, for example, on measurements of eleven skulls were being questioned. In short, the day of the Harvard anthropometric authority, who could survey a series of Hawaiian skulls and from the indices come up with statements as to their racial origin and relationships with other peoples, was about over.

The generalization that there was a relation between size of brain and intelligence had some biological facts on its side that could sound quite convincing if the negative instances were disregarded. It was true that prehistoric skulls from *Pithecanthropus erectus* upwards showed that along with increasing brain capacity went progress toward *Homo sapiens* status and development in civilization. More than that, it seemed to be fairly true that as these peoples became larger-headed they also became more "sapienter." For example, the negro race was predominantly narrower and smaller-headed than the self-styled Aryans. Australian aborigines, too, had small heads, but whether that had any effect on their low cultural level was at that time unprovable. Like the Anglo-Saxons, they were also among the long and narrow-headed. Ancient Cro-magnon people were much larger-headed than the Neanderthals, but the conclusion that this was related to their contributions to progress was founded on an uncertain assumption. How did we know that the Cromagnons were that much smarter? Esquimau people were reported to be big-headed, but the evidence even on that point was dubious. It didn't seem to be particularly smart of them to live where they do. Obviously, what was true of the mass might also not apply to the individual.

So I soon found myself merely the brake on the senior author's wagon. Thus I repeated my bike-riding experience, with the important difference that I could not dismount when the speed became excessive. As a brake I was ineffective. The faster Berry went down hill, the louder I squealed, but squealing merely advertised the fact that the brakes were defective.

This much I can offer in my colleague's support. We had measured approximately 10,000 heads, 200 of whom were in the extremes of brain size. I then proceeded to compare them mentally. I found that of those in the large-headed extremes, 25 per cent were above average in tested intelligence, whereas only 5 per cent of the small-headed were in that category. On the other hand, only 14 per cent of the large-headed (macrocephalic) were mentally inferior as against 50 per cent of the microcephalic.

We had to leave it at that, and as Berry was large-headed and I small-headed, both of us were content.

One other study should be mentioned, for I believe it had,

later on, a decided bearing on my managing to impress another anatomist when this was of crucial importance to me personally.

Head measurements were, of course, not brain measurements, and Lee's formula 14 tried to compensate for thickness of skull and scalp by making a standard deduction when trying to convert head size into brain capacity. One of the first things Berry suggested was that I test Lee's formula. Dr. Alice Lee, by the way, was a co-worker of Karl Pearson in London.

So for a time I worked on old-time methods of arriving at skull capacities by filling them with shot, dried peas, sand, etc., and then measuring the cubic capacity of the filling material. This was then compared with the figure obtained by using Lee's formula 14, by which 11 millimetres were indiscriminately subtracted from head length, breadth, and height. I still remember the formula: Length − 11, Breadth − 11, Height − 11 × .000337 + 406 c.c. This seemed to me a very haphazard approximation, but that was not the main trouble. There was no satisfactory reliability in repeated experiments, no matter what filling material we used in the skull. Damp sand gave the best approach to uniformity, but that also was extremely variable. It was difficult indeed to pack a skull with any kind of measurable material.

I then became associated in this work with a medical colleague, Dr. A. W. D. Robertson, and together we decided that if we could secure fresh brains before injection with formalin (which changed their specific gravity), remove them from the skulls and determine the volume of water displacement, we could test the formula. With the cooperation of the City Coroner and the Melbourne Hospital, we obtained access to all unclaimed bodies. Since time for various reasons was indeed of the essence of the matter, we both became very adept at the post-mortem method of removing the brain by sawing through the skull along the standard line of dissection of the scalp, lifting up the skull cap and cutting the brain stem. Suspended by a string, the brain was then carefully lowered into a full glass container and the overflow measured. Over a period of almost two years, we accumulated a series of over thirty brains. It was a very unpleasant job. The work was left unfinished when I departed for America, but at that point the average error of Lee's formula 14 was about 9 per cent. When I was at the Vineland Laboratory, I continued some experimental work, using material lent me by the Wistar Institute of Anatomy in Philadelphia, and this could well have resulted in my taking an involuntary dip in the ocean.

The brother-in-law of one of my Vineland friends was program chairman of the Kiwanis Club at Atlantic City, and one day he rang me in great distress. Would I help him by taking at instant notice the place of the noon-day speaker, who had suddenly found himself unable to fulfill his engagement?

"But I haven't the slightest idea of what I could talk about," I objected, "and I'm a very busy man, with no time to prepare a talk."

"What are you busy at?"

"Well," I said, "at the moment I'm playing around with some skulls trying to find out something about the brains that once inhabited them."

"Fine!" said my caller. "Tell the Kiwanis members all about the job. I'll bet they've never heard anything like that before. They don't know a scull from a skiff. I'll pick you and your skulls up in fifteen minutes."

There was no help for it. An hour and a half later I was seated at the speakers' table on a raised dais, looking down on an assemblage of about three hundred of the Kiwanis brethren, engaged noisily with their soup. I was used by then to a Rotary Club gathering, with its good fellowship, foolish songs, noisy talk, and good-natured laughter. I noted the sudden pause in soup ladling and a different buzz to the conversation when I opened my handbag and placed a white skull beside my plate.

Announcements and introductions over, I rose to my feet.

"Gentlemen," I began, "I have been brought, somewhat against my will, to tell you in some detail what I am doing with this and other human skulls. I thought it might be interesting to you to know what a scientist can tell about the one-time owner of this skull, who and what he or she was, where he or she lived and when. You will have, I am sure, some great surprises, but I will guarantee that what I have to tell are facts, and, moreover, at the end I shall tell you exactly how I know them to be facts. Science, you see, has no secrets. To begin with, the owner was a woman."

With that, I talked awhile about the smaller average head size, the finer bone structure of the lower jaw, and about the difficulty I should have had in sexing the skull if the individual had been a young male, etc. I looked carefully at the teeth and announced:

"No difficulty here about the age. She was about 75 years old when she died." Then I talked awhile about the grinding down of molars, the closing of the skull sutures after the need for keeping them open to allow of brain growth had ceased. With the practice of having personally measured 10,000 heads, I was able to estimate within a few millimetres the length, breadth, and height of the skull cap, wrote the formula on a blackboard, produced my slide rule and worked out for them the cubic capacity of the brain by Lee's formula, which, if I remember correctly, was about 1300 c.c.

By this time, watching a scientist at work was so engrossing that the ice-cream was melting and the coffee growing cold. Three hundred pairs of eyes followed my every move and their owners listened avidly while I threw in a little data about comparative brain size.

"But now," I said, "come some of the surprises I promised you. I can even tell you some of the things this woman was thinking about in her last years."

This time there was more than a buzz of disbelief. I quickly calculated her cranial index (the ratio of head breadth to head length) and threw in a little patter about the cranial indices of racial groups.

"So," I said, "I believe that she was a French Canadian. This skull has been out of her body over eighty years and that means she was born 160 years ago, or about 1765, some years before the American Revolution. It does not take much of a guess to say that she was interested in what was happening across the border. All Canadians were concerned, and you can be sure, if you know French Canadians, that they talked about it a blue streak."

That I got by with, but there was more derision than amazement when after another close look at the skull, I announced: "She was married and had five children." By this time it began to dawn on my audience that they were being taken for a chair ride along the Atlantic City Boardwalk.

When the laughter died down, I reminded them of my introduction: "But I told you that I would inform you exactly how I discovered these facts, for facts they are. You see, science does have no secrets. Gentlemen, I read it all in the Museum catalogue at Wistar Institute of Anatomy where this skull belongs. This merely goes to show you that any individual who can read a museum catalogue will know more about the one-time owner of a skull than a scientist can discover if he relies solely on his science."

I really believe that if a motion had been proposed that I be carried out and thrown into the sea from the Steel Pier, where the lunch was being held, it would have carried with only one dissenting voice.

But this anecdote is ahead of my story. By June 1915 my tests had been fairly launched in both England and America in Professor Green's *Journal of Experimental Pedagogy*, and the *American Journal of Psycho-Asthenics*. There were slight variations in the two reports. At that time the Binet Scale had attained such vogue that it served as a touchstone of validity for any newly proposed measure of intelligence. I also followed the pattern. So each article showed the case-by-case levels in both the Maze and Binet, the group reported in the British journal numbering 92 defectives, those in the American publication 120 cases. The graphs showed that the Maze gave somewhat higher test ages throughout, with the differences widening at the higher age levels. These superior scores for reputed defectives did not worry me unduly as I thought it important for the feebleminded to appear in the most favorable light, and thus increase the chances of children at Binet borderline levels of escaping the stigma of feeblemindedness and possibly commitment to institutions for life.

Nonetheless, the close relation of the two measures was important, the British journal article rather triumphantly disclosing that in 69 per cent of cases the two scores were within a year of each other. Not until later was I bold enough to claim that the Maze verdict should stand on its own feet as a measure of abilities not examined by the Binet. The two measures might correlate rather closely, but the Maze had its own independent validity—in short, both verdicts should be given equal weight in diagnosis. This contention is now well validated and widely accepted. Meanwhile, the small differences between the two scores invested the Maze with an aura of respectability. Though I did not know it, through these and other articles my way to America was being smoothed. In 1917, I had extended my interest beyond the mental defectives to what was then considered to be a closely related problem, juvenile delinquency. An article in the *American Psychological Review* reported briefly several rather important studies. One of these concerned inmates of the Burwood Boys' Home, many of whom had delinquent records. At that time the social effects of mental dullness were not clearly understood, and as a consequence some of the boys were, at the best, borderline defectives. A group of 22 cases tested only 2 years 4 months below their chronological age. Another 20 cases examined at the Royal Park Reformatory for confirmed delinquents showed a five-year deficiency of Maze scores compared with their average chronological age of 15 years. Some of this group were definitely feebleminded. One had decapitated a hunting companion with an axe because of some unimportant disagreement. At this time, too, there was technical uncertainty as to what was to be taken as the test average. The fifteen-year level that I had used was undoubtedly too high, and so the deficiency in test age development was exaggerated for the older boys.

This tendency to lump together delinquents and defectives was an expression of the belief, very common at the time, that feeblemindedness was the "root cause" of all social insufficiency. In 1912, when Goddard published his startling *Kallikak Family*, this idea was almost unquestionably accepted. Hence, when poorly trained social workers were gathering data for Goddard on descendants of a reputedly feebleminded girl and a Revolutionary officer, any social dereliction, such as horse stealing, prostitution, having illegitimate children, chronic unemployment, alcoholism, etc., was considered proof that the individual concerned was mentally defective, and was so classified on the Kallikak family tree. The result was that it was loaded with black squares and circles denoting "feebleminded," leading to the conclusion that heredity was the determining factor in mental defect.

It was a most impressive demonstration, and Australians, including Berry, were fully convinced that if legislative action could stop the propagation of such cases, a host of social problems would be solved. When I discovered later that only a very few of the Kallikak children had been given mental tests, I was very dubious about this conclusion. However, I was undoubtedly overimpressed by Goddard's authority. It was not until the publication of Healy's book, *The Individual Delinquent,* that serious doubts arose with regard to considering mental defect to be a main causative factor. Though the Maze results did not give Goddard's theories as definite support as did the Binet, they certainly warranted the conclusion that temperamental weaknesses, such as impulsivity, were largely to blame for social maladjustment. This demonstration certainly was a factor in my later invitation to go to America to carry on further research.

In the *American Psychological Review* article mentioned above, I also reported an initial study in a field that was ultimately to become one of my major life interests. It was important because at that time no one else except Woodworth and to some extent the members of the Cambridge Anthropological Expedition to northern Australia had shown any real concern with measuring the mental abilities of primitive peoples. In 1904, Woodworth had used the opportunity to test, mainly with the Seguin Form Board, some varied ethnic specimens gathered together for exhibition and study in the Chicago Exposition. Also in 1904, the Cambridge Expedition, which included men such as Rivers, Seligman, McDougall, and Myers, reported some studies, but their observations of Torres Strait islanders were physiological rather than psychological, and their subjects were not typical aborigines.

In 1915, I had been invited by the South Australian government to visit that state and in conjunction with Dr. Gertrude Halley, medical officer of the Adelaide Education Department, to report on the work of the Minda Home, an institution for mental defectives. As I had expressed interest in the aborigines, a visit was arranged to a government station at Point McLeay Mission near the mouth of the Murray River. The results, which were reported in the *Review* article, showed that the children, mainly half-castes at the Mission school, were at about the Maze Test level of white children, with some tendency to fall behind at the upper age levels. Further results were also reported for deaf children.

Meanwhile, work was proceeding with the standardization of the Maze with large groups, one of 1,000 school children, followed up by another group of 1,250. At that time, investigations with such large groups were rare.

During 1915 I entered into correspondence with Professor Lewis Terman of Stanford University, and he very kindly sent me in advance of publication the text of his Stanford Revision of the Binet, an obvious improvement on the Goddard form. This gave me an opportunity to apply Terman's revision to large groups of Australian children. In 1918, the *Journal of Educational Psychology* published my results under the title "The Measurement of Intelligence: Six Hundred and Fifty-Three Children Examined by the Binet and Porteus Tests." This number included 200 defectives, 190 normals tested by the Goddard Scale, and 263 by the Terman.

Tables also showed results with delinquents, and with the deaf, the effects of repetition of the Mazes after a year's interval (47 cases), and where errors occurred throughout the series in 100 normal children. Boys were shown to score better than girls of equal age, indicating small but constant differences. Maze changes after a year's interval were found to be irregular, and this apparent low reliability was due to the fact that the test itself was measuring the ability to profit by practice and that this varied in different individuals. This should have led to the conclusion that the ordinary coefficient of reliability, which reflects the tendency to make near-uniform changes, was not really applicable. However, this view was not generally recognized for many years, and occasionally some young worker will still come up with the discovery that the coefficient of test-retest reliability for the Maze is low, ignoring altogether the fact that if the test measured what it was supposed to measure, namely differences in ability to improve with practice, the coefficient should not be high.

The samples of cases mentioned above were, as previously mentioned, very large for that time, and are cited by way of illustrating the fact that by 1918 the Maze tests were already known in America and England and were in use in such unlikely places as Portugal, the Netherlands, and South Africa. Nevertheless, I was astonished to receive a ring from the Registrar's office in August, 1918, to say that there was a cablegram for me from America. It said simply, "Would you accept one year's appointment to the research department here. Letter follows." This was signed by E. R. Johnstone, Director of the famous Vineland Training School.

I caught the first train home, walked in and announced to my wife: "We're going to America!"

By that time she was getting used to surprises, and in any case adopted a matter-of-fact attitude to my rather grandiose plans, so she merely said calmly:

"Is that so? When?"

However, all was not that simple. The letter when it arrived spelled out the details of the offer in the following very moderate terms:

> I have been able to get the plans through, at least to the extent of offering you $2,000 and a year's engagement. I am not now able to make plans beyond that point. If you come alone, we can accommodate you at the Training School; if you bring your family, it will be advisable to live in Vineland, which would of course add greatly to your expense. From the institution standpoint, there is no objection to your living off the grounds. Dr. Goddard did this while he was with us.

This, I believe, was the first intimation I had received that Dr. Goddard was no longer head of the Vineland Laboratory. As to plans for work, Johnstone wrote:

> I do not want to lay down any requirements that may hamper you . . . but I should like your line of research, whatever it may be, to connect as closely as possible with that being carried on by our men at Wistar Institute of Anatomy. Two men there are now occupied—the one with the morphology, the other with the chemistry of the brain, using our clinical material.
>
> I am looking forward with a great deal of pleasure and expectation to having you with us, and I am sure it will be of mutual help and benefit. Dr. Goddard and Mr. Doll are both delighted and will probably write you.

Reading between the lines this seemed like an offer of a free hand for research. To be sure, $2,000 was rather a shoestring proposition, but as money was in those days, it was a fairly stout string. In any case, things like salary seemed to me of minor importance compared with the chance of having a year in America.

My wife and I put our heads together, consulted my wife's people, and found that they had no objection to my parking my family with them for a year. We decided further that if we sold our furniture and let our house, the receipts would about cover my travelling expenses. So I accepted. An exchange of letters followed, and I received congratulatory word from various people in the States, among them letters from Goddard and Doll and one from Dr. Harold Williams, professor at U.C.L.A. and psychologist at the Nelles School for delinquents at Riverside, asking me to lecture in Los Angeles and to stay with him and Mrs. Williams while in California.

But I was still at a loss to figure out where Dr. Goddard fitted into the picture. It took me almost two years to piece together the whole story. That must wait for the next chapter.

CHAPTER 5

Learning from the Feebleminded

THE VINELAND setup was peculiar. The Research Department, housed in a special laboratory building, differed in one important aspect from the rest of the Training School; it was supported by special funds donated by Samuel Fels, the well-known philanthropist from Philadelphia. He was also a large contributor to the research work of the Wistar Institute of Anatomy. As far as the Training School was concerned, he made it clear that his sole interest was research. His concern with the feebleminded was not with their training and welfare, but as he frankly put it—in getting them off the earth.

About 1905, I believe, there had been a meeting at Vineland of educators, medical men, and scientists, members of what was rather facetiously called the Feebleminded Club. Earl Barnes, noted educator, and Dr. H. H. Goddard, psychologist at State College, Westchester County, New York, were two of the members. Goddard addressed the group and put forward his view that scientific investigators were neglecting a wonderful opportunity to study human development by focussing attention on the mentally defective. He used the parallel of the advantage of observing a slow freight passing along a railway line in contrast with an express train. Its very slowness offered a chance to see how it was made up and what it carried. The express, on the other hand, went too fast for accurate study, and that was analogous to the rate of development in normal children. Mental progress in the defective child was so painfully slow that a psychologist might learn a lot by its systematic observation.

Someone in the group challenged him. "If that is so, Goddard, why don't you do it?"

"I couldn't afford it," was the reply. "I am dependent on my position at Westchester."

"Would you do it if you had the funds?" asked Fels.

When Goddard answered affirmatively, Fels said: "I will pay for setting up a Research Department here under your direction and support it just as long as you can present a satisfactory program of work."

Someone suggested that a committee be formed consisting of Fels, Dr. M. Greenman, Director of Wistar Institute of Anatomy, and E. R. Johnstone, Director of the Vineland Training School. Fels at once accepted with the understanding that the Training School as an institution should lie outside his sphere of interest. He would meet quarterly with Goddard and Johnstone, who were to be responsible for drawing up for approval the program of research. He also indicated that his contributions would be made four times a year and that continuance from year to year would be dependent on results.

As one of America's leading soap manufacturers, Fels was a hard-headed business man. His support was most generous, but he never visited the institution. The committee came to the mountain to report to Mahomet, who stayed at home. Goddard's first project was to visit Europe, where Binet was at work on the problem of the recognition of the mentally defective.

If I were asked to nominate the forgotten man in American psychology, I would suggest Goddard's name. The Vineland Committee had no idea of what kind of a snowball they had set rolling downhill, or that it would develop into an avalanche that, for a time, almost buried psychology. I do not know whether the two men ever met, but Goddard was the one who introduced Binet's work to America and so to the world. Goddard, however, did visit Decroly and Degand in their Belgian laboratory, where they were experimenting with the new tests. Goddard recognized the potential usefulness of these tests, brought them back to Vineland in translated form, applied them to the inmates, then to normals, and adapted them for American use. Departments of psychology at universities were almost wholly experimental in those days, with a strong "brass-instrument" orientation. Goddard brought psychology down to earth, applying it to nationwide problems, and soon Vineland's research department became a Mecca to which all faces turned. Terman, for his work in 1916 and for many years afterwards, has been adequately recognized, but Goddard, the pioneer in this field, has been ignored by the chroniclers. The American Psychological Association has, as far as I know, never made any public recognition of the debt their profession owes to Goddard. Possibly if his work had been identified with a university instead of a school for the feebleminded, the case might have stood differently. It may be that academic psychologists believed that he had stolen their private thunder, but no one between the years 1912 and 1918 could have failed to hear its reverberations, for they literally circled the earth. It has probably been forgotten that it was at Vineland that the committee met which devised or adapted the Army Alpha and Beta Tests. It was not a case of the mountain laboring and bringing forth a mouse. The progeny was rather a mastodon, which left great tracks visible to this day. Krakatoa is still remembered for its violent eruption, and it took fifteen years, I believe, before its dust subsided. The eruption that Goddard caused is now buried in its own dust.

For those interested in the history of psychology in the United States, it might be advisable to add a footnote outlining briefly its development at the time when I entered the field. It was a period of greatly increasing social awareness. The era ushered in by the new century was still dominated by German psychologists, such as Wundt, who mainly through Titchener had extended his influence to America. It has rather appropriately been called the age of psychological instrumentation. But suddenly the brass was no longer brightly polished. Just outside the laboratory doors lay a welter of human problems—mental and social maladjustment, in individual terms the feebleminded, the delinquent, the industrially incompetent, the confused adolescent—and for these the universities of the day offered but little help. Whatever was being done was done outside the academic walls. The big names were Cattell, G. Stanley Hall, Binet, Goddard, Cyril Burt, Woodworth, Whipple, Terman. Psychological clinics were indeed rare, for the number of clinical psychologists capable of staffing them was small. One of the earliest reports by Witmer, dealing with progress in training a "backward" boy, had been published at the University of Pennsylvania. Witmer's work, like that of Montessori, suffered from too great optimism in exaggerating the therapeutic results of intensive training of alleged defectives. At any rate, I found it impossible to match his success with individual cases. Probably the degree of "backwardness" had been over-estimated in both Witmer's and Goddard's cases.

By 1918, four years had passed since the publication of *The Kallikak Family,* years that had been rewarding in terms of publicity for Goddard and the Training School. This small volume had been followed by a much larger book, *Feeblemindedness: Its Causes and Consequences.* The response across the country was remarkable. Some state legislatures hastened to set up the legal machinery to bring about the sterilization of defectives. The first step had been over-confidently taken toward attacking the evil at its source. More than this, public interest had been aroused, and institutions for the welfare of mentally handicapped children had sprung up in various parts of the country. The use of mental tests spread like wildfire. Suddenly people were awakened to the fact that the number of defectives was much greater than anyone had believed possible. The use of the new intelligence quotient, or IQ as it was called, made possible, so it was believed, the quick determination of comparative mental status. All that was needed was to apply the Binet tests, work out the relation of chronological to mental age, and diagnosis was easy. If an individual had made less than three-quarters of the average progress in mental development, he was judged feebleminded and handicapped for life. Social data, hastily gathered, came flooding in, supporting the view that mental defect was indeed the nation's most ubiquitous problem. Examination of inmates of "houses of refuge," committed for prostitution, or groups of illegitimate children, showed a horrifying percentage of cases below the bar sinister, now reduced to 70 IQ. Similar surveys of corrective institutions repeated the story. Invasion of the schools by educational psychologists, many of them inexperienced in the pitfalls that attended mental test devising and procedures, showed an alarming percentage of very dull children. The estimates of the incidence of mental defect rose from a very modest one-half of one per cent to two per cent, and later to as high as six per cent. Nowadays, the careless use of the term "mental retardation," without any definition of its meaning or degree, has again resulted in greatly exaggerated estimates of its incidence.

The wholesale application of the Army Tests to hundreds of thousands of recruits during America's World War I effort showed an unbelievably large segment of the population, particularly rural draftees, to be sub-standard to a serious degree. Throughout the country controversy raged. Through the columns of *The Nation*, Professor Terman and Walter Lippmann carried on a long and sometimes bitter discussion of the interpretation of the Army Test scores. It came as a profound shock to find that the general application of the Stanford Revision of the Binet would have classified about one-third of the white draft below IQ 75, and therefore, by then prevalent standards, to be *feebleminded*.[1] That would indeed have meant a national blight, if true. Fortunately, that interpretation was ill-founded. The Binet scale and the Army Tests were undeserving of such diagnostic trust.

About 1917, doubts began to creep in regarding the validity of the evidence gathered for Goddard, on which he based his book *The Kallikak Family*. It is quite possible that Dr. Greenman was one of those who decided Goddard's findings were both too good and too bad to be true; the descendants of the Revolutionary officer through marriage with a woman of his own social class included *no* feebleminded as compared with the terrific load of mental defectives that hung from the limbs of the Kallikak family tree. Up to this point the majority of the informed public had accepted the Kallikak demonstration.

Whether Greenman communicated his doubts to Fels cannot now be proved, but when an invitation came to Goddard to head the newly established Bureau of Juvenile Research in Ohio, an offer carrying with it the then princely salary of $7,500 a year, this demand for his services was no great surprise. That came when Goddard laid the flattering proposal in the Vineland Committee's lap. Instead of meeting those terms, as he no doubt expected they would, Greenman and Fels congratulated him on the honor and suggested that he accept. To clinch matters, they asked him to select a suitable man to take his position as director of research.

The rest of the story must be filled in mainly by conjectures on my part. As my theories shed no particular glory on myself, perhaps they may be considered acceptable.

I assume that it may have helped Goddard's self-esteem to foster the idea that the Committee would have to go to the ends of the earth to find a man to take his place. I do know that Johnstone, like everyone else who knew Goddard well, was deeply

[1] See Milton S. Gurvitz, "Intelligence Test Standardization." *The Encyclopedia of Psychology,* 1st edition, p. 286.

disappointed at his imminent departure. It may also have occurred to him that an offer to me of $2,000 a year would be turned down promptly, and that even double that salary would not attract anyone else with decent qualifications. A stop-gap appointment would allow the dust to settle, and perhaps Mr. Fels might change his attitude. Any arrangement that would make it possible for the laboratory to continue was better than nothing.

Meanwhile, Goddard had accepted the Ohio offer and departed. Perhaps Johnstone thought I would refuse, which would still leave the matter open, but if the host was lukewarm, he was reckoning without a very willing guest. Once the Committee had approved my appointment, he could only pray that matters would turn out all right. In any case, Dr. Greenman seemed pleased with my coming, for in another letter Johnstone said: "I am taking the liberty of publishing in our little Bulletin, which comes out monthly, your paper from the *Australian Medical Journal.* I wanted to make some mention of your coming, and thought this might well go with it."

It so happened that the Rockefeller Fund was supporting medical research on hookworm, and Dr. J. H. Waite, who had been sent out to North Queensland, had applied both the Binet and the Porteus Maze to measure the extent of the retardation that resulted from the infestation. This had been published in 1918 in the *Australian Medical Journal.* I had also attended Dr. Waite's lecture on his experiences given at the Melbourne Anatomy Department, and the personal appearance of the author of one of the tests relied upon may have helped. Possibly I might be just what the doctor ordered.

It looked as if some cross-currents were involved, for no sooner had I arrived than Johnstone informed me that by some strange mistake on the part of a stenographer my salary had been misstated as $2,000 instead of $3,000, to be paid from the date of my departure from Australia. He added that Fels, who undoubtedly had talked matters over with Greenman, had been delighted with the prospect of my coming. This surely meant that the cracks in Goddard's position had been quietly widening.

A few weeks after my arrival from Melbourne, we had a dinner at Mr. Fels' house, and I was given a chance to outline my program of research; result, a retroactive raise in my salary to $5,000 and advice from Mr. Fels that I should at once send for my wife and family. Moreover, because of the circumstances, he would for the first time make his contribution for research an annual obligation. Everyone seemed pleased; I was delighted. No matter who else had been lost in the shuffle, I had gained.

Earlier I had learned from a note in a psychological journal that I had been named director to succeed Goddard. I remember also one item of casual conversation that bore unexpected fruit.

Dr. Harold Williams, with whom I stayed in Los Angeles, was enamored of the West, and like all good Angelinos not only talked enthusiastically about California, but showed me a good deal of it. Then came the inevitable question. How did it all impress me?

"Well, Dr. Williams," I said, "I've made up my mind that if anyone in Hawaii or California ever offered me a job for six months, I'd take it."

That chance remark led to a forty-year stay in the Islands, where this is being penned. Life has stored up for me some strange turns, and this was one. In California I had been flattered to find that my name was not unknown, and I received a very warm welcome from Professors Warner Brown at Berkeley and Lewis Terman at Stanford, both of whom remained my friends for life. On my return to the Vineland Laboratory from Canada, where I had gone to welcome my family, I was met with the welcome news that at the end of the year I would be paid the same salary as Goddard had been. For the first time I had the feeling that I was really his successor.

As for my financial situation, my pay was the equivalent of the full professor's salary in Australia, and well above the level of that paid to professors in the state universities in the United States.

Ed Johnstone, known to everyone as Professor Johnstone, was a man with extraordinary personal magnetism, plus high intelligence, and unsparing devotion to a cause. This last was the welfare of the mentally deficient. Vineland's institution motto was "Devoted to those whose minds have not developed normally"; its slogan, "Happiness first—all else follows."

With visitors, staff, and even pupils, Ed Johnstone, director of the institution to which the Research Department was attached, labored ceaselessly to instill what he called "the spirit of Vineland." It was akin to what is known in Hawaii as "the Aloha spirit." Like all slogans, it is easy to talk about but difficult to define, and may mean much or little in terms of the social behavior of individuals. But slogans are for utterance, not analysis.

This remarkable man certainly inspired devotion, and he soon realized that loyalty gathers about persons rather than about causes or movements; consequently, Johnstonism became a cult and an extremely well-knit one. The result was that his staff offered more earnest, dedicated, less well-paid service than could be easily imagined. He was the great leader, the veiled prophet, and like Feisal in Arabia, that devotion was in a sense a product of the aridity of his people's personal lives. Any institution is a world unto itself, and sometimes a dull world at that.

The Research Laboratory, shown here about 1925, at the Vineland Training School, New Jersey. The author succeeded Dr. H. H. Goddard as director of research here in 1919.

As a psychologist in residence, I had the privilege, if I wished, of attending the weekly staff meetings. Had I thought of it then, I had before me all the material for a novel of human interaction. There were all kinds of personalities involved, but all diminished by the magnitude of Johnstone's shadow, with eddies and crosscurrents circling around him. The rewards were the occasional "well-done," the individual's punishment, the public confession of responsibility when something did not turn out as well as expected. In consequence, there were cliques and schisms, feuds, love and hate affairs, and a fierce rivalry for the Director's smiles. One of the institution rules was that you could pat anyone on the back but not below the belt. Some of Johnstone's pats, it seemed to me, came perilously close to the foul line. I must say I enjoyed the situation of being a privileged outsider. The institution was indeed a microcosm, but except for its eddies of joys and conflict, it would perhaps have been a monotonous situation.

All this was of great interest to me as an onlooker, but as a matter of self-interest, my cue was to keep up my contacts with the other two members of the triumvirate, Fels and Greenman. As I have already indicated, Fels was a philanthropist, but he had a practical urge to see that he got value for his money. The best way to deal with him, I found, was to keep him thoroughly informed as to the difficulties and complexities as well as the successes of my program. He enjoyed the feeling of being the partner as well as the financial angel in our common enterprise.

Meanwhile, I was seized with the importance of filling a serious gap in the mental-test movement, the woeful lack of any worthwhile external criterion, through which we might discover what mental age meant in terms of social behavior. Vineland seemed to offer a splendid opportunity to answer this question.

Fortunately, in Alice M. Nash, educational and industrial director of the institution, I found an essential collaborator. She not only scheduled an educational program for each inmate, if he were young enough to attend classes, but also assigned all the industrial jobs for those who were older. The central institution, which had been using over 200 acres of land near Vineland, also had recently taken over 400 acres of swamp and undeveloped agricultural territory at Menantico, four miles distant. As Mrs. Nash received weekly reports from instructors on all the inmates, no one knew better than she of their practical progress and abilities. With this store of information at hand, this conventional business of comparing individual scores for diagnostic purposes when we did not know what we were actually measuring seemed to me a sinful waste of time. What we needed was not more testing but more careful research.

As it happened, I came to Vineland with first-hand experience, rare among psychologists, in the handling and training of defectives. Just as I found it of great advantage to be able to talk the language of anatomy and neurology with Dr. Greenman, my knowledge of the frustrations common to the training of the feebleminded helped my standing with Mrs. Nash. Admired, almost venerated as Dr. Goddard was, he was somewhat detached from close contact with his human subjects. With them his observation was clinical and intermittent. In November, 1919, Alice Nash and I put our experiences together in a booklet entitled *Educational Treatment of Defectives,* which had an excellent reception, especially in the United States and Canada.

Hence, I had no difficulty in obtaining Mrs. Nash's wholehearted assistance in the next step—that of making up a social rating scale for defectives, which was essentially a study of their comparative social adjustability. It was obvious that there were more ways in which intelligence could express itself than by performance in mental tests, based mainly on ordinary scholastic abilities. In talking matters over with Fels, I found that as an employer he was greatly interested, not only in his employees' abilities but also in their temperamental traits.

For illustrative purposes, it might be useful to present a brief outline of the steps taken in setting up the social ratings scale. First of all, I gathered from the literature all the terms I could find descriptive of the social behavior of defectives, and by eliminating duplications and vague generalizations, narrowed the list to eleven. Next we set up what we called a general social estimate, which reflected the chances of social adjustment of each inmate, if he were released from institutional supervision. These estimates ranged in a five-point range of social adjustability from excellent to hopeless. Mrs. Nash and the supervisor of cottage life (Ed Arnade) then rated all inmates with regard to the eleven behavioral categories.

Thus we were able on the basis of correlation indices to reduce the list of social traits to seven. Too low coefficients indicated irrelevance, too high that we were measuring the same trait twice. Individual scores were then correlated with the general social estimates. We found, unexpectedly, that while a trait such as disobedience was very frequently observed, its correlation with estimated social adjustability was low. Mrs. Nash and Mr. Arnade, who was the hospital and cottage supervisor, did not give the placid, malleable, irresolute, suggestible type of child as good a chance of returning to the community as the more aggressive child with initiative and self-determination. Such an individual might not be able to avoid delinquency, but his failure would not be due to mental deficiency. The seven traits finally selected for the scale were planfulness, resistance to suggestibility, irresolution, excitability, impulsivity, instability of moods, and obtrusiveness. These were weighted in the scale according to the size of correlations with the general social estimates.

The final step was the correlation of the rating scores of all inmates in the seven traits with the mental tests, and this was left in the capable hands of my assistant, Dr. Marjorie Babcock. Results were reported and discussed in my first book, *Vineland Studies,* which consisted of articles and monographs completed at Vineland and bound together for convenience in a single volume.

It is not particularly pertinent to discuss these results here as they were also treated in detail in *Studies in Mental Deviations*—published in Vineland in 1922—except to emphasize that the wide variation of mental test correlations depended entirely on the sample examined. For example, when the sample consisted of defective males with long institution experience and industrial training, the Maze correlated .7 with social ratings, the Binet only .32. These were temperamentally a very well-stabilized group.

With cases over 14 years of age, the Stanford-Binet correlated .60, the Maze .67. What was most interesting was the fact that when Binet and Porteus scores were pooled and averaged, the correlation rose to .73, proving conclusively that if temperamental and intellectual factors are given equal weight, the combination is the more reliable. Quite obviously, too, estimates of the number of mentally defective persons would be lowered considerably by balancing the high Maze performances against the low Binet scores, supporting my contention that important segments of intelligence were neglected in Binet examinations.

What was important from my personal standpoint was the negligible impact of these findings on psychological practice. Apparently many clinicians were unwilling to modify any procedure with which they had become, by training and experience, familiar. In plain language, they were in what is commonly described as a rut. Psychologists in practice are sometimes very slow learners.

Briefly stated, the situation was that while they decried the lack of external criteria with which to examine the validity of tests, when it *was* available, they neglected to use it. For a profession reportedly founded on and devoted to research, they were most remarkably indifferent to its findings.

This can hardly be excused by the statement that psychologists are now so much better trained and informed than we were in 1922. As we shall see, thirty years later, in 1953, military psychologists were declaring men unfit for basic training in aviation because they failed to pass at a 70% level in a six-hour mental examination. Then Lt. Colonel Jensen, who was in charge of the testing of candidates for basic air training, decided to admit to military service many individuals who had failed the comprehensive psychological examination but had normal performances in the Maze Test. He followed these men's records and found that they did almost as well as those who passed the psychological examination.

By 1922, three full years of work had been completed at Vineland, and I was beginning to feel that I had garnered about all that I could from this experience. Perhaps I felt like Samuel Fels. I knew much more than I had known about the feebleminded, but until science provided new approaches, I doubted whether I saw any clear advances toward the ultimate goal of getting them off the earth.

I did feel, however, that before I moved on to some new phase in my self-selected education, I should make some account of my stewardship. I had published a monograph describing the Maze Test, another under the title of *A Condensed Guide to the Binet Test,* and an article on *Sex Differences in the Maze,* written in collaboration with Dorothy Bassett. But I believed that the Social Rating Scale was my most important contribution to the understanding of personality. I was deeply conscious of my debt to the Training School, and more particularly to Alice Nash. As for Johnstone, I owed him my thanks for the fullest opportunities to do independent research, free from any demands for institution service.

CHAPTER 6

Isles of the Near-blessed

On my journey to America the day spent in Honolulu remained in memory as an exceptionally pleasurable experience. In 1919 there was no Tourists' Bureau, no road around the island, Waikiki was isolated from the rest of Honolulu by duck ponds and taro patches. For one accustomed to the ninety-mile stretches of golden sand to be found in Australia, the beach at Waikiki, of which we had heard and read so much, was a great disappointment, a tiny patch of beauty, but only a patch. But I was completely unused to green valleys tucked away between forested mountains, on the sides of which drifting clouds gathered and dispersed. A tram journey past the University and up Manoa Valley impressed me with its views of houses set well back from the streets, leaving room for almost continuous lawns of smooth, well-tended verdure. This, I thought was spacious living that could naturally become gracious. Looking toward thė upper valley, I was greatly intrigued by the thought of having a green thousand-foot cliff almost in one's backyard.

My rather casual remark to Dr. Williams about my willingness to take a half-year's job in Honolulu or California was merely wishful thinking. It was the kind of thing which was easy to say, seeing that no such chance was ever likely to occur. But once again the lightning struck unexpectedly. A cablegram from President Arthur Dean brought me an invitation to come to Hawaii for a year in order to set up a Psychological and Psychopathic Clinic at the University. And once again I closed my desk at the laboratory, walked across to our house a half-mile away, and announced expansively:

"Start packing! We're going to Honolulu." My wife was coming slowly to the realization that hers was a family in which anything might happen.

The circumstances were indeed unusual. Dr. Arthur Andrews, professor of English, had read with fascination Goddard's *Kallikak Family*, but was horrified to be told how neglect of the problem of the feebleminded threatened to lead the nation to the threshold of ultimate disaster. On a trip back East, he had visited Dr. Fernald's institution at Waverley, Massachusetts, and suffered a second mental vaccination. It seemed to him and his wife, a lady of exceptional resolution and a keen sense of public responsibility, that Hawaii could set the whole nation an object lesson in this matter of taking the timely stitch that in the end could save ninety-nine. The Andrews were filled with missionary zeal, and they gathered together a group of like-minded, transplanted New Englanders, who brought pressure to bear on the local legislature to set up Waimano Home for the Feebleminded and, as auxiliary organizations, a Venereal Clinic and a Psychological and Psychopathic Clinic as well. The prime movers in this effort were not themselves of missionary stock, but this seemed a logical extension of missionary influence.

The story of the arrival in 1820 of the first of several missionary companies who came to Hawaii and their long struggle against rum, sexuality, and the Hawaiian temperament has been told many times, once at least by my own pen. They brought with them round the Horn the Bible, some wonderful cabinets and bureaus, and, by their own admission, thick slices of the "New England conscience." They also imported sewing machines.

The missionary ladies were so shocked at the casual display of native charms that they sold feminine Hawaiian royalty on the idea of an over-modest concealment. Because of the constant starting and stopping action the natives called the new sewing contrivance a holo-ku, or "stop-go" machine, and the name was transferred to the product. With bright colors and a long train it looked like royal attire. But the missionary ladies laid on the modesty a bit too thick, for the holoku concealed *everything*, leaving no clue whatsoever as to what might lie underneath.

In other directions as well, the New England conscience began to operate, and a high degree of public morality was enjoined, extending even to the prohibition of riding horseback on Sundays. The legislators, being mainly Hawaiians, followed along nicely when it came to initiating reforms, but showed considerable disposition to forget their institution completely soon afterwards.

Thus they voted the funds to build Waimano Home, but worried not at all about any reliable methods for assembling those individuals that belonged there. The social workers promptly filled the place with a miscellaneous group of social misfits, delinquents and otherwise. Dr. Andrews and his group decided that there should also be established at the University an examining and diagnostic agency, and Dr. Harold Williams was invited to visit Honolulu from U.C.L.A. to report on the situation. By request, he submitted three names of persons who might fill the directorship and included mine.

I believe that he told the group that it would be very unlikely that I would agree to give up a better job at Vineland to come to Hawaii. The University administrators, like the Legislature, were not too keen on the whole project, but decided that if they set up the plan, by the end of a year everybody would be interested in some other scheme and the whole thing could be quietly forgotten. Hawaii was the one place where social problems, if carefully concealed, really seemed to fade away.

In my case there were several uncertainties that had to be resolved before I could accept Dr. Dean's offer, but an interview with Dr. Greenman smoothed the way. I had been continuously at work at Vineland for three years and had built up the staff by the addition of some competent psychological people. In addition, Dr. George Stephenson had been appointed as psychiatrist. I felt that they could carry on with our research program. Greenman was cooperative, and informed me that he had told the Committee that if Porteus wanted to measure the head of the man in the moon, let him do so.

I quickly came to terms with Hawaii's President Dean. The University would pay my expenses back and forth and I could appoint my own assistant. The Board of Regents proved to be most sympathetic, believing no doubt that the move to establish a University Clinic would furnish some kind of cushion or buffer that would absorb some of the shocks that the New England conscience had suffered. Chief among these had been the statement, now oft repeated, that the sons of the missionaries had forgotten their parents' social and moral purposes and had become too busy making money to bother themselves about the welfare of the Hawaiian society. Here was a chance to demonstrate, by proxy, their own interest in civic affairs. I had little difficulty in persuading influential people that the Clinic's work in various fields would be an outstanding contribution to social welfare. It would help to take the sting out of the oft-repeated charge that the missionaries came to Hawaii to do good and did well.

Actually, the Clinic's program was well ahead of most mainland efforts of its kind. The most pressing problem was educational backwardness. Mental examinations in schools could serve to pinpoint those who were not making normal progress. My assistant, Dr. Babcock, and I made a Binet survey. This showed that even if the verbal tests were modified to suit local conditions, the average intelligence quotient would be very little above 80. Because of the over-emphasis on such findings on the mainland, my policy was to avoid newspaper headlines. This was an easy decision, since we could demonstrate that the use of the Maze Tests, on the contrary, indicated a very normal distribution of scores. I could tell the newspaper reporters, when questioned, that, considering language and other cultural handicaps, Hawaii's school population were doing as well as could be expected. Comparison of the Binet scores showed that the Chinese tended to be slightly ahead, with Japanese, Portuguese, and Hawaiians very close behind. It was evident that language difficulties in general depressed the scores rather evenly.

In the Maze Test, where verbal facility did not count, the average test quotient of mainland white boys (*N* 182) was 99, three points below the Japanese with 102 (*N* 208). We had to use a Vineland public school comparative mean, as in Hawaii we had no middle- or lower-class white industrial groups. Our local population was beginning to break away from plantation labor to infiltrate the skilled and semi-skilled occupations. Chinese males (*N* 200) averaged 95 points in the Maze Test, while Portuguese (*N* 97) had a mean score of 92. A part-Hawaiian group (*N* 95) scored 100 in test quotients. The latest arrivals in the Territory of Hawaii were the Filipinos (*N* 150), who averaged 98 points. Thus it was very evident that ethnic differences, when the measuring rod was least affected by language, were slight, but as has been pointed out in my other publications, this does not mean that they were insignificant. If those differences are consistent, then they may be considered reliable for the purposes of ethnic comparisons, no matter what the coefficient of reliability (so-called) might be. I have argued that, just as in athletic contests, the team that wins consistently is the best, even though the margin of victory may be small.

The immediate result of the finding that the Maze offered a far better chance to demonstrate practical ability was extremely important. It meant that the chances of such cases being committed to the feebleminded Home were greatly reduced. My experience at Vineland had convinced me that from 15 to 20 per cent of the inmates were feebleminded only in relation to their Binet scores. With some training many would have been able to support and manage themselves in the community outside. Unfortunately, residence in an institution was often in itself adduced as evidence of mental deficiency. "If they weren't feebleminded," I was told, "they wouldn't be here."

Moreover, even in the best of institutions (and the Training School was one of the best in the world), it was sometimes easier to get a child enrolled than it was to get him out again. Certain individuals welcomed the discipline and support that an institution afforded, and settled down there quite happily.

Jan Masaryk, who was sent by his father to Vineland for six months, made himself such a nuisance that everyone was glad to be rid of him. Long after, when Jan was representing Czechoslovakia in Washington, he sent a postcard to the laboratory wishing to be remembered to all those at Vineland who did not believe that a Binet examination provided a proper estimate of intelligence. I am happy to say that Jan Masaryk was admitted before I became director of research at the Training School. He was an excellent, if unfortunate, political representative of his country.

At Waimano in Hawaii, once we had weeded out the earliest inmates, there were very few, if any, improper commitments. This may be credited to the use of the Maze as a diagnostic tool. Our reports on cases referred by the social agencies frequently contained the statement that the individual concerned might be a chronic delinquent but was not a mental defective.

As to our mixed ethnic population, if their classification by Binet mental age was unclear, their standing in terms of social adjustment as measured by the Social Ratings Scale was something different. As reported forty years ago, the results are of interest today. These data were fully discussed in a book *Temperament and Race* written in collaboration with Dr. Babcock and published in

Boston in 1926. Had its conclusions been well pondered, accepted, and applied, the whole course of our national policy in the Far East might well have been changed. This is indeed a broad claim, and its justification demands support.

When I had first reported the Social Ratings Scale in Philadelphia, newspaper editors had seized on the catchy headline "Seven Keys to Failure." They concluded that avoidance of these types of behavior would, conversely, mean success. Whether this conversion of a negative to a positive scale was legitimate or not did not seem to matter. For a time I was bothered with letters from business concerns throughout the country inviting me to set up my social rating system in factories and other industrial ventures. Many executives informed me that lack of planning, irresolution, instability of purpose, poor initiative, impulsive decisions, and the like among employees plagued their businesses, and if this type of scale could be used in selection, the money saved would be tremendous. Moreover, they believed that these failings were not confined to the lower echelons, but that square pegs in round holes were numerous at the upper levels. Apparently businessmen are attracted by this type of efficiency bait! I had to tell my correspondents that I wasn't fishing.

But in Hawaii I could concern myself with groups rather than with individuals and here the Scale seemed to have a valid application. I secured 25 raters, individuals reputed to be of good judgment plus long experience and contact with the ethnic groups that were to be rated. No less than sixteen were sugar plantation managers, so that industrial relations would undoubtedly bias their ratings. As a partial offset, the other nine judges included educators, physicians, head workers of a couple of social settlements. Some men I contacted refused to participate—they were too busy. Others admitted that recent happenings on the plantations might influence their opinions, but after I had taken the time to discuss thoroughly the nature of the Scale, they took the keenest interest in its application. Some even suggested that the whole study would have greatly increased value if it could be repeated twenty years later. This was not done, but the light of subsequent history is revealing, especially with regard to the Japanese.

The traits most commonly ascribed to them as a group were tenacity of purpose, planning and organizing ability, secrecy in relation to long-term future plans, and loyalty to the idea of their advancement as a group rather than as individuals. This organizing ability paid off in terms of bargaining with management, a fact which did not add to their personal popularity. Heightened race consciousness was evinced by their avoidance of intermarriage with other groups. In this they were taking the long view. Their family cohesion was indicated by very low juvenile and adult delinquency rates, their foresight by the sacrifices they were willing to make to ensure the education of their children. I summed up the situation in these words:

"In short, they were adaptable, but not suggestible. As a group they have not learned to conciliate and are, in fact, somewhat aggressive and unscrupulous in pursuing an advantage." In this summary it must be remembered that these were not the researchers' judgments, but were those of the raters who applied the scale.

Other more generalized opinions are reflected in the following extract:

> Their ambitions, unlike those of the Chinese, extend to the social standing of the group as a whole. They are extremely sensitive to any imputation of inferiority. Politically speaking, they follow a policy of biding their time. In this respect they have shown considerable astuteness in refraining from registering as voters. . . . There is little doubt that it is no part of their plan to waste their strength in futile action before the period when their full weight can be brought to bear.

Another predictive observation stated that with time there might develop "a fairly wide gulf between the ideas and policies of the Hawaiian Japanese and the Japanese in Japan."

So much for the raters' judgments. As for our own conclusions, we wrote:

> While we are not alarmists, we recognize that a serious situation confronts the dominant white race. . . . In the very important question of the dominance of the Pacific, Japanese competition is very much to be reckoned with. . . . Despite all of Japan's protestations, we believe that her ambition is by no means dormant and that her policies are very shrewdly shaped and hidden behind a mask of inscrutability.

In the national sphere, such forebodings were of course amply justified fifteen years later when the bombs were dropping on Pearl Harbor. These warnings, it should be noted, were not actuated by hostility but were founded on our very healthy respect for the national strength and the high mental and temperamental abilities of our great Pacific neighbor, as evinced by our local sample.

This is being wise both before and after the event—a very unusual kind of wisdom, if things work out as predicted. National and local history has provided proof of Japanese resourcefulness, planning, and adaptability, indicated on the one hand by the challenge Japan was able to hurl against Britain and America in World War II, but also locally in their sudden take-over of domestic government in Hawaii. It would be indeed presumptuous to expect that a book written so long ago as 1926 could predict as explicitly and accurately the course of events in other, more general, directions.

In this early volume we put forth a summary review of conflicting theories regarding racial equalities or differences. The controversy was represented on the one hand by such writers as McDougall and Boas, on the other by Griffith Taylor and Ellsworth Huntington; the one group designated as race levellers, the other race dogmatists. In 1926 we took pains to assert that we favored the middle ground, and I should like, forty years later, to re-affirm that position.

We said then:

> The progress of races is not entirely a matter of chance circumstances nor is it entirely related to racial intelligence. To borrow an apt analogy, heredity deals the player the cards, but experience teaches him how to play them. . . . Mental endowment is the primary or basic factor. If the individual lacks a certain basic level of ability, you may surround him with all the cultural or environmental stimuli that you will, and there is no progress. . . . Where opportunity is denied or environmental stimuli are restricted, there can be little progress even in the well-endowed.

From this general discussion we turned to Hawaii.

> The fact that in one or two generations the descendants of coolie laborers, imported under contract to do the most arduous and unskilled work in the cane fields, are filling high school and university classes, gaining records in scholarship equal to those of the sons and daughters of a highly selected and intelligent group of whites, and making their way by every possible loophole of opportunity into the skilled professions—surely this seems like the strongest proof that, given educational advantages, even the (apparently) most poorly endowed racial groups may make their way despite all handicaps of colour, custom and language.

The three tests for selecting suitable contract laborers for Hawaii were popularly supposed to be—bare feet, calloused hands, and ignorance of English—the first indicating low social status, the second willingness to work, the third freedom from the influence of labor agitators. And we summed up the situation that "these barefooted, horny-handed, ignorant laborers were *not* poorly endowed but rich in an inheritance of temperamental or *psychosynergic* traits that only needed the opportunity to make their weight felt in interracial and social competition." Personally, I still like the term psychosynergic as signifying the dynamic mental forces, even though it was not generally adopted.

As to that burning question of today, the position of the Negro in America, I believe that it is not the skin color that counts for progress but the individual possession of those same psychosynergic traits—a combination of planning, initiative, self-control, drive, and prudence—that will finally determine the social status of any group in the community. By all means strengthen civil rights but let us not delude ourselves into thinking that having the vote, living in fine houses, or gaining a better education is going to work any miracles of social development. We might as well approve a policy of gradual improvement, for that is all we are going to get under any circumstances. Stupidity is not going to be corrected, prejudices removed, poverty abolished, nor intelligence achieved by act of Congress. A "head start" for young children will be fine, provided it is in the right direction.

In Hawaii the picture as outlined forty years ago has not been radically changed, but the shading is different. The long-term foresight of our largest Oriental group, as predicted, caused them to oppose the Pacific policies of the leaders of their homeland. Nevertheless, the orientalization of our community has grown apace, with Japanese films and theaters, sister cities in Japan, radio broadcasts, language schools, and airplane services, etc.—all part of our daily lives. Group stability of purpose is still remarkably impressive. The material affluence of the Japanese is evident, their zest for higher education undiminished. Their record as regards crime and delinquency, though not as excellent as it was, is still good.

Undeniably, the Chinese, with their business acumen, industriousness, and accumulating wealth, wield a power and influence beyond their quota of population. It is significant that our senior senator in Congress is a millionaire Chinese, while our three other representatives are Japanese. The pure, or predominantly Polynesian, Hawaiians, in spite of their friendliness, tact, and happy-go-lucky background, have lost ground politically. Their index of law violations is not good. As we wrote in *Temperament and Race,* "In business the average Hawaiian is rarely successful. He seems to be devoid of the trading impulse." The Portuguese have sustained their reputation for thrift and industriousness, but they are still somewhat unstable emotionally. They are, however, good home-builders. As a result of the high organizing ability of their leaders, the Portuguese have continued to occupy public positions quite out of proportion to their voting strength, though as regards educational attainments they cannot match the orientals. Politically, the Filipinos have not made much of a dent. They are not considered "trouble-makers" but do not achieve leadership readily. So far their educational record has not been impressive. Like the Hawaiians they have lived too long in the tropics to attain toughness of mental fiber. As to the various mixed groups, Hawaii's experience seems to contradict any theories that racial admixture of blood has any deleterious effects. The Neo-Pacific life stream seems to have been strengthened rather than weakened by its many different tributaries.

The missionaries and their descendants brought with them native shrewdness and enterprise, though absolutely none of their first generation died rich. As a group they still carry a strong sense of civic responsibility, which, however, does not interfere with their resolution to build a strong business structure. Undoubtedly the Hawaiians with their Polynesian background of easy tolerance and good humor helped to soften Yankee temperament, making it less rigid and uncompromising. Chinese waters run deep so that their gifts to the community are not so easily summated; possibly, a keen individualism, a sense of family dignity, and an artistic background that even generations of coolie status could not efface have been in their gift.

Sociologists are fond of calling Hawaii a social laboratory and speak as if credit should somehow be due to us for our racial tolerance, muted prejudices, the Aloha spirit, and the like. All I can say is that, if Hawaii is a laboratory, it is one without either definite plan or direction. None of our social permissiveness is of our conscious planning. Even the ingredients of our melting pot are chance contributions, thrown in at random, the determining factor in immigration being merely willingness to work in our sugar and pineapple fields. Moreover, expediency dictated the number of arrivals, so that no one group constitutes a majority, and none probably ever will. Hawaii, to my mind, is one of the greatest unplanned, but fortunate experiments in human history, in the sense of being almost a casual agglomeration of peoples drawn here by a variety of motives, mainly economic. If I were put to it to state the most important factor in our history, I would list the impact of the missionary groups, who came with the noble if somewhat ineffective purpose of lifting the moral tone of a Polynesian people. Puritanism may be as out of date as the dodo, or the neck-to-ankle bathing suit, but it left a very salutary mark on public behavior.

Meanwhile, the happy situation of the University of Hawaii at the slow-moving center of the ethnic whirlpool had not gone unrealized. Dr. Dean, whose Yale background included training at Sheffield Institute, had managed to interest the heads of the Rockefeller Foundation in the potential value of research in and about Hawaii. He had been told that the Foundation would support financially any attempt to strengthen the University faculty. The Foundation also suggested that an important step forward would be an endeavor to recruit one of the leading physical anthropologists in the world, Dr. Frederic Wood Jones, at that time Professor of Anatomy in the University of Adelaide, South Australia. It was suggested that the position might be made attractive to him if assurance could be given that the job would not include teaching duties, but would be full-time research. Two other legs of the investigative tripod were to be Dr. Romanzo Adams, sociologist, and myself.

The publication of *Temperament and Race,* though it occasioned considerable controversy and criticism, gave prominence to my own program, which, with Wood Jones' arrival, I hoped to see greatly extended. He and I soon discovered common interests; I could at least speak the language of neurology and physical anthropology. The Rockefeller people, who knew of his great British reputation, had guessed right. For long he had been mulling over the project of a book outlining the story of the evolution of the brain, but since the brain had a mind he felt some inadequacy in dealing with psychological functions. After long discussions, we decided to collaborate on a book for which I supplied the concluding chapters and the title *The Matrix of the Mind.*

This association was indeed of great advantage to me for Wood Jones possessed the medical knowledge that I lacked, and up-to-date paleontological information. For my part, I had the advantage of the purposive viewpoint, and he agreed that it would be impossible to tell the story of the brain without reference to functions set up in response to environmental stimuli. Teleology, the theory of adaptation to ends, because of its theological implications of an over-all creative design, had fallen into disrepute. Wood Jones and I believed that it was incorrect only because of its emphasis on predetermined or external design. To us, structure and function were contemporaneous in development. It seemed, in our view, that purposes and designs proceeded together, hand in hand.

For a book with the avowed object of blending the viewpoints of psychology and anatomy, it met with extraordinary success. Wood Jones had, I'm afraid, to take my knowledge of psychology on trust, but my contribution got by with really a minimum of criticism, illustrating the fact that such a blending was novel. Those whose business it was to teach and write about the mind did very little thinking about the neural structures that formed the mental matrix and vice versa. Had they known more about both, their criticisms would have been more weighty.

My former assistant at the Clinic, Dr. C. M. Louttit, later a well-known psychologist, complained to Wood Jones that I had manufactured my psychological contribution "out of whole cloth," to which my collaborator innocently replied that he did not know that there was so much material loose or lying around unused. As to the mixture itself, reviewers again and again approved of this bold attempt. Said one medical review:

"A book written by an anatomist and a psychologist, in which one has to look at the table of contents before he can be sure whether it is the anatomist or the psychologist whose words one is reading on any particular page, is unknown."

Actually, many times the reviewers guessed wrong as to the individual authorship. In many pages of appraisal the term and topic of "the relevant stimulus" were credited to my collaborator, whereas the idea, as an essential modification of the biologist's *adequate stimulus,* was my own. It formed the basis of our theory of the most essential role of the pallium, namely, the selection of the stimulus to which the organism chooses to respond. This, too, was the foundation for my own definition of intelligence as "the ability to respond to a wide range of relevant stimuli."

The temptation is strong to quote largely from the reviews written from both sides of the wall that separated the medical and the psychological aspects. These comments were not all laudatory, for our opinions on psychoanalysis as practice or art rather than science drew some very heated comments, but on the whole reviewers were markedly appreciative. At least our effort did not go unnoticed. Reviews, of which I have copies, would fill at least five chapters of this book. Whether our labors succeeded in building a footbridge between the two disciplines is, I'm afraid, a matter for doubt. The first edition of *The Matrix of the Mind* appeared in 1929, thirty-nine years ago. A swift survey of the field does not reveal any very outstanding discoveries of new relationships since that time. Actually, as we shall see later, many of the results of recent research are mainly of doubtful interpretation. Some later facts as to the organization of portions of the brain for certain functions contradict our earlier assumptions, notably the predominance of the frontal lobes.

In an article of mine in the *British Journal of Medical Psychology* in 1955, some of these changes in viewpoint are briefly elaborated.

"The consistent principle in brain building, I would like to suggest, is that the more directly an area is connected with the self-preservative upper brain stem and its associated nuclei, the more primitive or fundamental will be the behavior that it mediates."

Wilder Penfield, noted Canadian (McGill University) neurosurgeon and neurologist had already put forth a similar viewpoint when he suggested that "the master motor area may be found at the level of the upper brain stem where all the necessary sensory and mnemonic information is readily available." My own conclusion was founded on the data afforded by lobotomy, which showed that the more closely brain injuries approached the center of the frontal brain (areas 4, 5, 6, and 8, which constitute a vertical extension of the mid-brain) the more the abilities of foresight and prudence were adversely affected. In sum, this indicates that the matrix of the mind is situated much lower in the central nervous system than had been supposed.

All this is borne out by the modern concept of the central nervous system as being par excellence the organ of rapid and effective communication, in short, the command post into which all pathways of intelligence converge. In line with this principle, I have suggested that the fissuring of the brain's surface, which in Professor Berry's time was supposed to have been developed solely to increase space for the grey matter without unduly enlarging the cerebral hemispheres, could more logically be considered as Nature's design to bring the bases of these convolutions of fissures nearer to the main streams of mental communication.

If Wood Jones were alive now and we could have rewritten *The Matrix,* that suggestion could have been put forward as another feature of the blending of anatomy and psychology in the direction of mapping out the means of proprioception throughout the whole human organism.

CHAPTER 7

Back to the Bush

A BRIEF chronological insertion may help to keep the record straight. In 1923, after I had refused the Board of Regents' request that I remain in Hawaii, Dr. Dean came up with a counter-proposal that I divide my time between Honolulu and Vineland. I told him that if I could get Vineland's consent, I should be quite willing. Again, Greenman and Fels were most sympathetic, so that for four years we travelled back and forth at somewhat irregular intervals between Hawaii and the eastern seaboard.

Finally, holding two jobs almost six thousand miles apart began to be like trying to keep three balls in the air at once, an adroit juggling trick, but one that needed constant practice; hence, I resigned my Vineland position. Unfortunately, for the Research Department, Fels at once discontinued his support, though Johnstone, with Dr. Edgar Doll as an efficient director, continued its operations, and did very useful work. What was not then fully realized was the fact that the tide of interest set in motion by Goddard was at its ebb.

Apparently, *Temperament and Race* did stimulate some interest in ethnic comparisons, for in 1928 I received a letter from the Australian National Research Council, inviting me to visit the universities of the Commonwealth and lay, before those interested, suggestions for research among Australian aborigines.

In the ensuing correspondence I made it clear that in the state of my current knowledge I had little to lecture about, but that I should be glad to spend the greater part of 1929 in field work; by that time I might have some first-hand experience. This plan was accepted, so by April of that year I was travelling with my friend Clinton S. Childs of Maui on the East-West railway line to Fremantle, where we would catch the coastal steamer *Koolinda* that would take us north to Broome. This town, then the center of the pearl fishing industry along the northwestern coast, would serve as a convenient base for my operations in the little-travelled Kimberley region where aborigines might be most conveniently met with and studied.

The plans called for a five-man expedition, driving by truck along the single ribbon of travel that connected Derby and Wyndham, tiny settlements of whites which served as centers for the cattle industry. To reach Derby from Broome meant 140 miles of

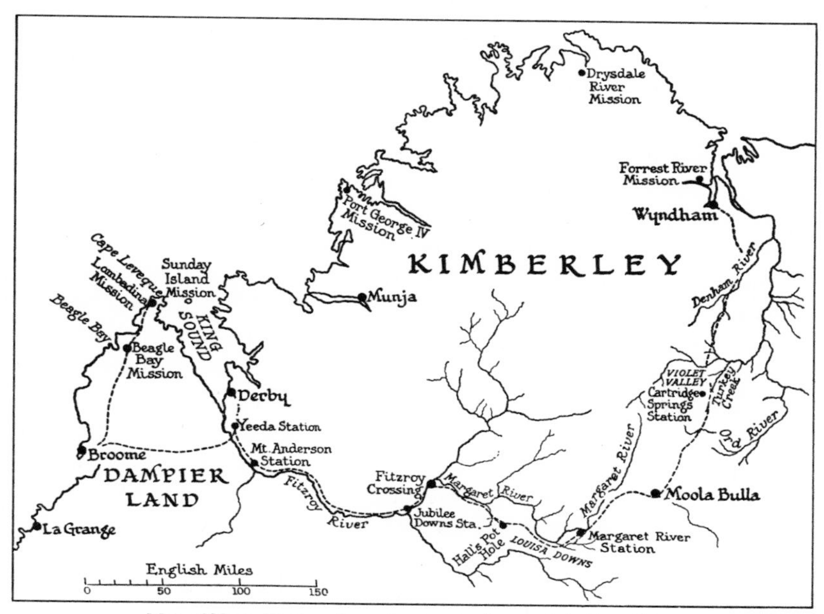

Map of North-Western Area, showing the Route of the Expedition

The broken line traces the author's 1929 expedition in northwest Australia to do research among the aborigines.

grinding progress along a sand track through the low forest locally known as "pindan," until we came to the Fitzroy River, thence another 750 miles by road to Wyndham. Strung like infrequent beads on a loose string were about five cattle stations, the road connecting them being by local consensus of opinion the worst in the world.

Before leaving Honolulu, I had arranged with Dr. Paul Withington, medical man and noted Eastern University athlete and coach, to join us at Broome. At the last minute he sought the interest of a group of Honolulu businessmen who backed the venture with funds sufficient to purchase a Chevrolet truck, and to employ a former Hollywood photographer with an assistant, who were to join us a month later at Broome.

Meanwhile, Childs, who had majored in sociology, agreed to work with me at the Beagle Bay Mission, where we also hoped to arrange for picture-taking. The agreement was that all the pictures I needed were to be taken first and that afterwards the photographer could put together a movie for commercial purposes. There was, however, a strict proviso that this should be submitted to my personal censorship. Dr. Withington was to act as medical attendant, but as happened later, he proved to be his own most serious patient, and very nearly lost his life by misadventure. Otherwise, the agreement was honored more in its breach than its observance.

The Australian Research Council had nothing to do with the film, and since arrangements for it were completed after I left Honolulu, I had no written agreement controlling its disposal and exhibition. This finally caused me so much concern that eventually I had to withdraw all connection with the film project, and to threaten with legal proceedings the movie company, who bought it from the local backers, if my name was mentioned therewith. I also took steps to ban its showing in Australia. My objection was that Hollywood insisted on an ending of the story that was completely unauthentic.

Actually, as a pictorial record of the everyday life of the aborigines it was excellent, except that Hollywood dubbed in a phony episode to give it some "sex appeal." The script editors had us discovering a mythical white woman, sole survivor of a vessel wrecked on the coast, captured by aborigines and living with her half-caste children and aboriginal chief so happily that she turned down our offer to return with us to civilization. The movie people undressed a white girl and dressed up a colored man and photographed them in some caves in California to complete the story. Strangely enough, this was the only episode that was objected to by critics as fictitious. When the picture was exhibited under the title "The Blonde Captive," it received otherwise excellent reviews. The local financial supporters made no profit, even though the movie was credited with grossing several millions of dollars. But that, as Kipling was wont to remark, is another story, and a rather sad one at that. The only lesson I learned was not to put my trust in moving picture princes with regard to truthful narration.

In Perth, Childs and I laid in three months' supplies for our expedition, with the help of the manager of the main department store. Unfortunately, he included only one can-opener, which we promptly lost at our first camp site. One other article that would have saved us interminable arguments was an encyclopedia. It is astonishing what extraordinary controversies crop up among five men confined to close quarters for several months. I cannot say which was the worse, cut fingers from opening cans with a penknife, or the petty abrasions of temper due to verbal disputes.

Since full professors are so scarce in Australia, the title brought me deference and helpful attention in Perth, but at the gangplank of the *S.S. Koolinda,* its magic disappeared. No one without compelling business was on the ship, the first to ply this coast since the end of the cyclone or "cock-eyed Bob" season. Everybody on board knew all about his neighbor's cattle and private business, how many half-caste children he was reputed to have fathered, how much he owed the banks, whether his wife was expecting or expected to return from the south, how much he was drinking, or how close to bankruptcy he happened to be.

But whatever reason Childs and I had for going to the Kimberleys was a matter for wonder and even suspicion. It was certainly of no use explaining that I was a psychologist going out to the vast Kimberley region to study the natives. In the first place no one on board except ourselves could even spell psychology; and in the second my announced purpose merely excited unseemly mirth. Blackfellows, by common consent, had no mentality. Any old-timer could tell you that.

It took them some days, several hundred drinks in the saloon bar, and floods of drunken or half-sober conversation before the ship's company evolved a satisfactory theory as to why we were on board. Everybody in Western Australia believed implicitly that this wilderness, arid though it seemed, was literally floating on huge untapped pools of oil. The only professors that had ever visited these parts were geologists who, if not interested in oil, had secret information about vast stores of gold, silver, tin, copper, uranium, etc., the common slogan being—"You name it, we've got it."

Only Americans had the money to uncover this Aladdin's lamp of untold wealth, and we were from America, so obviously this silly story of studying the natives was just a smoke screen to conceal tremendous commercial designs. Apparently no one trusted Americans, and any denials of any hidden intent simply confirmed suspicion. Actually, I never shook off the idea that I was a geologist in disguise; in fact, I gave up trying.

So our ship made its way north, past grim red cliffs, brown rocky headlands, and broken islands. There I saw what I had thought could not exist—a mirage at sea. When the sun was in the right position some of the islands appeared to float as if suspended in mid-air. In an oily calm, schools of sporting porpoises broached the surface, while whales in pairs headed towards us or suddenly sheered away from the ship as if distrustful of this new monster. At one point in the middle of a bay between two low headlands lay the rusting hull of a large steamer, thrust up against a shelving foreshore. No break of land or river-mouth lay ahead of its pointing bows, nor was there any appearance or promise of a waiting harbor. Here, I thought, was a plain case of a ship's suicide. Perhaps it had been lost too long in a weary waste of waters and had given up. It looked as if, of its own volition, it had driven itself ashore.

By the time we had reached Port Hedland, last stop on our way to Broome, the ship's company from the captain down had decided that if we wished to persist in foolish tales about our mysterious mission, that was our business. My participation in a cricket match—the ship versus the shore—in which in spite of not having seen a cricket bat for ten years I made the top score, plus Childs' ludicrous attempt to play the game as if it were baseball added greatly to our popularity. American oil spies or not, we must have had a dozen invitations to stay at various cattle stations for a year at least, with offers to line up the whole available aboriginal population if I still wanted to play silly games such as testing blackfellows' mentalities. Among these offers of extended hospitality was a cordial invitation from one of the owners of Go Go station at

Fitzroy River Crossing, some 259 miles southwest of the little seaside town of Derby. This I was very glad to accept, as it was on our route to Wyndham. The station was of only moderate size, a mere five million acres, carrying 85,000 head of cattle.

Mr. Neville, State Protector of Aborigines in Perth, had supplied me with maps, containing many dotted lines signifying unexplored territory, but the best obtainable. Our purpose was to travel 150 miles north from Broome on a shakedown trip to Cape Leveque and a brief visit to the Sunday Island Mission. On our

An aborigine paddling a type of catamaran near Broome in 1929, showing the possible means of arrival of these natives in northwest Australia.

return we would strike west 150 miles to Derby, then continue along the Fitzroy Valley, a twenty-mile-wide estuary in "The Wet" [1] and a chain of deep waterholes and subsidiary lagoons in the dry season.

The only memories that remain to me of Broome in 1929 are of a rather haphazardly planned town built beside a creek in which the pearl fishing fleet lay at anchor; stone buildings, the roofs of which, if they had any hope of permanency, being literally chained

[1] This is the name universally applied throughout northwestern Australia to the three months' period of torrential monsoonal downpours, during which all ordinary roads are impassable. Complete drought is the usual condition during the rest of the year.

to the ground against the malevolence of recurrent cyclones; huge bloated baobabs, also known as cream of tartar trees; and, caged on the veranda of the Governor Broome Hotel, birds of an unbelievable metallic sheen, locally known as blood-wing parrots because of the splash of brilliant crimson each wore on its wings. Possibly my clearest recollection was of a gang of aborigines chained together, who under the ready rifles of the police guard shuffled along the dusty road on their way back to the local jail. They had been out all day repairing roads and bridges. They probably represented the season's catch of cattle spearers, with a ritual murderer or two thrown in for good measure.

Otherwise the point of greatest interest to us was the mile-long pier pointing straight into Roebuck Bay, built so that unloading steamers would not have to wait out the tides. The expanse of the Indian Ocean looked as if someone had tipped into it a few hundred tons of pale blue washing powder, which provided a strong contrast with the black teredo- or ship-worm–proof piles. Except for this jetty the bay probably looked just as it did when Dampier, buccaneer and navigator, saw and named it 250 years before.

My book, *The Psychology of a Primitive People,* into which I am dipping to refresh my memory, appeals to me now as a great waste, in some places, of rather fine writing. I'm afraid my colleagues valued it none too highly. Like my fellow passengers on the *Koolinda,* they probably wondered what the psychology of primitive man amounted to, anyhow! However, an increasing number of anthropologists were impressed. In 1940, Hooton of Harvard [2] wrote:

> The study of Australian social psychology is as basic and indispensable to the student of society as a knowledge of the openings to the learning of chess. Many features of Australian social organization and religion are by no means unique, and some of them are not primitive, but they are woven together into a complicated pattern, which is found nowhere else, and is as much Australian as their cranial morphology.

To examine these patterns of social anthropology was my main purpose, leaving to better scholars than myself, such as A. P. Elkin and his co-workers, the working out of the threads of understanding of the system of blood relationships that governed their intra-

[2] Earnest A. Hooton, *Why Men Behave Like Apes and Vice Versa* (Princeton: Princeton University Press, 1940).

tribal marriages. In that field Dr. Elkin and his co-workers did a thoroughly competent job. My concern, however, was with the wider psychological patterns of social adjustment, such as dominance of elders and other factors making for aboriginal survival.

In a later section of his book, Hooton referred to my second volume, *Primitive Intelligence and Environment.*

> At this point we may fittingly discuss together the available evidence concerning the psychological traits of the Bushmen, the Australians, the Negritos, especially since they have been made the subjects of careful studies by one of the most experienced psychologists who have investigated this problem, Dr. S. D. Porteus.

The reader of the present book will recognize how meager, at that point, the writer's experience was, and, actually, how little was known by *anyone* of this subject. If indeed, as Hooton said, the results of such studies were indispensable, it was strange that social psychology seemed to get along so well without them.

Since my avowed purpose was to measure and observe man's attempts to come to terms with a most repressive environment, my work began with Childs' and my departure from Broome along the single track that ran through the pindan to reach the outpost of civilization that the Brothers of the Pallottine order had inherited from the Trappist monks some fifty years before our visit to Beagle Bay.

There is little need to repeat here the details of that missionary effort except to underline the burdens that life itself imposed in that environment. All the work that could be done was confined to the winter season, for in "the Wet" nothing moved except on its belly; the region was a green hell where only snakes, centipedes, leeches, and other vermin prospered. In the dry winter months the Pallottine Brothers consolidated their petty gains. Donkey teams with rawhide harness, wagons with circular sections sawn from tree trunks to serve as wheels hauled clay to be made into sun-dried bricks; kerosene cans had to be hammered out for roofs; church pews had to be hand-hewn; mother-of-pearl shells were gathered to make an altar, and here in these wastes rose an imposing church, with tower and steeple. Its white walls were a bold affirmation of faith, a challenge to the wilderness.

Most interesting to a psychologist was the significance of all this to the natives. Strangely enough, the mysteries of the Mass with its swinging censers, its altar boys, its unknown tongue, its deep-voiced responses from the congregation had a special appeal to these simple people, whose life was already rooted in tradition, for the whole philosophy of the aborigines was based on belief in the legends handed down to them from the past. This new faith, they found, could be readily grafted on to the old, and any restraints it imposed could be easily sloughed off outside the mission boundaries. The same men who knelt in church carried on their secret rites and ceremonies not a mile from its shadows, and their spiritual mentors found it wiser not to enquire too closely as to what went on. The Brothers' attitude seemed to be that if they labored all the daylight hours for Mother Church, the dark could look after itself. The natives soon learned that we belonged to a different breed of white men, and in my case I think they decided I was about as unregenerate as they themselves.

In my personal luggage I carried Baldwin Spencer's two volumes on the Arunta, well illustrated with photos and drawings of Central Australian *churinga,* sacred objects incised with designs related to their totemic life. Hiding the book carefully under my shirt so that no woman or uninitiated youth could see it, I showed it to old Felix, the acknowledged headman of the tribe. Pictures of men decorating themselves with vegetable down and feathers in preparation for secret ceremonies drew excited laughter from Felix and some of his friends of the tribal council. But when they turned the pages and discovered line drawings of the churinga patterns, silence fell. They excitedly whispered to me *"Minburr,"* then with a careful glance around to be sure that none of the Brothers were in sight, they drew their shoulders closely together and, one by one, with all the signs of reverence, each man traced the mystic design with the tip of his finger. Then in low tones, Felix confided to me:

"Mine got same fella *minburr*. Tomorrow we show."

Alick, one of the group who had been a pearl-diver and spoke English, then passed on to me a request from Felix that I lend him the book to show some of the absent elders. My admonitions as to the need to keep it out of sight were met with nods of approval and the comment "Him properly savee," before the group quietly melted away.

The next afternoon was Saturday and Alick took Childs and me by a devious route to a small clearing hidden in the pindan. Then from different directions about twenty men quietly drifted in, among them Felix, who led the way to a cajeput tree, where hidden in the branches was a bundle wrapped about with a piece of sail cloth. A couple of the younger men were sent out as sentinels, and then old Felix reverently spread out the sacred wooden symbols, bearing similar designs to those of the Arunta churinga from 700 miles away to the south. Each man picked out his individual "minburr," held my finger and we reverently traced the incised pattern.

Each time I ejaculated, "Kallilipe, Kallilipe [very good]" I met with friendly smiles, while Felix murmured, "This waipella [white fellow] him plenty savee all right." Then the performance was repeated with Childs. My companion suggested to me that when we went to Broome to meet Dr. Withington and the truck that was being shipped from Fremantle, we should buy a canvas bag, treat it chemically so as to repel white ants, and present it to the tribe for storing their sacred belongings. This we did and on the morning when our truck finally departed from Beagle Bay, Childs and I were led aside and presented with a fine bundle of *minburr,* which Alick explained we could give to the tribes down south. Had we known it, this was also a guarantee of safe conduct throughout inland Australia, for this put us in the position of tribal messengers, whose persons were sacred.

One "cobba-cobba" or dance that the natives showed us was very interesting. Out of the brush appeared two men decorated with pipe-clay designs, which with a large mother-of-pearl shell as a pubic ornament made up their only attire. Each man carried a green bough with which he swept the ground to obliterate any tell-tale tracks. At intervals the men dropped their branches and rotated their hands quickly near the ground while the chorus of onlookers sang excitedly and rattled their "kylies" or boomerangs in accompaniment. Alick explained to us that the rotating of the dancers' hands would have the effect of twisting a woman's insides to such an extent that she would wander away from the camp where her would-be lover would find her completely unresisting. In most of the public dances women took no active part other than carrying on an ecstatic quivering of lower abdominal and thigh muscles, a very suggestive "belly dance." The rotating of the performer's hands might work magic, but it was quite apparent that the women kept themselves in practice. Moreover, the older men saw to it that any females subjected to the magic spell were of the right moiety or subsection for marriage with the charmer. Amorous

Bush natives on the Kimberley Coast, showing decorative scars indicating initiation.

intrigues were not lacking, although the mission authorities discountenanced any such heathen practices. According to Father Healy, specially appointed to the supervision of the Mission during our stay, the aboriginal women needed no artificial or magic means to stimulate their appetites. His opinion of female aboriginality was low, and he was much averse to the filming of any dances in which women took part.

There was no doubt at all of the dramatic appeal of any collective performance. The old men at Lombadina, fifty miles distant, had promised us that they would arrange a night dance, for which our photographers were prepared with magnesium flares, etc. Lombadina was an annex of the main mission, and Father Healy gave rather grudging assent to filming dances there, rather than at Beagle Bay. If there was to be any letting down of hair or relaxation of Mission rules, he preferred it to take place not under his direct observation. I gathered the impression that we had at least his unofficial blessing.

Woman showing mourning scars inflicted after the death of a relative.

At Lombadina there was no native camp as at Beagle Bay, merely a collection of sand dunes, each surmounted by a family "wurley," a brush shelter roofed in the wet seasons by sheets of bark or in a few cases with flattened kerosene cans. In the dry winter time no one bothered with any more protection than a hollow

A family "wurley" or brush shelter, roofed in the wet seasons with sheets of bark or in a few cases with flattened kerosene cans.

in the sand beside a small fire, where adults, children, and dogs could all huddle together, just as they did in Dampier's day. When we arrived at a little hollow that was to serve as a dance ground, we could see the fires winking on the dunes but not a native in sight; so Childs and I sought out our intermediary to whom we had already given an advance payment of a shilling for the entertainment. We had been informed at the Mission that this must be our own show, the best they could offer being a benevolent neutrality.

Our man seemed at first to have lost interest and informed us it was too cold for blackfellows to leave their home fires. No one felt like dancing anyhow. But with another shilling in hand, he said he would confer with his fellows. This sounded to us as if it was too late to call a tribal meeting, but we found that consultation was easy. Our friend faced each point of the compass in turn, shouting an enquiry and listening to each reply. If I were any judge of the tone of these answers, they sounded like a downright refusal with, in many cases, rude injunctions to the white men to go to hell and take all their schemes and purposes with them.

Our hearts sank into our boots, for this had seemed a wonderful opportunity to film a night dance or "cobba-cobba." But after listening silently to a particularly vociferous outburst, he turned to us and said, "Them fella bin say orl right."

Soon from the dance ground came the beat of the kylies (boomerangs), accompanying the first high notes of the old men's chorus, descending bar by bar to a long sustained deep bass ending, only to be lifted again an octave higher by the leader, with all the other men joining in with such emphasis as almost to shake the song loose from their chests. Over to one side sat all the women, providing a lighter accompaniment by clapping their hands on their inner thighs.

Then out of the dark came the dancers, their now naked bodies bearing bars of pipe-clay outlining their limbs like living skeletons. Then we discovered that each man had already painted on his bare skin white pigment designs that must have taken hours to apply, so that their apparent unwillingness to put on the dance was merely for effect. In fact, they would have been disappointed if I had not made a show of persuasion.

All this is set forth in *The Psychology of a Primitive People* and need not be repeated here except for a note as to the psychological values of the dance. It must be remembered what a tiny assemblage of souls this was in a vast solitude, where survival meant incessant daily individual effort. Now in contrast was unity, identification of the individual with the purpose and tempo of group action. For an hour or two the fires were heaped high while song and rhythm thrust back the threatening shadows, thus warding off the fears, the loneliness that beset them. I doubt if even the oldest men knew the significance of the words they sang, only that these songs and stylized motions had been handed down almost since time began. These and a great store of legends made up the psychic life of the tribe, the possession of which distinguished men from the animals, and insured the people's sanity. For all these things constituted a rallying point, a firmly driven peg that held their otherwise shaky society together.

During our stay, Childs and I were busy carrying out examinations of the natives. Our days began early, for by six in the morning the bird chorus was so loud and insistent that sleep was out of the question. So at dawn each day he and I walked along the creek where it emptied into the bay, trying to make a bird list. Apparently the clearing of land around the Mission provided a feeding ground for bush birds, while the creek's small estuary was crowded with wild fowl. Along a mile and a half stretch we recorded fifty bird species.

Their first curiosity about our testing procedures having subsided, the good Brothers left us to our own devices. After our truck arrived, we set out for Cape Leveque, where we intended to cross the twelve-mile strait to Sunday Island. We were already packed to leave Lombadina when an old bleary-eyed elder complained that "the teacher" had not given him any of the tests. As we needed his good will for picture-taking on our return, there was nothing to do but unload the truck, set up my testing apparatus, and get to work. At once one of the Brothers rushed up to warn me that a heavy cloud threatened a most unexpected winter rain, and that if three-quarters of an inch fell we would be unable to cross the black soil plains to the south for at least three weeks. But when in my hurry I tried to help the old man with the tests, he objected that I was only giving him "the baby plays." As I did not dare offend the old fellow I had to sit an hour and a half until he could find his way out of the mazes, while I and my companions were in danger of being bogged down in a maze of mud instead of one of paper. Fortunately, after a few big drops the skies cleared and we could proceed; but after this experience, I never mis-estimated the interest of primitive people in a maze test.

At the Cape Leveque lighthouse we waited for Mr. Collier, the Mission superintendent, to ferry us across to Sunday Island, but he did not appear. On our return from a kangaroo hunt, the lighthouse keepers told us that the *Koolinda*'s engines must have broken down, for she had anchored for several hours about three miles out, presumably to make repairs. Actually, the ship lay there trying to send me a flag signal to say that Mr. Collier would be delayed three days, having broken the rudder of his ketch.

But it so happened that neither the lighthouse keeper nor his assistant had their spyglasses handy and as it was a sixty-yard walk up to the lighthouse the message went undelivered.

CHAPTER 8

Our Stone-Age Poor Relations

JUST AS we had loaded the truck for our return to Broome, the beginning of our cross-country trip through the southern Kimberley region, Mr. Collier arrived to convey us across to Sunday Island. Much to his disappointment our time schedule would not allow of any further stay, but Dr. Withington was already contemplating a lugger trip up the coast and promised to visit the mission then. On his return trip he was able to redeem his promise.

I have not previously mentioned that a mounted trooper, Constable Dewar, had accompanied us to Cape Leveque, and as police movements are of intense interest to the natives, we had some demonstration of the efficacy of the "bush telegraph." Our projected date and time of arrival had not been made known to the lighthouse keepers—the last traveller overland having reached there two years earlier. Two hours before we appeared, the natives had told the lighthouse people that five white men would reach there that afternoon. Similarly, when we reached Lombadina on our return, the mission people were expecting us. Whether the fifty-mile gap in ordinary communications had been bridged by smoke signals or by a native runner with a "message stick," the hours of our sittings down and uprisings were all correctly reported.

My earliest plans had included a comparison of the well-watered temperate southeastern segment of the continent, which I knew well, and the vast hinterland, which was quite new to me. The writings of Spencer and Gillen, together with those of the early explorers, had made everyone aware that aridity and food sparsity sharpened the struggle for existence imposed on aboriginal inhabitants, but the abundance of nutritional resources in the monsoonal regions of the northwest was a tremendous surprise to me. The bird life was prodigious, the marine life from rock oysters to dugongs (sea-cows), fish, and turtles was prolific, while kangaroos, wallabies, and other marsupials, together with snakes and huge lizards were easily found. Except for its terrific summer heat and humidity, this region was the antithesis of desert. Gradually it dawned on me that if these conditions changed materially from those of the coastal areas, then my problem could be redefined. If monsoonal regions and the arid center provided entirely different environments, these must leave a varied impress on the mentalities of the two sets of aboriginal inhabitants. According to sociological theories, the harsh, repressive desert conditions would result in lower intelligence, more primitive social organization, and generally depressed cultural development. It was a case of the weakest being driven to the wall—and what a wall!

I am afraid I can make no claims to prescience, certainly not in the way of proving any preconceived theories. My change of ideas came gradually as we travelled.

Our first hundred miles of travel east from Broome brought home to us the realization that northwest Australia was a land of striking contrasts, and that running water, like magic, changed the face of the whole country. Near Beagle Bay there was nothing to see except the grey-green monotony of the pindan, with hardly any signs of life. However, a great bush fire was burning to the south and the presence of hundreds of kites swooping around the columns of smoke indicated that the pindan must be full of Shakespearean "small deer," hidden by the brush but routed from concealment by the flames. The kites were evidently reaping a harvest.

But when we swung down into the valley of the Fitzroy there was a truly remarkable change. Here were huge trees overhanging sheets of bright water, the surface broken by movement of all kinds of wildfowl—teal, widgeon, mallards, pied geese, and black duck—while in the shallows stood two five-foot jabiru, magnificent black and white cranes, betraying only passing interest in our arrival.

Then a couple of wallabies hopped up a tributary gully, while a yellow dingo, whirling behind a bush, melted into the landscape and quickly disappeared. A swiftly moving cloud obscured the sun

—a flight of several thousand galahs—birds of the parrot family, pink and white, as they flashed in the sunlight. Only one thing spelled menace; a swirl in the river betrayed a sea-going crocodile rapidly getting out of rifle range to hide in the reeds of the opposite bank. From Derby, thirty miles downstream, we traversed 250 miles of river valley, along flats where we could travel 35 miles an hour between the white gums, past mesa-like bastions detached from the parallel Leopold ranges. From monotony and concealment of life we had passed into infinite variety.

Arrived at the Fitzroy River Crossing we faced a mile of deep sand to the opposite riverbank, but no sign of Millard, the Go Go station manager, who was to meet us on June 2nd with a team of horses to pull our truck across. The inn-keeper seemed to think his non-arrival to be a matter of no importance, and assured me that no one hereabouts was slave to a calendar; June 2nd would merely mean about that time, give or take a couple of days. Everyone in the Kimberleys, I was assured, thought that being three days late was just as good as being on time. Time was elastic anyhow.

Seventy-five miles back on the track I had resisted firmly the entreaties of a six-months' bridegroom who wanted us to detour fifty miles to stay a week or so at his station, where his wife, having no one but blacks around her, would be overjoyed to see five unexpected white visitors. He promised to gather up for us blackfellows galore, who would put on cobba-cobbas—the local name for corroborees—water sports, kangaroo hunts, even initiation ceremonies for our edification. Now, I realize, I might just as well have accepted rather than put him off with solemn promises to stay with him on our return—if ever that happened.

However, in a couple of days our host, Mr. Millard, arrived at the Crossing and took us to the station homestead. Here he and half a dozen white stockmen—there are no "cowboys" in Australia—supervised his five million-acre station with its estimated 85,000 head of cattle. Millard told us that he never expected to see all of this immense holding and that without aboriginal help he could not have run the place. His only complaint about native stockmen was that they overrode their mounts, without any consideration for their condition or welfare. However, the station kept plenty of horses and the blacks could afford to ride some to death. His policy was to try to keep the natives camped near the homestead, where he could keep them under his eye.

As to their intelligence, Mr. Millard had the highest opinion.

He had no hesitation in outlining to them, in pidgin English, plans with regard to shifting hundreds of cattle from one part of this huge extent of country to another, relying in the main on their reports on the cattle's condition and the grazing available.

Knowing my interest in native food supplies, he took a day off for us to visit a large bend in the river where, he said, kangaroos by the thousand collected in the dry season. We loaded half a dozen men into our truck, while Millard himself drove me and the camera men in his new utility wagon. Where a river bend narrowed between the fringes of forest, we unloaded the camera and the two photographers, while we drove downstream about three miles. There the blacks and I formed a line to beat the game past the cameras. In two miles of this drive, by shouting and shots, we must have set up a stampede of a couple of thousand kangaroos and wallabies, the latter of a species called "agile," which were sheltering from the sun in the shade of the forest.

In a little while the whole scene seemed to be alive with a moving tide of animals. At one point several hundred broke out of the cover attempting to dash back across the plain, so Dr. Withington tried to head off this minor stampede and turn the animals toward the camera. I have never seen such a sight—the doctor huddled over the wheel driving forty miles an hour with a fine disregard of his own life and the safety of our truck, in pursuit of a "mob" of kangaroos of all sizes and lengths of hops, streaking across the plain. Whites and blacks alike collapsed on the ground in gales of mirth.

By this time our line of beaters had been pierced in scores of places. I found myself kicking desperately at wallabies or jumping sideways to escape being bowled over by a flying kangaroo. As for the natives, who had not understood the moving-picture plan, the more purposeless the whole performance seemed, the funnier it was. There was evidently no limit to the white man's foolishness, especially when after such a hunt we did not bother taking a single dead wallaby back home with us. As for our picture-taking, we found that with the first rush of kangaroos the operator had made the mistake of trying to "pan" the camera, following individual groups, so that by the time the tripod was moved to cover a clear space, the main body of the driven animals had passed by. What the aboriginal men told their women after their return we did not know, but I am sure no item of absurdity was overlooked, including my own near-collision with a kangaroo. That the natives had their own viewpoint as regards white men's behavior and a wonderful mimicking power had already been demonstrated to me.

One day I was watching a group of *gins* (women) clustered about Mr. Millard's utility truck. One old hag sat in the driver's seat, hands on the wheel, while the rest gave vent to an extraordinary series of grunts, squeaks, and rattles, ending in a most realistic splutter of an imaginary engine. When silence fell, the mock driver fiddled with all the knobs on the dashboard, gave a signal to her companions, who then repeated the performance with great enthusiasm. When this failed to start the car, the old woman descended, walked to the front of the station wagon, kicked the front tire viciously, and then in the exact tones of Millard's voice said loudly, "I wonder what's wrong with the bloody bastard now!" The response of the native onlookers was uninhibited.

One other note illustrating the ways of aboriginal women impressed me. I saw a group of them sitting on the ground knitting. As soon as they saw me approaching, each one put her piece of work down and sat on it. Only when I talked to them about other things and made as if to depart did they one by one produce their knitting and present it eagerly for my admiring inspection. Their attitude said plainly: "We women have our secrets too." They even wanted to give me the best samples of their skill, and seemed disappointed when I declined to accept them.

From Go Go we drove north and west through a chain of stations—Christmas Creek, Margaret Downs, through Hall's Gap and on to Moola Boola and Violet Valley. We were warned that we would meet with some of the worst roads in Australia, but discovered that travellers here had another set of values. A "good" road was often beset with boulders or clung precariously to rocky "sidings," or was pockmarked with abysmal potholes. What made a good road here was a hard, even craggy foundation; badness in a road depended on the number of dry river beds it crossed, where the truck sank to the axles, wheels spinning vainly in dry sand. Passage of one of these stream beds could easily take a half-day of almost superhuman effort to gain perhaps 200 yards of progress.

On several occasions we came on native encampments, where our arrival was the signal for a mad dash for the bushes, from which all the adults emerged, arrayed in various scraps and remnants of clothing. It didn't matter so long as each individual had one piece of covering, no matter how inadequate. A tattered blouse or shirt with nothing else below it was quite satisfactory. We soon learned that this rush to appear clothed had as its purpose the protection of *our* modesty, not theirs. I was already familiar with the gay abandon with which every stitch of clothing was discarded within half a mile of a mission, when a group went "walkabout." Older children up to 12 or 13 years were not expected to go otherwise than stark naked. No one paid them any attention.

Our progress, as we had been warned, was greatly delayed by the passage of the sandy beds of the Laura, the Margaret, the Mary, and the Violet, all feminine names. Two reasons were suggested for this; the one was that women were so scarce in the Kimberleys that the earliest settlers wanted to remind themselves that such beings existed; the other explanation, less flattering, was that these rivers were of such uncertain temperaments that one never knew whether they would present a raging flood or be empty of everything except sand.

Finally, in about three days of covering either forty miles or forty yards in an hour, we reached the government station at Moola Boola.

This represented an experiment, initiated, I believe, by Mr. Neville of the Aborigines Protection Department. The Kimberley natives had always "enjoyed" the reputation of being among the most untamed tribes. As a consequence, this area for forty years had been an extremely dangerous district, with the blacks deliberately scattering the cattle and spearing them later at their leisure. Moola Boola, with three to four thousand head, was set up as if under aboriginal ownership, the cattle being bred there and slaughtered at intervals when the blacks needed beef. In time the natives recognized this as their own cattle preserve and did what they could to hold off raiding parties of wild or bush aborigines into the district, and, indeed, helping the police to track down or drive away any intruders.

Since news of movements of groups or individuals required nothing better in the way of communications than smoke signals, the station managers of Moola Boola and Violet Valley encouraged the holding of inter-tribal gatherings. At the time of our visit a very large and important cobba-cobba was being planned. Already the message sticks, which served as invitations, had been sent out by couriers to the men of the Gregory Ranges, 200 miles north, country where ordinary police patrols never ventured. The corroboree was to be held a few miles from the station, where the station natives planned to drive half a dozen cattle for slaughtering. Mr. Woodlands, the manager, told us that on such occasions there would be many quarrels, fights, and some blood-letting, but all this was part of the show, which served as a social escape valve. The police patrol would have business elsewhere and with the station providing the beef, pacification of the region was greatly furthered. Woodlands informed us that this was the main reason why a party of newcomers like ourselves could now travel with safety through the southern Kimberleys. Only a well-armed police party would venture farther into the northwest. Mission stations on the coast were tolerated by the blacks provided the whites stayed close by home. In time Moola Boola's permissive policy would, he thought, modify the distrust and hostility of the aborigines. His optimism has now been fully justified.

However, the cobba-cobba (or corroboree) situation was not helpful to my plans. Most of the men were up north gathering bamboo for spears, while the women were ranging the bush, collecting and storing supplies of vegetable food, mainly edible seeds, yams, etc. that would not deteriorate swiftly. The local Keidja tribe was acting as hosts for the big get-together, and if food ran short, it would be greatly to their discredit. This was the only instance of foresight on the part of the natives that I was able to observe. Because of the presence of blow-flies, meat could not be dried and preserved. Seeds however could be gathered and kept in dilly-bags and at the same time the local aborigines marked down the positions of "bee-trees" so that they could be raided for honey when the visitors arrived. These gatherings were so infrequent that such instances of foresight had never been, as far as I knew, recorded.

This failure to provide for infrequent emergencies was doubtless the reason for the accusation that the aborigines did not know how to anticipate the future by building huts or weather-proof shelters. In the Wet, when the mosquitoes are a plague, or in unseasonable rains, the natives will build excellent bark huts. These, with smoke from a fire in the center, effectively kept mosquitoes at bay.

At one time when subjects were scarce, I tried to test the oft-reported claim that natives could unfailingly identify the footprints of any individual in the camp. Each man in turn was blindfolded while one by one the others in the group walked across a dusty spot of ground. With the blindfolds removed, the natives then identified the tracks.

There was considerable variability in the skill displayed. I have since wondered whether there was not some unwillingness on the part of the station natives to recognize the tracks of certain men who had bad police records. No one knew when a blood feud might arise involving police attention. It might then be the case that ignorance, if not exactly blissful, could be very convenient, for in that case man-tracks told no tales.

Of demonstrations of ordinary tracking ability, we had had plenty of evidence. Our own clumsy efforts to conceal our tracks were vain, but even when natives tried to disguise their tracks by walking on clumps of grass or rocky ground or jumping on and off logs, the trackers solved every problem quickly. As there was no water, the old Indian trick of walking in a stream could not be used.

For the benefit of other investigators, I would hazard the opinion that tests either completely familiar or unfamiliar are likely to be unsuitable. Any examining device adopted from their own cultural background may seem to them like child's play and be given only perfunctory attention. This might have been the case with my "footprints test," in which subjects were asked to pair photos of identical footprints. It certainly explained the ineffectiveness of the Thurstone Hand Test, in which the subjects were asked to sort out drawings of hands as right or left according to the position of thumbs and fingers. For a people familiar with a sign language, this was so easy as to be unworthy of any special attention. On the other hand, any test which required long or complex instructions was likely to be considered white men's business, and therefore rejected. Failure to succeed was then immaterial.

The ready acceptance by practically all aborigines of the Porteus Maze is due, I believe, to the fact that finding their way about by means of a most careful examination of the whole terrain and recognition of land marks was usual, and therefore the Maze appeared to them to be a genuine trial of individual ability. The *gins* (women) were frequently called upon by the old men to demonstrate all kinds of animal spoors, and hence their comparative failure in the Maze was unexpected. But here again there were unlooked-for factors in performance. The fact that the examiner chose the men for examination before the women indicated, to their minds, that this game was essentially men's business. To do better than the men might cause them trouble; to appear to be a little stupid might be wise. A show of mental obtuseness is a favorite native smokescreen.

In tracking demonstrations there was always one imitation that "brought down the house," so to speak, especially in Central Australia. The spoor of a camel is like two circular depressions divided by a line separating the two halves of the pad-marks. An old woman would carry an infant, held "honey-pot" fashion, and lightly press the baby's bottom on the dusty surface to make an excellent camel track. With great glee, the old men would assure me that a baby girl's backside was better than a boy's since it required no touching up to complete the picture. A kangaroo track was one of the easiest —pressing down the heel of the palm first, then adding the three toe marks with the finger nail.

After leaving Moola Boola, I spent a very interesting time in the jail at Wyndham, where three murderers and a group of material witnesses were incarcerated, awaiting the arrival of a police magistrate to try the cases. This, of course, might mean a delay of as long as three months. Release on bail would be followed, of course, by instant and protracted disappearance of both accused and material witnesses. For safekeeping, the accused—and the witnesses —were kept in chains and heavily guarded. The prize prisoner was a man named Gurug, who was known to have committed several murders and to have made a couple of remarkable jail escapes. He wore leg shackles plus a chain around his neck, padlocked to a post. Two other men were being held for ritual murders, which they freely admitted, the victim being a man who had eloped with a woman not of the proper marriage group or tribal sub-division. Thus he had laid himself and the woman under double jeopardy for this aboriginal crime. The old men in tribal council picked out Wattie and Grant, two very alert and likeable young men employed at a cattle station, as tribal avengers. Spearing the offender through the thigh or arm, plus some battering over the head with a club or "nulla nulla" would have been acceptable punishment, but the man unwisely made such effective resistance that they drove a spear through his chest. His death, of course, brought the police into the case. Wattie and Grant fled north over the Ord River, knowing that the white man's law stopped at the stream bed and that further pursuit would mean attack by tribespeople of that untamed land.

But the police, knowing that intruders of any color would be unwelcome, merely camped on the river for a few days waiting for the murderers to come out. The presence of strangers would be bitterly resented by the local tribes, so after three or four days of dodging the wild blacks, Wattie and Grant decided that the white man's law constituted the lesser danger and they surrendered. It was quite possible that Dr. Cotton, the local magistrate, with his knowledge of tribal customs, would consider that by "blackfellow law" the two young men were merely executioners. Together with the fact that they were already marked for punishment, possibly death, at the hands of the dead man's relatives, Dr. Cotton might conclude that a year or two in the chain gang at Broome would allow the situation to simmer down, though some kind of native retribution must ensue.

That this region was not wholly "pacified" had been brought to our minds on the occasion of our kangaroo film-making at Go Go. To drive the game ahead of us, we had put up an awful racket, including a mild gun-shot cannonade, which undoubtedly alerted the blacks for miles around. They at once moved in closer to the station where Mr. Millard could report their presence to the police, the very best alibi, if there was a serious affray, they could possibly arrange.

As far as my earlier experience with natives was concerned, my knowledge of aboriginal customs, though scanty, was useful. I was made most welcome at the Wyndham jail by both witnesses and murderers, who made up a most interesting and interested testing group. For the first session an armed constable sat at my side during Gurug's examination, but he was able to report to the police sergeant that the prisoner was so interested that it would be difficult to drive him away from the prison.

"If you would stick around for a couple of weeks, Professor," said the sergeant, "you would make our job of watching these fellows much easier. We could arrest a dozen more if you need them, and hold them on suspicion of cattle spearing. That's the standard charge around here."

However, the *Koolinda* was due any day on her return from Java to Darwin, and Dr. Withington and I had replanned our objectives. He was to hire a lugger with a half-caste aboriginal skipper to take him and his camera crew up the coast between Broome and Wyndham, where he would pick up our truck, with additional supplies, and set off across the north of the continent to Brisbane and Sydney. Meanwhile, Childs and I were to continue south to Perth, and take the transcontinental train over to Adelaide. There

I would catch the initial trip of the "Ghan," as they called the train to Alice Springs, while Childs returned to Honolulu. My visit to Central Australia (always referred to locally as "the Centre") with accommodations at the Finke River Mission station, 90 miles west of Alice Springs, had been arranged with the help of the late Dr. T. D. Campbell, who had made several trips there for anthropological purposes.

We then boarded the *Koolinda,* disembarked Withington in Broome to make arrangements for his wildly adventurous trip, which would take him up this uncharted coast, past such seldom-seen spots as Walcott Inlet, Port George, and the Drysdale River Missions.

The dangers were mainly two, the most immediate being tides of 30 feet rising to 45 feet in the long narrow Walcott Inlet, and the next, aborigines of very uncertain temper. On their actual itinerary, they proceeded by rule-of-thumb navigation on the part of their half-caste skipper, taking pictures as they went. As to the natives, the party made several contacts and attained a most exciting pictorial record of dances, etc.

The only trouble that really threatened was when they landed to obtain fresh water and were accosted by a party of natives who, in their usual hospitable fashion, offered them the use of their women. The old leader was deeply insulted at the white men's refusal, but while the aborigines scattered to retrieve their spears hidden in the brush, Withington hurried his men into their outboard motor boat and back to the lugger, while their offended hosts danced angrily on the beach and shook their spears at their unappreciative guests. They had merely adopted the usual way to cement friendship with strangers, and to have their hospitality treated so contemptuously was a deep affront.

CHAPTER 9

The Center of Nowhere

I AM enamored of journeys, for it always seems to me that what you pass through in reaching your goal is much more interesting than what you do when you get there. Body and spirit should make good fellow-travellers, but so many wayfarers leave their spirits behind. My venture into the interior of Australia was undertaken with zest.

Missing the first "Ghan," as the train had been called, was a blessing, for it made it possible for me to fill the gap in companionship occasioned by Clinton Childs' return to Hawaii. Since the next train for the Centre did not leave Adelaide for two weeks, I had time to visit my family, temporarily living in East Gippsland, Victoria.

I was passing along Collins Street in Melbourne when I met an old friend of my Victorian walking days. Robert Croll, Bob to a crowd of friends and readers, was an Australian nature writer of note. Two of his popular books had been devoted to experiences gathered on holiday "walkabouts" in the bush. Along with an eye for nature, Bob had an ear for the right word and the well-turned phrase. Just one word of invitation to accompany me to Central Australia was enough, and shortly we found ourselves racketing over the railway ties on our thousand-mile journey from Adelaide north.

Had I waited twenty years for a greater contrast between the well-watered Kimberley districts and the vast arid expanse that has been often called the dead heart of Australia, I could not have chosen a better time for our visit.

From Adelaide north the land was in the grip of drought. Even in the districts near the coast we saw just a trace of green surrounding each gum tree, marking the limits of the noonday shade. Here unshorn sheep huddled like a dirty grey blanket, or they shuffled along, noses to the ground, from one dry bent of grass to the next. But as the train rattled and clanked northward all signs of life disappeared. Between the brown of the ranges and the faded yellow of the plains there was little to choose. The hills looked as if they had been staked out for torture under the unpitying sun, but whether it were brown slope, shallow valley, or "gibber plain," a stony brown expanse of rocks, like a pavement, flattened by the wind, everything alike gasped for rain.

In our compartment there was a Catholic priest returning to some inland mission and a grizzled cattleman. The latter told us that in his country west of Alice Springs no "decent" rain had fallen for nine years, and all his stock except a few animals that he had herded close to bore-hole water were dead. Incredible as it seemed, he was still optimistic about his prospects.

"My word, Perfessor," he assured me, "this country has a great future. You should see what one good season does—grass to your horses' bellies. All it needs is water, an' you wouldn't know the place."

The priest agreed, but where the water was to come from, and where it could be held in reservoirs when the rains came, was indeed a problem.

As the hours slid by and we proceeded north through the little sun-baked townships of Marree and Oodnadatta, the country everywhere bore the marks of the drought. Isolated rocky hills, their summits wind-eroded like windowed battlements, their lower slopes partly hidden by dead mulga trees and tufts of spinifex grass, marched with the railway line. A railway trestle carried us over the dry stream bed of the Finke River, a red and yellow ribbon of sand meandering south between double lines of white "ghost gums" to its final obliteration under the desert sands. No water had filled its lower reaches for fifty years. South of us 300 miles lay a great gypsum and dried mud-bed that was called Lake Eyre.

I must confine myself to several incidents that together told the grim story of drought. The first nearly brought us to a permanent halt. Two days before our passage a great desert wind sprang up from somewhere and laid down a stifling blanket of red sand and dust over the countryside. Twenty-seven drifts covered the railway line in ten miles, some of them a couple of feet deep. Gangs of men had been working at either end to clear the line so that our train could proceed. Water and food were conveyed to them by trolley. Fortunately it was midwinter or this second trip of the "Ghan" might have been its last.

However, the work went slowly, so train crew and passengers, armed with shovels, set to work on the last remaining drift. The priest shed his clerical garb and our friend the rancher acted as foreman. After a couple of hours' shovelling, our foreman drew the priest and me aside for tactful consultation. He evidently represented management, the Father and I the "upper ten" of the passenger population.

"Look," he said, "do you know wot I think? Youse fellers could do a sight more good if yer dropped yer shovels, slipped back to the train and made a coupla buckets of 'ot tea an' brung 'em 'ere."

This seemed to both of us to make supreme sense, so the Father with Croll and myself went back to the engine, obtained supplies of boiling water from the engine-driver and carried buckets of steaming tea back to the work gang. I have never received so enthusiastic a reception in my whole life, and certainly have never before or since been made to feel like a ministering angel. The reverend Father was perhaps more used to the role, but from the encomiums heaped on Croll and me anyone would have thought that, practically speaking, we personally had cleared the line ourselves. Since our friend the rancher appointed himself spokesman, I found it difficult to obtain for him due recognition as the initiator of the idea. After an hour or two, the last sand heaps had been shovelled away and the train puffed slowly along between two cheering lines of the work gang, heartened by the hand-clapping of our fellow passengers. No train ever bore such a load of undeserved good will. After the wheels had ground through the final drift, the engine-driver and fireman stopped the train to come back and express their thanks in large enamel mugs of warm beer.

A second experience carried with it the threat of human tragedy. After some weeks of work at the Finke River Mission at Hermannsburg, Croll and I "went bush" in search of a group of natives who, under the oversight of an old man, had been encouraged by the Mission people to "go walkabout" on a foraging excursion which would lessen the strain on the Mission food supplies, already near the breaking point because of a new influx of population. The arrivals were a tribe of Pitjandjara, who belonged to the southwest in the Luritcha group, a complex similar to that of the Arunta for whose spiritual and bodily welfare Hermannsburg Mission had been established.

These people came from about 250 miles over the mountains west of Lake Amadeus, a huge salt bed now completely dry. The waterholes in their home country were exhausted, food supplies depleted, and when in some mysterious fashion news filtered through the desert that white men were distributing food at the Mission, the old men gathered the group together for the long trek to Hermannsburg.

I was indeed fortunate, for otherwise I would never have seen a completely primitive set of aborigines existing in their original way of life. There were 38 of them, men, women and children, with not a shred of clothing among the lot. This tribal horde was equipped with spears, spear-throwers (woomeras), boomerangs, stone knives, adzes, and spear points. But their arrival put a heavy strain on food resources at the Mission and Mr. Albrecht, the missionary in charge, picked out of the population a group of newer arrivals who could be more equal to the problem of gathering enough sustenance from the desert to ensure their temporary survival. As they grew

Luritcha boys and girls as they arrived at the Finke River Mission in 1929.

weak they were replaced by others who had gained strength on Mission rations. It was a plan to distribute, not supplies, but the great hunger more equitably.

Under the guidance of Mr. Heinrich, the Mission schoolmaster, we drove out into the area where Lame Woppity, leader of the foragers, was operating. Here we had opportunity to gain some insight into the life-and-death struggle that a drought in this region imposes.

There were about 30 in Woppity's group, whose headquarters were close by a tiny spring, well screened by a thicket of green brush, on the side of a dry range overlooking what is known as the Horn Valley, discovered by the Expedition of that name. It was a rockhole about eighteen inches deep, full of sweet water, which overflowed in a thin trickle a few feet down the slope. Overlooking the spring was a cunningly constructed blind, behind which two of Woppity's best young spearmen took turns in a night and day watch for rock wallabies visiting the spot.

The rest of the foraging party was scattered about, the old and feeble ranging close to camp, the younger, more active men further afield, and outside them a thin screen of the tribe's most experienced hunters. We came on one man who was actually running, turning over rocks and decaying logs, gathering anything that moved—ants, grubs, beetles—into a skin receptacle. His only word of English was "hongry, hongry" illustrated by an expressive rubbing of his flattened stomach. We gave him the remains of our lunch, which he carefully stowed away without tasting it. At night the group would reassemble at the camp spot, where Woppity distributed the day's catch in the one meal of the day. When the pangs of hunger were too persistent, the natives would still them by swallowing the inner bark of trees, unnutritious but filling.

Here was first-hand evidence of the discipline exerted by the old men, without which only the most athletic young men could possibly have survived. Under this beneficent control, the integrity of the tribe was preserved and the wisdom and experience of the old leaders perpetuated. Thus was ensured not only the survival of the hardiest in the group, but also, through the old men, the continuity of aboriginal psychic inheritance—the songs, the dances, the legends, the whole philosophy of existence. There, in front of me, was an exposition of social psychology that no university course could possibly offer. My education was indeed proceeding. I had to remind myself that I had just come from the Fitzroy River waterholes, where game was so plentiful that I had literally to kick it out of my way.

Though the evidence of the vicissitudes of life faced by the Australian people was everywhere apparent, it took a massive demonstration such as this to impress me in its overwhelming detail. I was actually watching a battle similar to those waged through a hundred centuries—a naked people striving to maintain itself in this, the loneliest of all continents.

On another excursion that Croll and I made into the Western McDonnell ranges, we climbed up an elevation where a large soakage was supposed to exist. Under the rim of a saucer-shaped shallow depression springs had dampened several acres of ground. At one time vegetation had surrounded the spot, but now the springs had been plugged by the trampling hooves of cattle.

The original herbage had long been eaten so that the cattle had to range further and further afield for sustenance during the day, coming in to drink or at least lick the damp earth each night. Finally, the weaker beasts could no longer travel away to graze and scores of them died alongside the middle of the springs. Starvation and thirst finally took their toll of the stronger animals until they, too, fell in their tracks.

The little hollow became a place of death. For a radius of more than a hundred yards we could not walk except on sun-dried carcasses. There was not even room to put a foot to the ground. Only on the periphery was there actually space left for the cattle to die, while far back on the rim of the depression lay the scattered bodies of those that survived the longest.

Miles away in the bush there were still many bodies. Apparently because the air was so dry and the sun so hot, each carcass was an unbroken bag of bones. Beside our track to the Mission someone with a macabre sense of humor had picked up the desiccated remains of a bay colt with white forefeet, and stood it up against a tree. With its tail swinging in the breeze and its legs in trotting position it looked almost alive.

C. T. Madigan, Central Australian air-explorer and author, records seeing in 1927 cattle by the tracks to Alice Springs, two years before our visit, i.e., with two more years of drought to go. "These," he wrote, "stood perfectly still, even when we had to swerve to avoid them; it seemed uncanny, and we stopped to examine them. To our horror, we found that they were standing in a kind of trance, staring ahead with glazed eyes, neither hearing

Standley Chasm, first traversed and named by the author in 1929, is located in the Chewings Ranges thirty-three miles west of Alice Springs in Central Australia. The 250-foot high walls of this remarkable chasm spring into blazing color as the sun strikes the rocky floor around midday. The chasm was named after a Mrs. Standley on account of the services she rendered for many years to half-caste children in Alice Springs.

nor seeing, dead on their feet. They would fall down in time and never rise again." The travellers wanted to shoot them, but this was against the code. No one knew when a shower of rain might fall and save the strongest. There were, however, no showers for over twenty months.

The author and Robert Croll with their string of camels in Palm Valley amphitheatre in 1929.

While we were at the Mission, we were allowed to take the children on a camel trip to bring drinking water from Koparilya Springs seven or eight miles back in the mountains. At one time there was a wild cry of "snakes" from two ten-year-old boys, but they proved to be only five-inch earthworms living in the grass by the side of the spring. None of the children with us had seen a worm since the drought began.

Though even the crows were dying for lack of carrion, the natives were still surviving. Government flour without greens of any kind brought on scurvy, and eleven people had died at the Mission before two medical men from an Adelaide University party diagnosed the disease. A supply of fresh oranges from Adelaide soon corrected the malady.

Thus my purpose of testing the mental reactions and abilities of people of the same race and cultural status, but living in regions differing strikingly in regard to ease of subsistence, was greatly furthered, though I would joyfully have suffered any detriment to my work if only the Centre could have had rain. But willy-nilly, I was presented with extremes beyond any I could have foreseen or even imagined. The arrival of the Pitjandjara tribe set us eagerly at work to make the best of our opportunity to test and measure aboriginal male abilities. I was able to donate all our excess food stocks to the Mission. Here I was to receive a lesson in courtesy that these desert dwellers could extend to the white man.

It so happened that there were eight men in the University party, organized by my friend Dr. T. D. Campbell for anthropological studies at Hermannsburg. They had preceded us by a very short time. Because of their obvious interest in the Arunta, the old men considered them honorary members of the tribe just as Spencer and Gillen had been twenty years previously.

When Croll and I arrived, we were similarly recognized and, more or less jocularly, each of us was assigned to an exogamic division of the tribe. My subsection was Pungata, which made all the other Pungata men my brothers and all the Mbitjana women eligible to me as wives. It also determined my classificatory relation to everyone else in camp, and prescribed the appropriate types of behavior between us. For example, I was supposed to completely avoid all the women whom the Mbitjana called *mia* or mother, since these could be my prospective mothers-in-law. Similarly I owed certain obligations to my potential fathers-in-law, and even the place I occupied at a campfire was predetermined.

As I was too busy to concern myself with social amenities, I went blithely on my way, speaking to anyone regardless of the rules. Croll, however, took the induction much more seriously and did his best to do the right thing. Though every small child knew his relationship to everyone else, it was difficult indeed for a white man to work out the system. Consequently, Croll was always in trouble and decided to lay a complaint before the tribal elders.

"This fella Porteus," he said, "him all the time silly fella, but nobody laugh at him. Me try all the time, but everyone laugh. Whaffor?"

"Oh," the old men assured him, as far as their limited English would allow, "take no notice of him—that fella feebleminded."

Later we were allotted our secret *knaninja* or totems. I was an *ilya* or emu man. Croll was of a different "skin," as they called it, and was assigned to the *achilpa,* or wild cat totem.

When the Luritcha arrived at the Mission, they were informed that I was an *ilya* man but completely ignorant. Nevertheless, I still owned plenty of flour and thus I should be given instructions

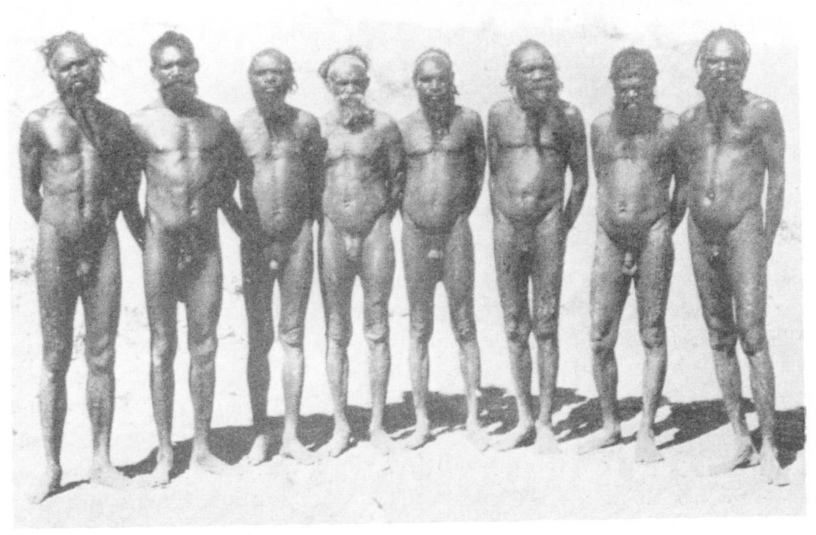

Luritcha men of the author's totem, 1929.

as to my obligations to these, my totemic brothers, who also happened to be *ilya* men. So the leader of the Pitjandjara suggested they take me down to the creek bed for a day's schooling to show me some of my ancestral secret ceremonies. However, since Croll was an *achilpa* (wild cat), he could not be present, and even our friend Heinrich was not reckoned a member of the tribe, so he, too, was excluded.

Early on a Saturday morning, armed with a pistol and two words of Luritcha, *ballalinka* (very good) and *itchi* (no), I was escorted to a spot out of sight of the Mission, where the rest of the men were already decorating themselves with a triple line of white extending from their shoulders to their lower chests, thence down the thighs to knee level, the whole suggesting the markings of the emu.

The ceremonial ground had been carefully swept with a eucalyptus bough and consecrated with blood drawn from a young man's vein and then scattered around the spot. A ball of hair string was covered with blood so that white feathers and vegetable down would adhere to it. This was hung around the neck of the old

The author and some of his "blood brothers" of the Central Arunta tribe in 1929.

leader of the totemic group. Three round stones from the creek were similarly decorated and placed on a bare spot, representing the nest and eggs of our mythical ancestor, the emu.

Then from the bushes emerged the chief performers, peering this way and that, at the same time imitating the call of the emu to attract the other *ilya* spirits. The men approached in line, each bent with hands locked behind his back to represent the emu's tail. Then they knelt down in a close ring around the older men who stood above the nest. I had been sitting on the ground a few feet away, but at this stage I was beckoned to come close and watch from a gap in the line left for me. All of the group then rhythmically contracted their shoulder and abdominal muscles, universally accepted by natives as a sign of great emotion. I had been informed by Mr. Love of Port George Mission that the phrase for emotional excitement is "my belly is boiling." It will also be remembered that the rotation of the hands in the love-magic scene at Beagle Bay was to bring about the play of abdominal muscles, the concomitant of sexual excitement to be aroused in the woman whom the dance was supposed to stimulate and bring to the spot. In this case, the ceremony was performed in a most reverent fashion, while the emu "heart" swung rhythmically from the old man's neck.

Then for some hours the group ran through a whole series which I judged to be bits and pieces of rites and ceremonies related to the magical increase of the birds and animals. One remarkable performance was for the eight men to form a line, standing with legs slightly spread and quickly vibrated in unison, so that the line retreated by means of the backward shuffling of the feet, a few inches at a time.

At only one period did I feel any disquiet. A small portion of the ground was cleared again and the old man, using a sharp splinter of stone, stabbed himself in that portion of his penis which had been the site of the sub-incision operation performed after he was first initiated, the blood being vigorously splattered around.

Then the whole group sat in a ring singing with rising excitement and tempo the *lartna* or circumcision song, at the same time beating sticks and woomeras on the ground.

Two men knelt on their hands and knees so that their backs formed a human platform, on each side of which stood two men, the oldest with a stone circumcision knife in hand. When I was urgently invited to approach, I wondered for the moment whether the initiation to be conferred on me might be actually earned rather than honorary. My hearty *ballalinka* (very good) changed suddenly to a fervent *"itchi, itchi"* (no, no).

But the men, sensing my misgivings, merely laughed, patted my arm gently and pointed to my camera, the purpose of which they had evidently learned from the Arunta. A young man lay back on the surgical table and while the assistant held him by the arm, the chief operator imitated the cutting of the foreskin accompanied by the loud chanting of the *lartna* song.

Another very solemn activity was the making of ceremonial

waningas by winding hair string on a wooden cross, following a very careful design. A song initiated the winding, which was interrupted at several stages while all the group gathered and sang together in very reverential tones. I regretted that I could not follow the words of the song, but was informed later by an authority on the Arunta language that the words used would be traditional and that many of the celebrants would not themselves understand their full meaning.

But I was learning—learning to appreciate how many of the ceremonial forms of savage living, though at first sight seemingly capricious, were actually part of an on-going, inherited social system that was traditional. True, many of these procedures were repeated simply because things had always been done that way, and possessed values not easily apparent. In this land of sparse population and infrequent contacts, it was important to strengthen and preserve what social bonds had already been forged through the ages. I had seen for myself one instance of what Goldenweiser called "the tragic emergencies of savage life," at which time tribal discipline was essential if their society were to survive.

Quite obviously those who had lived through other crises, or had met similar emergencies, were the most fitted to govern, and everything that would support this authority was valued. Thus the initiatory rites, cruel and bloody though they were, bolstered that authority. Then, too, if something more than mere animal survival were needed, the elders' knowledge of songs, ceremonies, and legends together constituted a communicable philosophy of life, the transmission of which was most essential. If the old men took unto themselves some compensatory privileges, particularly as regards food and women, that was not to be wondered at.

In our own culture we have an example of the elevation of the old and experienced to posts of command in times of national crisis. Indeed, the tendency to rely on elderly leaders may be overdone, so that world wars sometimes provide the graves of great reputations.

All this might be considered as social foresight far beyond the range of vision of the aborigines. These are, however, devices that possibly are not directly the result of deliberate planning, but if so, they are remarkable instances of fortuity that somehow worked out to these people's advantage. Such, for example, is the making of the totemic ceremonial grounds and *churinga* hiding places so sacrosanct that not only are tribal offenders safe from punishment there, but animals also will not be killed within their limits.

The region around Palm Springs in the James or Krichauff Ranges was just such a spot, and its sanctity was reinforced by the fact that the owners of this particular region had died out, but their spirits still would be supposed to defend the place. Hence, the animals and birds were safe from hunting parties so that, with the final breaking of the drought, the Springs would serve as a distributing center of wild life for miles around.

Another measure that made for social cohesion was the division of the tribe into exogamic subdivisions, which meant that only one-eighth of the women were eligible to individual old men as wives. Diminishing the number of sexual competitors certainly would prevent quarrels or antagonism among the real rulers of the horde—the old men. Another precautionary provision was that the children of a union were not of the same "skin" as either of the parents, but returned to the subsection of the grandfather. The result was that no section or subsection would become numerically so important through superior fertility as to outnumber those belonging to other divisions. This, in my opinion, was a far more logical reason for exogamy than fear of incest, which in turn would imply a knowledge of genetics far beyond aboriginal understanding. These notions were, of course, put forward by me in my writings, but the intrusion of a social psychologist into the field of anthropology was not exactly pleasing.

Actually, I was merely giving an added emphasis to the ideas of other students, whose standing in anthropology was much more assured than my own. For example, Eyre had promulgated the theory that the first aboriginal landing place and later dispersion area was northwest Australia, a view which I adopted and held despite criticism. Now it seems that carbon datings appear to indicate the presence of Australids in the northwest at a period antedating that of natives in the east and south by some thousands of years. Torres Strait, at the tip of northeast Queensland, has been called by ethnographers the front door of aboriginal immigration, but I prefer to regard it as the side door, or tradesmen's entrance.

Similarly, my emphasis on old-man government as the dominant feature throughout the continent had previously been often remarked upon, but what students failed to do was to recognize that this might be the key to the understanding of Australid social organization in general. Nor do I think that students nowadays should support the idea that the use of skins for clothing and the building of bark shelters and canoes constituted proof that the tribes who lived in the temperate southeast were superior in general culture and ability to the Central peoples. Actually, the Central aborigines lived at a much more complex social organization level.

We can now return to the original purpose of my work undertaken in Australia in 1929—to obtain an answer to the question as to the influence of a harsh physical environment on the comparative intelligence of primitive groups, specifically aborigines living in the northwest of the continent, where food was plentiful, as against those living in Central Australia, where the struggle merely to survive was unceasing.

Contrary to all previous expectations, the natives in the Centre scored relatively higher in the Porteus Maze Tests. In the northwest, 65 males scored 10.48 years, while those in the Centre averaged 12.08 years, a quite significant superiority.

As to the relation of the Maze to intelligence, especially of a practical nature, there was at the time of the study by no means as much evidence of the sensitivity of the test as at present. Not until 15 years later was there a clear demonstration of the fact that Maze test performance was closely related to damage to the frontal lobes of the brain. Still later, other proof of its reliability as a "brain test" became available. Though these conclusions could only be demonstrated in civilized patients, there is no reason to doubt that they would also apply to primitive peoples.

Not only was Maze performance in the Centre superior to that of natives in the northwest, but in practically all the other measures used (Form and Assembling, Form Board, Digit Memory, Xylophone Memory, and Goodenough Drawing) the Arunta held a constant if lesser advantage.

Apparently, the keener struggle for existence brought about a greater demand for mental alertness and planning capacity. However, it was eventually shown that the Arunta constituted a superior sample of aborigines. Their success in the tests was probably not by any means wholly due to closer acculturation with whites. It is true that at the Finke River Mission the natives had been under somewhat longer and closer mission supervision, but at Beagle Bay, Lombadina, Moola Boola, Violet Valley, and Wyndham contact with whites had been almost as intimate. But the Arunta at Hermannsburg represented a concentration of males of superior practical abilities.

From all of my experiences with the aborigines, I came away with the highest opinion of their ability to adjust to their own environment, but I steadfastly refused to make comparisons between aboriginal and white intelligence. To my mind such comparisons take us back to an outmoded psychological viewpoint, namely, that intelligence is "a unit character." Surely the simplest survey of man's achievements, in our own or any other culture, would show the futility of that conception. We have a hundred instances to prove that intelligence is "a many-splendored thing."

The author writing *The Psychology of a Primitive People* in 1931 after his return from Central Australia.

It is like national currency, of full value in one set of financial circumstances, but useless in another. In other words, intelligence has no gold standard with which its value can be equated.

Elsewhere I have pointed out that intelligence is a complex of abilities with perhaps a strong tendency to cluster together in constellations. Apparently *verbal* facility is one of the most interchangeable of many such constellations, one that the poet, the novelist, the playwright, the teacher must each possess to a high degree. But a genius like Shakespeare needed much more than verbal facility; he possessed superlative empathy, the ability to enter into the minds of men, to think as they think, to speak as they speak in many imagined situations involving many emotions. He was the social psychologist par excellence.

There is another constellation of abilities that involves the sound of music, and this requires quite another type of insight and expression. It would be utterly foolish to compare a Beethoven and a Shakespeare, or even an Einstein with a Michelangelo.

Similarly, at a very simple level, it seems purposeless to compare aboriginal with white intelligence. This is a mistake made, I think, by some of the best friends of the native. A review of a book quoted by the ethnologist Mountford (Walkabout, May 1966), stated that the reasonableness of the aboriginal way of life "is evidence enough of well-trained intelligence of such calibre as white man's." The conclusion would have been unassailable if the quotation had stopped at the word "intelligence." We have no single measure of intelligence calibre that is applicable. The fact that these primitive people are our living contemporaries is proof of intelligent behavior in their own environment. It proves nothing as to their ability to compete with whites in an environment largely of the latter's making.

All that my studies showed was that man's adjustment to a repressive environment depends largely on what strength he could draw from within. If using his own resources for survival were the sole criterion, then the aboriginal is greatly superior.

CHAPTER 10

Africa: Wonderland or Blunderland

IN MID-1933, after a breakdown in arrangements to effect an academic exchange with the University of Natal, I received a cable from Dr. Francis Keppel, President of the Carnegie Foundation, offering me a visitor's grant to enable me to carry out studies in South Africa. I presume that this interest in my research had been stimulated by the selection of my Australian book *The Psychology of a Primitive People* by the Scientific Book of the Month Club. Approval by its prestigious Selection Committee—Edward L. Thorndike of Columbia; Arthur H. Compton, Carnegie Institute; Harlan T. Stetson, astronomer, M.I.T.; Edwin G. Conklin, biologist, Princeton; Kirtley F. Mather, geologist, Harvard—was very encouraging.

My wife likes to tell the story that she was engaged in remodelling our house. The plan involved raising the roof over one section, and this looked to me to be beyond our financial resources. She says that I phoned from the University and announced: "You can raise the roof—my book has been selected by the Scientific Book Club." My comment was that if this had not occurred she would have been raising the roof ever since.

Of course, the Carnegie offer was accepted, and March 1934 saw us on our way to Durban. Our visit was noteworthy because it marked one of at least two occasions when, quite by inadvertence, I told the truth.

On our campus, after the trip had been announced, I met a friend who was a geologist-geographer, and had quite a passion for exact information.

"Where are you going?" he asked. "Now don't tell me 'Africa.' I want to know just where in Africa you will be."

I really had no settled plans except that I hoped to visit the Kalahari Desert in Bechuanaland, so as to compare the habitat of the Bushmen with that of the Australids. However, in looking over maps, my eye happened to light on the town of Molepolole, a name which, like Mesopotamia, seemed to come trippingly off the tongue; so quite hopefully I told him, Molepolole. My friend was satisfied, looked it up, and informed me next day that it was within a couple of hundred miles of the exact antipodes of Honolulu.

"If you want to know the shortest way," he said, "you could start burrowing straight down there," pointing at the ground between his feet.

To my pleased surprise when I landed in Durban, I received a letter from the South African Council that Mr. John Knobel had agreed to accompany our party as guide, philosopher, and friend, and that he had suggested as a base of Kalahari operations the native store he operated at Molepolole. For the purposes of our expedition—we soon found that *safari* was considered a Nairobi affectation—I had ordered a Chevrolet engine and chassis from New York, the truck body to be built in South Africa. The front seat provided more or less comfortable sitting room for John Knobel and my friend Dr. Kuhns, who was to be our medical officer. As he was also to be the main hunter of the party, I allotted him the outside seat. That left me about 9 inches of space in the center on which I could stuff a cushion for my own sitting accommodation. Travel in the Kalahari added up to nine hours' daily discomfort, for I was literally falling between two stools with scant support from either. All I could do for relief was to turn the other cheek.

In the building of the truck body, I had specified a space of 6 feet 6 inches behind the cab, just room enough for a three-quarter mattress on which we could sleep if lions became too troublesome. After we had traversed the Kalahari, my wife was to join me at Victoria Falls and we would then travel down to Cape Town together, while Dr. Kuhns and Knobel returned by train. John's inclusion in our party was the happiest possible circumstance. He had lived 27 years at Molepolole, just inside the edge of the desert, spoke Sechuana fluently, and had a university degree. More than that, he was, like his Boer forefathers, consumed with curiosity as to what lay beyond his immediate frontiers—in short, he was an authentic pioneer. After the first hundred and fifty miles the route of our excursion would be new to him, but his background of veldt experience was of utmost value to us. Besides his hunting skills, he had a scientific outlook; but his outstanding value lay in his thorough understanding of native intelligence and temperament. His availability and interest in my purposes were to me the most fortunate circumstances in an extremely lucky life. His kindly yet firm handling of the natives changed all my ideas as to the wisdom of Boer policies, at least in this vast undeveloped region of the Kalahari.

As to my special quest, the situation reminded me of the gold prospector's observation—gold is where you find it. The same was true of the Bushmen. It was like the old recipe for jugged hare, which began with the admonition—first catch your hare before you cook it. Catching up with the most elusive people in the world was a matter of chance rather than of good planning.

After outfitting in Johannesburg, we drove to Mafeking, picked up Knobel, then travelled 100 miles north to Gaberones, and thence west to Molepolole. Mafeking, of course, was famous for its long siege in the Boer War, but its monotony left me wondering why the Boers coveted such a desert outpost, and why the British chose to defend it. Apparently its possession had psychological, if not military value. Fortunately, no one talked of psychological warfare at that time.

Knobel met us with the bad news that Bechuanaland had been declared afflicted with hoof-and-mouth disease and that Colonel Ray, the resident director and chief administrator, had clamped down on any intrusion of visitors from the rest of South Africa. He was particularly opposed to hunting parties. The Crown Prince of Sweden, though armed with all kinds of documents from the British Home Office in London, had been stopped in his tracks by a firm refusal to be allowed to enter the Kalahari. Our prospects looked desperate, since letters from the Government of South Africa, which I carried, would be a detriment rather than a help.

Fortunately, Colonel Ray had literary propensities and had just written a long article describing a recent trip through his protectorate. In Melbourne a friend, the state public librarian, had given me the issue of the *British Journal of Geography* in which the account had appeared. The Colonel was so delighted that I carried this with me when I walked into his office that I departed not only with his permission to enter the Kalahari, but also armed with an official letter to all resident magistrates, stating that I "was proceeding with the full support of the Government," and enjoining them to give me every assistance in their power. Perhaps I did exaggerate a little the impact of the Colonel's article on American geographers, but actually it was well written and of great value to me.

The journey north afforded just enough glimpses of the region and its inhabitants to nudge us into the realization that this was indeed Africa. The track wound about thickets of camel-thorn trees standing on the rises, their tops cropped level like ragged umbrellas blown inside out by the wind. Bird life was abundant, with flights of long-tailed weaver birds, and of starlings shining with a metallic gloss. Kalahari pheasants, each with its brood of young, ran across the track, while at intervals we heard the Go-Away birds crying a warning to everything within hearing on the veldt that strangers were abroad. Over to the east stood the rampart of the Lobatsi Hills, crowned above their green flanks by granite tors, white with vulture droppings. Occasional meerkats fled into their burrows at the noise of our car. Knobel told us that the rocks were the hiding places of leopards, whose cunning kept them alive when lions and other big game had disappeared.

Here, too, we realized the illimitability of Africa. Westward the sun was dipping beneath the sands of the Kalahari. Ahead of us the track went 300 miles north to Buluwayo, thence to the Zambezi and Tanganyika, while several thousand miles beyond lay Abyssinia, Libya, and the Mediterranean. Behind us stretched another thousand miles south to the Orange River, past Kimberley, until the veldt finally met the southern sweep of the Indian and Atlantic Oceans. Here, indeed, was Africa, land of mystery, lying like a black monster at the foot of Europe.

West from Gaberones we were in Livingstone's country, once one of the great big-game regions of the world. Eighty years before our visit, two Englishmen recorded shooting seventy-eight rhinos here in a single season. Livingstone himself described, with sad disapproval, the wholesale slaughter of kudu, eland, zebra, wildebeeste, impala by driving them between strong stockades, ending in pits where the animals were speared or smothered themselves, dying in heaps. Just thirty miles to the north, Livingstone was able to shoot buffalo from his own doorstep. Now the game is depleted almost to the point of extinction; yet to our unaccustomed eyes there was still plenty. The sun was setting in front of us as we proceeded west over the thirty-six miles that led from Gaberones to Molepolole, and what wild life was left was stirring on the veldt. Duiker and steenbok crossed the track in front of the truck, and we caught swift sight of a greater kudu, an antelope with a magnificent head of horns that would have been a trophy hunter's delight. However, Knobel wisely discouraged all shooting near his home, which we reached just at sundown.

His house nestled closely under a line of rocky kopjes or hills, and our introduction to Africa was completed by the sight of an old baboon parading up and down a rocky ledge, barking defiance at the humans below. Knobel had planted an orchard around his home and the baboons had been raiding it nightly. On a post his son had placed the white skull of one of the marauders as a warning to trespassers. Chained to a tree was a half-grown, partly tamed baboon named Jacky. When he slipped out of his collar, the natives made chase, armed with sacks and nets for his capture, a risky business as the beast's teeth were sharp and his jaws inordinately strong. But Elsa, Knobel's daughter, had just to appear and call him, and Jacky at once came to her quietly to have his collar and chain refastened. John complained that the natives made Jacky's escape a matter for hullabaloo and a mad scamper of pursuit, which they enjoyed so much that their attempts to catch Jacky were only half-hearted. Chasing a young baboon was much more fun than working in the garden.

Our time was spent profitably, checking with John Knobel the excess supplies which we had bought in Johannesburg. Our plan was to proceed west from Molepolole toward the center of the Kalahari, making contact with any Masarwa (Bushmen) that we could locate. There would be a wagon track of a kind for 150 miles, after which we must travel over unmapped, untravelled veldt, following as best we could a northwest direction with detours around sand hill areas. If in 400 miles we could reach the Boer settlement of Ghanzi, we had Knobel's assurance that ours would be the first wheeled vehicle to cross the Kalahari in this direction. He himself had been over only the first 100 miles of this journey, as far as Motate Pan. Colonel Rey had given me what purported to be War Office maps, almost empty of any details, and those which appeared were usually wrong.

I suspect that John was harboring a secret desire to be an explorer, like his Boer parents and grandparents who had followed the great trekking traditions of South Africa. I had, however, no special wish to establish any records of travel or desert adventure. My plan was, if possible, to find the Masarwa and then to get some first-hand knowledge of their habitat with its food and water resources, and thus compare for myself the Central Australian and Kalahari environments.

The testing and measuring part of my work was almost secondary in importance. I knew that any contact with Bushmen would be brief, and I did not have anything like complete faith in the applicability of the test measures to extremely primitive subjects. But with my recent Australian experience in mind, I believed that I could make fair judgments as to just what human traits of temperament and intelligence were needed for survival in both environmental situations. This African project would carry my studies a long step forward. Central Australia and the Kalahari were both classified as deserts, but it was already apparent that the two regions were, from the viewpoint of human ecology, very different. Though I was not far within the Kalahari desert fringe, I could already sense that once again something had gone wrong with my research plan. Five years previously I had set out to compare two groups of subjects of the same race but reared in varying environments. Now I was trying to find out what happened if two peoples of different races lived in similar environmental situations, both called desert. But I was beginning to realize that two habitats may both be classified as desert yet could be extremely different. I must, therefore, bring to bear every bit of observation I could command to understand just what varying demands life in the Kalahari made as regards human adjustment. That was my primary problem. The comparison of test performances must come later after I had set my first objective in proper perspective.

Having reduced our load by discarding surplus supplies as much as possible, we set out on an early April morning along a wagon spoor that wound somewhat uncertainly westward. I had thought the Australian inland scene featureless, but the Kalahari veldt was even more monotonous. There were no hills, merely a succession of sandy rises, up which we ground in second gear. Occasionally we appeared to be approaching a low hill, only to find that merely looking up a long slope gave that impression by appearing to thicken the vegetation, camel-thorn trees and the like, only to find them evenly spaced when we topped the rise.

The first difference between the Australian bush and the veldt was that while the tree growth was stunted, it covered the surface thinly but constantly. It was obvious at once that here was better cover for stalking game, provided always that the hunter stooped low enough to keep his head below about a three-foot level. The Australian aboriginal, with stature about the same as whites, would be at a disadvantage in his stalking approach. The Bushmen, or Masarwa as we should call them, could jack-knife themselves, holding their heads down so that the low brush provided excellent cover.

At first, I was misled into thinking that the veldt was as empty as the bush, until after fifty miles' travel we came to the edge of an ancient river course, in places obliterated by the drifting sand. Here the trees were larger and for the first time we saw rocks edging the banks of the vanished river. This shade provided extra cover and we saw a small group of gray apes chattering at us from the branches. Rattling over stones on the opposite bank, we ran into a flock of several hundred guinea fowl that ran ahead of the truck until with a noisy clatter of wings they rose in flight. Dr. Kuhns shot a couple for our supper.

As we ground on along the sketchy wagon trail, Knobel pointed out the spot where a year previously he had joined in a hunt for a lion that had been raiding the cattle kraals belonging to the natives of a Bakalahari village we were approaching. He had fired and missed the lion, but it was shot most unexpectedly by a native with an old-fashioned, smooth-bore gun. This was an extraordinarily lucky shot, as these desert Bechuana are notoriously bad marksmen, yet take great assurance from the noise of a gun. Later we found that a native would journey at night into lion country if he was allowed to carry an empty rifle.

However, the local medicine man was just as suspicious of the village hunter's aim, and so he attributed the hit to the white man's magic and the good fortune that Knobel's presence brought to the hunt. It probably was wise to do so, for otherwise the marksman might have attained prestige that would have threatened the old medicine man's own social standing and reputation.

The village was a small collection of huts ringed about by a rather flimsy lion fence. These people were of Bantu descent, who in the time of the great raids and wars when Zulus and Matabele were the scourge of the subcontinent, had fled into the desert for safety. They called themselves Ba-kalahari, or Bakalaghadi, the people of the Kalahari, and John Knobel knew their language perfectly because of his 27 years of experience as a trader in Molepolole. They welcomed his unlooked-for return and told him that if we would stay the night they would put on the best *ngama,* or dance, that such short notice would allow.

But we had another sixty miles to go before we would reach Motate Pan, where we expected to camp for three or four days to gather the news of the desert. This would include the movements of game, the presence of lions in the area, tidings of Bushmen, and most important of all, whether the crop of tsama melons was a good one, for that would determine the kind of hunting, whether of game or Masarwa, that we should experience. For where the melons were, there we should find game and natives also.

As the afternoon wore on, the desert lost its appearance of emptiness. As John told us, nothing moved in the midday heat; each pair of animals stayed immobilized in mottled shade, where sun and shadow provided perfect camouflage. But by four in the afternoon, the game were on the move looking for their evening meal. This was evidently the time when wariness was of extreme importance. This was how it impressed me, for I wrote:

> Darkness is near and it behooves every creature on the veldt to scout its immediate surroundings most carefully, for it is at this time that the night's ambushes are laid. Ceaseless vigilance is the price of life in the Kalahari. There are few deep thickets or secret coverts in the desert. To draw a wide circle of loneliness about you and to hold everything at eyes' length as it were—this is the desert system of defence. . . . The very largeness of the desert, threatening as it seems, provides the best protection. He travels furthest who travels alone, provided that the appearance of emptiness does not bring a false sense of security. Any thickening of shadow, any darker curtain of brush may hide an enemy.[1]

But during our three-day stay beside Motate Pan—a saucer-like shallow depression a mile wide, covered with an off-white deposit of salt—I had ample opportunity to judge that this was a desert only by reason of the absence of surface water. In the beginning of summer, thunderstorms criss-cross the Kalahari, but the sands soak it up greedily to the last drop. Only the pans hold a thin film of water too salt to drink. But the storms, though scattered, supported the desert's own peculiar vegetation well enough to keep the desert dwellers, whether man or beast, alive. The tsama melon, about five inches in diameter, is borne along trailing vines, and

[1] Quoted from *Primitive Intelligence and Environment* (New York: The Macmillan Co., 1937).

the game when thirsty break the dark green rind with their hooves and lick out the juicy contents.

There were two kinds of melons, one far too bitter for human consumption. We found it was impossible for anyone to distinguish the edible from the bitter variety. But the animals made no mistake, and the natives followed along, gathering all the melons on a vine that bore fruit which the game had broken. Many of these animals rarely drank, obtaining their moisture by licking the early morning dew. When the desert winds dried up these rather fortuitous supplies, everything followed the melons that sprang up along the path of the storms.

But there was no doubt in my mind as to which of the two "deserts" offered the best chances of animal and human survival. For though the Kalahari had no surface water, it was covered with a tenuous network, a thin curtain of life. Except near the Pan itself, where the creatures of the wild came to lick or "brack" the salt dust, game was not to be found in herds but rather in tiny groups or even pairs. Yet the variety was impressive. There were wildebeeste, hartebeeste, duiker, steenbok, ostriches, gemsbok, occasional giraffes—altogether a zoological variety entirely unmatched by anything I saw in Australia.

"Our aborigines would grow fat here," I remarked, "once they had mastered the trick of staying alive." But that, I realized, would take long experience, a complete ecological apprenticeship.

The Bakalaghadi represented the anthropologically thin spume of fugitives driven inland by invading hordes of superior Bakwena —the people who, in Knobel's phrase, "danced to Kwena the crocodile," as their tribal symbol. The fact that they were now a couple of hundred miles inland from any crocodile rivers bore witness to the terror in which these panic-stricken warriors had, in their turn, fled from the Makalolo or the Matabele of King Tshaka's day. Another hundred miles into the heart of the desert beyond Motate Pan marked the limits of Bakalaghadi flight. Beyond them, in a land that no one coveted even as an escape from death, lived the Bushmen, called by the Bechuana, Masarwa, "the abandoned people."

Every few yards we were reminded of the reasons why the Kalahari provided sanctuary for the desperate in spirit. As I wrote later,

> Nothing that grew in that region seemed to be without its thorns. We learned to know the hook-and-stick, so called because at the base

of each of its sharp spikes is a little barb that holds you while the thorn pierces; then there was the ape thorn, a tree with trunk set about with sharks' teeth; the wait-a-bit, whose name is sufficiently descriptive; the black thorn, which literally seems to reach out and catch you as you pass. All these ring the desert in, as though on guard against the intruder. It was easy to see why the Kalahari became a sanctuary for the hunted. It protects because it outdoes in savagery the enmity of the pursuer. Those who sought its refuge must accept its hazards—hunger, thirst, danger from wild beasts, loneliness.

As soon as we began shooting game at Motate Pan, natives appeared as if by magic from the apparently empty veldt. They informed us that for two months no lion spoor had been seen, but that 50 miles further on there were lions in plenty. More essential to my purpose was the news that Bushmen were also to be found in the Khutse veldt area. Whether they would still be there on our arrival no one could say.

"Masarwa," the men told Knobel, "are not people but things of the veldt, here today and gone tomorrow, no man knows whither. Why do not the *moreni* [white lords] stay at our kraal and shoot game? Then if the white teacher [myself] wanted to see and study real men, they would dance for him and do for him whatever he pleases. Who are the Masarwa, anyway?"

The absence of lions was reassuring, but there were two other things that prompted our early departure from Motate. The first, of course, was the news that Masarwa were within reach; the second was that by the fourth day, with the exception of a beautiful gemsbok, an antelope with horns like curved scimitars lying back along its neck, which we shot on the Pan, game suddenly disappeared. Even the vultures did not seem to keep us under as constant surveillance. The sudden emptiness of the veldt puzzled even the natives.

The next morning, just as we drove along a faint track skirting the northwest margin of the Pan, we found the reason. An apparent darker patch of shadow under a camel-thorn suddenly exploded into a pack of Cape hunting dogs, ugly beasts with blotched brown and black patches. Fortunately, they only ran fifty yards before stopping to look at us, and by this time the doctor and John were at work with their rifles; the result, five dogs dead out of a dozen.

These animals are indeed the scourge of the veldt. Everything flees in panic when a pack of dogs moves in, for they can run down almost any game and destroy it. John was delighted with our success. He said that our bag—if you may call five evil-smelling dogs a bag—would destroy more game than all we had shot since our arrival. Shooting would merely stir the veldt into activity, but a pack of wild dogs would set up a disturbance that would stampede everything for a radius of fifty miles. Even the jackals and hyenas, which follow lions, give the wild dogs a wide berth.

Through fifty more miles of hot Kalahari sunshine, grinding along in second gear when one wheel could no longer "half-spoor" the wagon track, we pressed forward with every nerve set against the constant jar and jostle of the truck. But we were at least cheered by the last word the natives brought us at Motate. It seemed that a very late storm had left water in a hole at Khutse, and Masarwa were camped near by the stadt or village of Bokhame, the local Bakalaghadi headman.

Had there been anything stout enough to make a shade, the evening shadows would have been long when we broke through the low brush alongside a twenty-yard hole, half filled with chalky but nevertheless drinkable liquid. That this water was a focal point for game was apparent when a herd of eland galloped by our truck. Two red hartebeeste gazed at us for a minute before making for the thickets that bounded the *vlei* or shallow valley. Then half a dozen ostriches paced slowly along its rim, silhouetted against the declining sun.

Here we picked up a new Bakalaghadi camp boy, Raumkavideo, who spoke English quite passably. He informed us that shooting one of these large, placid eland would keep the Masarwa near our camp as long as the fat lasted. Fat was what the Masarwa, like the Australian aborigines, dreamed about. The flesh of ordinary game and native cattle was stringy and tough. Eland provided the choicest meat, though there was also much spoor of other game. The best proof of that were fresh pug marks of lions around the waterhole.

We were indeed fortunate in finding surface water, for Knobel assured us that for the next 300 miles we would see none. We had already dipped into our jealously hoarded store of forty gallons, mainly to cool our engine, which boiled every twenty minutes on the last part of our journey. The seeds of the yellow Bushman grass, winnowed in our passage, had closely blanketed our radiator. Now we could pick out the seeds and fill one of our large twenty-gallon cans with this new supply.

As for the lions, Raumkavideo told us that the Masarwa had killed a hartebeeste which lions had mauled but not pulled down. They hung some of the meat in a tree at their *werft* or camp, and had been kept awake for two nights throwing lighted sticks from their campfire into the darkness to keep the lions at a respectful distance. Our boy said that the Masarwa admitted they had no business interfering with the lions' property. He assured us that we, being strangers, would be quite safe from annoyance for at least three or four days until the lions had looked us over and figured out our intentions. Knobel agreed, saying that lions were gentlemen and left anyone alone who did not interfere with them. We noted again that the natives spoke of lions just as if the latter were human.

In spite of such verbal assurances, I was glad to lend the Bakalaghadi our new small axe while they assisted Raumkavideo in building a *boma* or lion fence around our camp site. This we had selected about two hundred yards from the waterhole so as not to disturb the game. When I pointed out a wide gap in the thornbush barrier, Knobel told me not to worry—that was where Raumkavideo would sleep at night to keep our fire going.

Before we slept, I heard lions roaring for a time about a mile or less away, but I slept peacefully, snuggled against and slightly under a branch of thornbush. I consoled myself with the knowledge that both Doctor Kuhns and Knobel were far bigger and juicier than I, and that surely none but a feebleminded lion would choose me for a meal.

I noted, however, that before John rolled himself in his blanket, he reloaded his gun with buckshot and leaned it against a small bush near his hand.

"There's nothing like a gun loaded with buckshot to blow a hole in a lion at close quarters," he explained. "A rifle bullet will go clean through him without any immediate effect."

"But," I objected, "I thought you told us that lions were gentlemen, and would not attack unless interfered with."

"Well," he said, "they are really not dangerous unless they happen to be man-eaters, but in any case, it's always the unexpected that happens in Africa!"

As regards desert dwellers, one lesson I learned was that having no stake in the country, no ties, no abiding place, no responsibilities was possibly a happier state of existence than clinging to thin threads of civilization, maintaining a desperate hold on poor possessions, putting down such shallow roots that any winds can sweep the whole away. This was the plight of the Bakalaghari,[2] whose lives were cast "between the desert and the sown," belonging to neither. As Livingstone remarked, the Bushmen live in the desert by choice, the Bakalaghari by compulsion.

Of the people of the Kalahari, the less fortunate, I believe, were not the Masarwa, but the more recent arrivals, the Bakalaghadi, who lived precariously between two worlds. Many of them showed signs of mixture with the Bushmen, both in color, small stature, and pepper-corn hair. Their overlordship over wandering groups of Masarwa was of a perfunctory nature, though there was, so I was informed, a token tribute of animal skins occasionally paid to the headmen of kraals adjacent to Bushmen hunting grounds. The headman of the Khutse stadt, the Boer name for a settlement or kraal, spoke to us slightingly of the Masarwa. When there was meat available, he complained, they were always on hand, but when they were needed for any good purpose, they could never be found.

Incidentally, John had tried to explain my importance and my psychological mission, but not with too flattering results.

"This man," he told the Bakalaghadi, "is a big chief in his country. Every morning the young men gather in crowds at the door of his hut to hear his words of wisdom." The group considered this in silence for a time.

"Does he speak Sechuana [the language of the Bakwena]?" they asked. Knobel answered in the negative.

"Tell him," they said, "that we are very sorry for him."

This comment disposed completely of any question as to my importance.

At Lunakie, a typical werft or kraal, halfway to Khutse Pan, we had decided to off-load half our supplies, storing them there to be picked up on our return. John Knobel scoffed at my fears that the natives might not be trusted to look after our belongings. I realized that just a fraction of our temporary discards would represent untold wealth to these poverty-stricken people.

"Don't worry," he told me, "if we are away for a year, everything will be just as we left it. We'll give them an empty petrol drum as a reward. Filled with water, that could help save their lives until the rains come."

Incidentally, I found that Livingstone provided strong support for one of my theories as to the minor importance of environment. Of the first arrival of the Bakalaghari in this region, he wrote:

[2] Livingstone's spelling.

> Living ever since on the same plains with the Bushmen, subjected to the same influence of climate, enduring the same thirst and subsisting on the same food for centuries, they seem to supply a standing proof that locality is not always sufficient to account for differences in races. The Bakalaghari retain in undying vigor the Bechuana love for agriculture and domestic animals. They hoe their gardens annually, though all they can hope for is a supply of melons and pumpkins. They carefully rear small herds of goats, and I have seen them lift water for them out of small wells with a bit of ostrich shell, or by spoonfuls.

Livingstone was, I believe, saying just what I meant when I affirmed that environment is not the sole developing force in building ethnic character and personality. What is within as well as without is an equally powerful determinant of what manner of men, whether Bushmen or Bakalaghari, they will turn out to be. I am very much afraid that all this modern emphasis on the influence of environment is somewhat out of balance.

This is how Lunakie and its people impressed me:

> Hard pressed indeed must people be who would choose Lunakie as a home. As I remember it, the wilderness had already marched across the valley above and below, completely ringing it in. But for a mile across the depression not a shrub or a tree was to be seen. The natives had long ago swept it bare of everything that would burn.
>
> The huts were of the primitive beehive shape, surrounded by a fence of thornbush. They were built each with a framework of crooked poles set thickly together, the spaces being filled with a thatch of desert grass. On a fire between two huts was a three-legged Boer pot filled with melon strips, bubbling over the flame. On a springbok skin the melon seeds were being dried in the sun.
>
> It may be difficult to enter into the interests of these desert dwellers, but it is easy to understand their fears. A thorn fence seemed such a flimsy barrier to keep out the carnivorous beasts when these are about. The lion, as everyone knows, is usually not to be feared, but when there is a drought and game is scarce, it may be a different story. One may turn man-eater for various reasons—sometimes he becomes bad-tempered because of a porcupine quill stuck in his cheek, the festering wound preventing him from doing his ordinary hunting—and so he turns to man-killing. Then occurs a reign of terror, which lasts till the killer is hunted down and destroyed. The old men told Knobel of nights when they sat on guard, each man in his hut with assegai braced firmly in the ground, lest a bold paw tear down the flimsy mat barrier that forms the

> door and hides the cowering folk inside. Occasionally a child has been carried off by a hyena or a lion has sprung upon a woman emptying the ashes at the back of the hut, but these fatalities are rare. You may buy a man's skin kaross easily, his cattle rarely, even his wife, but his protective charms not at all.
>
> Against these and many other perils of forest and wayside, the prudent man will avail himself of magic. The claw of the lion, the whiskers of the leopard, the skin of a snake, the scrapings of bucks' horns, the toe nails of the hyena, if mixed together and burnt by the witch doctor, carry protection in their smoke. So the newborn babe must be held over the magic fire, the ashes of which, if mixed with the water he drinks, will give additional protection.

This is life in uncivilized Africa, and the question arises, why do the people not move away? The answer lies deep in their psychology. Nothing except direst necessity, or when death is the only other choice, will drive them away. This is their home, and home is the most meaningful word in any language. The Australian aborigines feel about it the same way. Each man has his own country to which, whenever possible, he will return.

CHAPTER 11

Okovango Sanctuary

If I were a hunter of lions instead of Bushmen, I could no doubt make this an interesting tale. I had a rifle but my tools were pencil and paper, so while the doctor and John scoured the veldt, I set up my bush laboratory in our camp. At first, prospects of work seemed dim. When John told Bokhame that I wanted to see and work with Bushmen, he was at first contemptuous and then indignant. Like our earlier visitors, he wanted to know, if I came so far to find out how clever people were, why did I want to look past him and his people? Masarwa, he assured John, are absolutely different from "us Bakwena"—they were nothing, not even as useful as animals.

"I have no authority over them," he said. "As well ask me to gather the jackals together! Yes, they do dance after a fashion, shuffling around and around in a circle while their women clap their hands, but if you want real entertainment [and he leered at us suggestively], the women of my stadt could supply it much better than these naked savages."

He did, however, condescend to show us the general direction of the Bushmen's *werft,* and with Raumkavideo as guide, we discovered, two miles away in the veldt, a huddle of small huts in the shape of half-domes, with one side wide open to intruders, lions or otherwise. These were skilfully placed on a sandy rise, not in a close or compact group, but scattered so that they blended very well with the veldt. A hundred yards away they were practically invisible. It has been said in Scripture that a city set upon a hill cannot be hid, but this is untrue of a Bushman village, which is so scattered on an open rise that it can easily be overlooked.

One hut seemed deserted but the ashes in front of it were warm, and an ostrich-eggshell at the back of the structure had some spoonfuls of water in it. Raumkavideo raised a strange ululating cry and presently above a slightly thicker patch of brush, three or

A Bushman hut—the wide opening offering no protection against lions, which were common in this locality.

four small black heads cautiously appeared. Their owners were poised for flight until Knobel called to them in Sechuana. He evidently knew what to say to them for they arose, giggling with astonishment and delight. There were six women clad in karosses or cloaks of skin, adorned with beads fashioned of bits of ostrich-eggshell. They were accompanied by a youth evidently part-Bakalaghadi, who appeared to be under their direction rather than the reverse. He exhibited for us a "Bushman violin," consisting of a partly hollowed piece of wood and a single string, cupped at one

Raumkavideo, the Bakalaghadi camp boy, with Bushman women and a youth.

end by a tin can, and with this he produced a monotonous, two-toned accompaniment to a song. Once having started the youth singing, I could not stop him, so everywhere I went in this little *werft* I was escorted by this one-stringed band.

Once the ice was broken, there was no doubt of our welcome. None of the women was more than four feet two inches in stature, and their small triangular-shaped faces, with sharp chins and high cheek bones, plus a light cinnamon skin color, marked them down as authentic desert Masarwa. They showed us their bracelets and ostrich-shell necklaces, and told Knobel that their men were away hunting. They seemed deliberately vague in indicating the direction they had gone. When Knobel tried to express my wish that they would come to our camp and dance, they merely laughed and chattered in their own language, the clicks following each other like a rattle of beads on a rosary. Since neither Raumkavideo nor Knobel had enough conversational Masarwa, John finally gave up in despair. One of the younger women had on a specially well-beaded kaross, which indicated, so Raumkavideo told us, that she was about to be married. In farewell, the oldest woman—not much beyond 30 years I would judge—stroked John's forearm gently as if to feel its texture. No one, except my musical escort, paid any attention to me. Well, I had found the Masarwa, but how I could persuade them to do what I wanted in the way of tests and measurements was beyond me. Bokhame had, as we have seen, shown no disposition to be helpful.

However, my prestige among Bokhame and the Bakalaghari was unexpectedly promoted. In northwest Australia I had achieved a reputation as a geologist simply by looking wise when presented with a mineral specimen, finding out what the enquirer thought it was, and then agreeing with him. This whole procedure obviated long, inadequate explanations of what a psychologist was and did. Now in the Kalahari I found myself suddenly acclaimed as a medicine man.

From the evening of our arrival, Bokhame had been asking the doctor for medicine to relieve his abdominal pains. Jay Kuhns, on the basis of his long medical experience on plantations in Hawaii, decided that constipation was the most likely trouble and gave the headman a couple of pills. Next morning Bokhame was at our camp very early with the same complaint and the doctor increased the dose, again with no results. On the third day, John, thinking it a good joke, took our friend Jay apart.

"Doctor," said he, "do you realize that you are lowering the white man's prestige seriously around these parts? Here I've been telling the natives what a great physician you are in your country and yet you cannot cure a simple belly ache!"

"I've given him triple doses of every laxative I've got in my bag, enough to move a horse. I can't do more."

"Perhaps," I suggested, "the patient needs a psychologist."

"Take him," Jay announced, "I give up—he's all yours. And I promise not to report you when you reach home for practising medicine without a license."

"That's not practising medicine," I objected. "That's merely like asking the patient to swallow or put out his tongue, and neither operation requires a medical diploma." But the doctor was disgusted and went on cleaning his gun.

Knowing a little about primitive psychology, I had come to the conclusion that Bokhame was merely building up his own private medicine chest to add to his own status as a magic healer after we had departed. So I took him to one side, dissolved a couple of cascara pills in a large mug of water, fortified it by a couple of packets of Epsom salts, then stood by while he drank the lot. After the nauseous draught went down, I noted that he eyed me with considerable respect, since native faith in any medicine increases in direct proportion to the nastiness of the remedy.

Apparently my diagnosis was correct. Bokhame did not appear near our camp for a couple of days; but he did send word by Raumkavideo that he would do anything about the Masarwa that I wanted, provided I would remove the powerful spell I had imposed on him. The next morning I stopped filling in time examining Raumkavideo and his fellow tribesmen and began work on eight Bushmen, who were personally escorted into camp by the headman himself. Moreover, Bokhame assured me that in a couple of days time it would be nearly full moon, and the Masarwa, being now well fed, would dance for us at his stadt. He seemed as much impressed by the quick lifting of the spell, as by the initial success of its operation. The only one not impressed was Jay Kuhns, M.D., who merely grunted when I told him that was merely professional jealousy on his part, and that he should employ some mental catharsis with his patients.

As a result of Bokhame's unexpected cooperation, I had a clear field for my testing program. In spite of the Masarwas' apparent interest in my Mazes, their performances were unexpectedly low. I felt that the women would have done better than the men, but since I had no comparative data on Australid women, I did not examine them. Physically speaking, there was evidence in several cases of mixture of blood with the Bakalaghari, but the group, while small, could be classed as authentic Bushmen. Judging by the many pits that had at one time been dug for the entrapment of game, I decided that Khutse had indeed once been a "place of plenty," which its name signified.

Meanwhile, John and Jay drove the truck on daily hunting excursions, which had as their joint purposes shooting and exploration. They reported that at Qusi Pan, fifty miles farther west, the trail disappeared completely and that further exploration must be across the untracked veldt. Moreover, the natives reported sandhill country ahead, which would slow our progress drastically. There was a rapidly drying soakage in Qusi where we might by digging find a little water. The natives there could give no clue to the whereabouts of Bushmen, as all beyond their kraal was "Bushman Land," which they penetrated warily in fear of the little hunters with their deadly poisoned arrows. For these weapons the Bakalaghari had the greatest respect. Our Masarwa friends at Khutse gave me a bow and a skin quiver, in which were a dozen arrows carefully fastened with their deadly poisoned tips set downward so as to avoid accidents. Each arrow had a small shaft of either ostrich bone or hard wood, which fitted into a hollow reed. This was done so that the poisoned section would remain in the wound while the arrow shaft dropped to the ground and could be recovered.

The poison was snake venom, squeezed from puff-adder poison sacs. When dried it was mixed either with euphorbia juice, or if great potency was desired, with the dried bodies of the *ngwa* grub, the body juices of which were highly venomous when the animal was in the pupal stage.

Their hunting strategy was clever. The game was cautiously stalked, the hunter frequently wearing a bunch of brush on his head. As soon as the arrow was discharged at short range, the hunter fell quickly to the ground and remained there. If not alarmed by the sight of men, the animal runs but a short distance, and then begins to feed again until it feels the effect of the poison. Then its instinct is to leave the herd and run as far as it can into the veldt. The hunter then takes up the trail until he finds his quarry dying or dead.

In the case of a large animal, such as a giraffe, the chase may take two or three days, and this calls for tremendous Bushman endurance. But this is not wanting. Well-attested cases have been reported where a Masarwa, to show his hunting ability, singled out a young animal from the herd and set off on its trail and actually ran it down. If the man is strong enough to head the animal in the direction of the *werft,* the meat does not need to be carried far. Thus the hunter gains great prestige as a good provider, especially among the eligible women.

A careful review of our gasoline and water situation made it apparent that if all went well, we should be at least sixty miles short of our goal, the Boer settlement of Ghansi, where I had arranged for 80 gallons of gasoline to be sent in from southwest Africa. This the Vacuum Oil Company in Johannesburg had promised to do. But there was no assurance that everything would go well. To drive over sandhills would mean losing precious mileage, and we might very well find ourselves stranded in the desert, perhaps a hundred miles short of our objective. Then our lives would depend on the narrow chance of locating Bushmen and persuading them to carry on a letter to Ghansi, asking for gasoline to be sent out to us by truck or wagon.

That seemed to me an unlikely gamble. John seemed anxious to try our luck, but I remembered what I had read in Madison's book on his journeys into Central Australia. Speaking of explorers' mishaps, he wrote:

"Adventures belong to the heroic days of exploration, when ways and means were undeveloped. They should not happen today. The Arctic explorer Steffanson very truly says, 'Adventures are a mark of incompetence.' "

The responsibility was mine. Regretfully, I decided to pull back to Molepolole, travel north for 300 miles to Serowe, then strike out across the northern Kalahari, another 400 miles, for the little town of Maun. There we could refit, and journey west either to Ghansi or north to Victoria Falls, seeking Masarwa as we went. I had been told that somewhere hidden in the vast Okovango swamps there was reputed to be a village of 300 Bushmen. So we fixed on the next Saturday night for our Masarwa dance, set aside Sunday for rest and packing up, so that we could set out on our return the next morning.

The dance can, I think, be disposed of briefly. We almost ruined the performance by setting off two rockets from those we carried with us in case any of our party was lost on the veldt. Whoever reached camp would set off a couple of flares at dark to give the wanderer the direction in which the camp lay. But the Bushmen and Bakalaghari were so frightened that the latter begged us not to shoot down any more stars or we should never see the Masarwa again.

The dance itself was hardly an inspiriting affair. The men merely shuffled around a small circle, using a short step and a little flick of the heels that left a groove in the sand. The dance was accompanied by the rhythmic hand-clapping of the women grouped on one side. The very monotony of the performance seemed to induce some kind of self-hypnosis, indicated by set faces and staring eyeballs reflecting the camp fire. At various points in the circle, the dancers emitted some low but forceful grunts, which seemed to stir the excitement of the onlookers.

This was a fertility dance and the men made stiff movements of their forearms, which we were told represented the sowing of tsama melon seeds or their scattering over the veldt by the wind. One other dance was in honor of the eland, with a slightly quicker rhythm, the performers making a little jump every now and then in the air, while the women contributed a shrill ululating cry.

The women did not dance, except one, who suddenly left the chorus to shuffle around at the side of one Bushman youth. This action and her frankly invitational glances caused great amusement until she slowed down and danced backwards to her former place in the chorus.

Judging by the girl's posterior wrigglings, she was being deliberately provocative to the Bushman dancer, and it was easy to understand how it came about that Masarwa features and skin color were to be commonly observed among the Bakalaghari. Probably these carefree, independent, rather mysterious wanderers on the veldt exerted considerable sex appeal to the stay-at-home, convention-bound women of the stadt. In much the same way thoroughly respectable girls in our own culture are often attracted to uninhibited, disrespectable males, who, temporarily at least, offer them the incitement "to throw their bonnets over the moon" in defiance of all social regulations. It seemed to me that the older women eyed the young social rebel enviously. Their chances of romance had been bound up with years of waiting, while their suitors slowly amassed the *bogadi,* or bride price to be paid in cattle to their families. It looked as if the gypsy-like, carefree band of Masarwa might find a new recruit.

As a great favor to me, the Bushmen, well fed with eland fat, next morning repeated the night's performance in daylight so that I could secure the first moving pictures ever taken of authentic Masarwa dances.

Soon we had packed up and were on our way back to Molepolole. We stopped at the waterhole to fill up our water cans and were interested to see fresh lion spoor in the mud. Evidently the Bushmen were right; the lions had looked us over and were ready for closer acquaintance, since our camp was just two hundred yards distant. A second stop was at Lunakie where our cache of canned food lay still untouched in a spare hut. The women of the kraal were overwhelmed by our gift of the promised petrol can. Evidently promises are shadowy things in the desert; only when the reward is in hand is it really appreciated. John Knobel assured us that if we had never come back, our stores would have lain intact until the

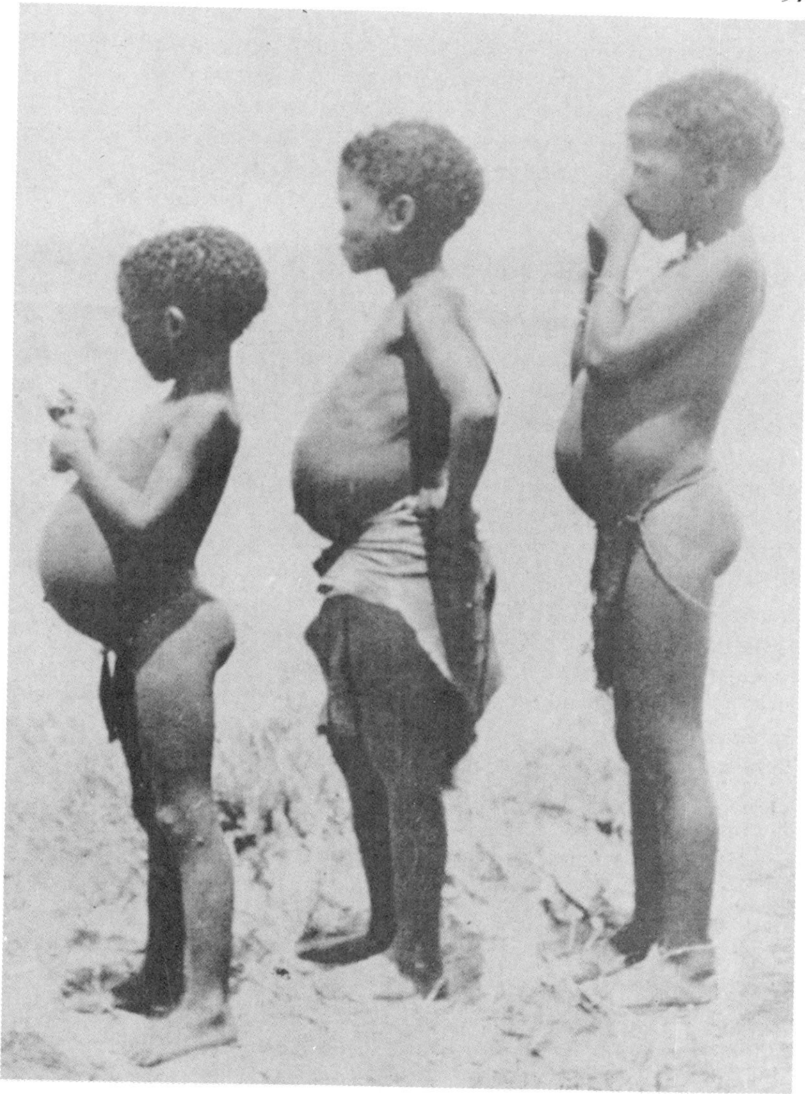

Bushman children after a feast of eland meat, 1934.

cans rusted.

After reaching and leaving Molepolole, our route north paralleled the railway line to Buluwayo. At the little wayside station of Debeete, we turned aside to pay a call on the station master. On the morning of our arrival he had been amazed to see a full-grown lion on the railway platform. During the night he had been kept awake by continued roaring. He pointed out to us his native assistant's hut, where the lions came so close that his dogs had rushed inside in terror and sought shelter under his bed.

The station master gave us a very warm invitation to stay the night at his two-roomed house, but Knobel had already picked out a grove of trees about a mile away where we could expect a much quieter night, out of sight and sound of natives. Knobel also felt that the station master might have tended to exaggerate the danger. White visitors, even complete strangers, offered both company and conversation, two social items very rare at Debeete. A trainload of passengers going through daily hardly counted; they didn't even pass the time of day with a fellow human being. So we turned a deaf ear to the proffered hospitality. We might as well be kept awake all night by lions as by a spate of dammed-up speech from a lonely Dutch station master. John knew his compatriots.

But there *were* lions. Early next morning we could see the pug marks of the two big cats which had circled our camp, apparently reconnoitering the situation very thoroughly. This would explain, on a windless night, a mysterious shaking of the Bushman grass that I had sleepily noted a dozen yards away when I got up to throw an armful of brush on our failing camp fire. Then and there I served notice that I intended to back our truck, with its rear doors open, close to my blankets, and that if the lions had anything to say in the night, my companions had about two minutes to join me before those doors were closed.

Just what a lion could do to a man was amply demonstrated to us a little later. On our further trek from Serowe, the one-time capital of Khama's kingdom, to the far-west small town of Maun on the Thamalakane River, we had just passed over what was known as the worst road in Ngamiland (which surely qualifies its inclusion among the worst roads in the world). By this time we had come to the Botletle River, a natural spillway into the desert of the annual overflow of the Thamalakane, which in turn was fed from the Okovango, the greatest of all West African rivers.

We had been told that we could save ourselves sixty miles of travel by cutting across the Haina Veldt, occupying a great bend of the river. Since this area was almost treeless and lions were particularly aggressive, we were advised to load our truck with firewood before we left the river valley, so that we could keep a good blaze going all night. Not only was the lion population thick, but it had once been one of the greatest hunting grounds in Africa. Elephants had been so common that native hunters used their tusks for building stockades when trees were scarce. In 1857, one party of whites killed 900 elephants in a single season. At the Rakops trading post, a man named Lyttleton showed us his month's bag of huge spotted-hyena skins. A hundred miles further on was the scene of one of our tragic experiences with a lion.

When within about 16 miles of Maun, we were stopped by a white man with a strange request. Could we carry two wounded men to the native hospital at Maun? Just then, two men emerged from the brush, one leading a donkey on which was a native chief, Gaeba, who had been terribly mauled by a lion.

He was a Damara, one of the people who had trekked out of southwest Africa to escape the Germans, who with characteristic thoroughness had set out to exterminate them. Lions had been killing the Damara cattle and the chief asked Johnson and his son, who were cutting a new track to Maun, to hunt down the marauders. The father refused, but told his son, a young man of 23, that he could go with the chief to shoot the lion.

Accompanied by a couple of hundred natives, several of them armed with antiquated firearms, they set out on the spoor of the lion at midday, knowing well that the animal would not travel far over the hot sand, but would make a stand as soon as he was tired and thirsty.

True enough, the lion holed up in a thicket. Young Johnson put a bullet through the beast's forepaw and the lion at once charged. All the natives, except Gaeba and one other man, fled. The second native tried, by running forward at an angle, to divert the lion's attention and at the same time to obtain a clear shot. When the lion leapt at him, he threw himself face down, so that the beast jumped over him and then continued its charge towards Gaeba and Johnson. The latter fired two shots from his army rifle and missed.

Just as the animal reared on its hind legs to seize Johnson, the chief, who was unarmed, threw himself right in front of the lion, which seized him, shaking him as a dog shakes a rat. Johnson fired three more shots at point-blank range before the beast rolled over, dead.

But Gaeba, with one eye torn from its socket, his shoulder and one arm mangled, and teeth wounds showing that the lion had actually had his head in his jaws, was in terrible shape.

We had no hot water, so that all the doctor could do was to bandage the wounds and inject morphine, while Johnson unloaded his truck and set off with the patient for Maun, which he reached a couple of hours before us. But in two days the wound in Gaeba's eye turned septic and he died. Young Johnson nearly succumbed from shock.

Tragic as this event was, it did not delay our stay in Maun. Colonel Rey's letter assured us of the District Officer's help in every way possible. Seeing I could not be dissuaded from entering the dreaded Okovango swamp, Captain Potts, the D.O., did all he could to help us. He attached a Basuto trooper to my service to be my personal escort, and provided me with a rough map of the ten thousand square mile Okovango area, drawn by Captain Stigand after his expedition twelve years before.

But the great problem was to secure paddlers. Captain Potts, our host, declared that Maun men were useless for this purpose, since they were lazy and did not know the Okovango swamp, except by reputation, which was essentially evil. This strangely enough, was due to the ferocity of the hippos, which in my ignorance I thought constituted a very minor hazard. Among big game hunters in Africa you can set up an argument any time as to which is the most dangerous animal, with judgments divided between lions, leopards, buffalo, and elephants, with hippos down at the bottom of the list. Yet in the Okovango neither canoes nor boats of any kind that ventured into deep water were free from danger of instant attack. This had been the experience of two expeditions into the swamp since Livingstone's day. Twelve years before our coming, Stigand, the first to cross the area, had a steel boat which was attacked so vigorously that it had to be beached on an island, and his men barely escaped with their lives. Ellenberger, another explorer, had had a similar experience, and on a couple of other occasions men had been bitten in half by these huge beasts. Neither lions, elephants, buffalo, nor tsetse flies were held in as much dread by the natives as the swamp hippos.

When I talked with Captain Potts, resident magistrate in Maun, I asked him about a report that had reached me that a village of about 300 Bushmen was located at the end of the sixty-mile-long Mathibe's Island in the swamp. He informed me that a rumor had reached him that these people had all been wiped out by some disease, either black-water fever or sleeping sickness. He himself had once penetrated the marshes for a distance of 50 miles when he went to bring out the body of a white hunter who had been killed by a lion, and to rescue his companion, who afterwards died of shock after trying to drag the lion by the tail away from the hunter. Their native guide had then seized his rifle and shot the animal at point-blank range.

Captain Potts, with Colonel Rey's letter in hand asking him to give me all possible assistance, made a most earnest plea to me to give up all idea of entering the Okovango. But he was trying to reason with a somewhat frustrated psychologist who had journeyed twelve thousand miles and had succeeded so far in locating only eight Bushmen males. It would be a long time, I felt sure, before anyone in my profession would desert laboratory and lecture hall to be paddled 120 miles into a wild and untracked region of Africa, which even the rest of the Dark Continent could not match as *terra incognita*. What the captain was really dealing with was the insatiable curiosity of a 12-year-old boy, a level which apparently I had never grown out of, aided and abetted by a middle-aged Boer, and an equally staid Hawaiian plantation doctor, both with a thirst for new experiences. I do not think that Potts relished the prospect of having to go and bring us out, dead or alive, with very heavy odds that it would be the former. If the hippos didn't get us, the tsetse flies must. Potts' misgivings were entirely justified. I'm afraid that it was only fools' luck that brought us back unharmed. If medals were granted for sheer stupidity, we would have been leading candidates. Looking back, I must admit that the whole plan was crazy and a most untypical lapse of my ordinary caution. I evidently suffered a mental lapse.

However, being unable to dissuade us, Captain Potts worked hard to further our plans in every way possible. He lent me the only government vessel in those waters, a rather dilapidated, flat-bottomed scow which he thought even hippos would find difficult to torpedo. He also gave me a letter which Knobel and I conveyed to Matseoakhumo, the headman of the Batawana tribe, whose kraal was about 25 miles upstream, asking him to supply us with a dozen paddlers and, if possible, to go with us himself. This headman had accompanied Stigand's expedition and was the only man who could claim to know anything about the swamp. Potts also gave my personal guard, Sakai, strict, if impossible, instructions not to let me out of his sight. The Basuto trooper was a very intelligent young man and did his utmost to guard me closely, although it was doubtless his private opinion that all Americans and Australians were mad.

We had planned a mere shakedown cruise of about 14 miles before camping, with an early start on the next morning to meet the headman and his party. None of the natives except an older native named Madomo had ever been inside the ten thousand square mile swamp, and some of our excitement evidently overflowed from us to them. They boasted loudly of how they would return to their villages in *makoras,* or dugout canoes, loaded with skins of pythons, with which, so they said, the place was literally crawling. That night with the full moon tracing the huge limbs of motsweri trees overhead, and the pulsating rhythm of drums sounding from a nearby kraal hidden in the forest, I had no need to remind myself that I was in Africa. The only sobering thought came when we shone our flashlights on the quiet river to reveal a score or more of crocodile eyes shining like double light globes on its surface, reminding us that the Thamalakane and probably the swamp also were awaiting new victims. Swimming, we realized, was definitely *out.*

Next morning our flotilla reached the rendezvous, but there was no sign of the headman and his men. After wasting the rest of the morning, a pause utilized by my two companions to zero in their guns on a target, I decided to leave one man with a *makora* to await Matseoakhumo and proceed some miles farther into the swamp, and camp. The Santantadibe looked to be little more than a large creek about twenty yards wide. When John asked Madomo why we did not go up the Gomoto, a large river marked on the map Captain Potts had given me, which emptied into the Thamalakane a few miles to the north, he was horrified at the idea. If we ventured into deep water, he explained, the hippos would attack us on sight. When John argued that the large size of the scow would provide protection, the old hunter merely poked his finger into a hole near our waterline. Then he counted on his fingers the nine men in the scow and four more in *makoras.* We followed this mental arithmetic and came up with the answer—if the scow were sunk, five men would be left over with no place to go. By the time rescue could be organized they could die in the swamp.

In the course of our consultation, John enquired from Madomo the reason for hippo hostility and learned that for many years there had been a ready market for the huge teeth of the animals; the ancient Chinese ground up the ivory as they did rhinoceros horns, believing it to be a powerful aphrodisiac. Whether this was fact or superstition, it was certainly true that the thick hippo hide could be cut into whips, or sjamboks, that gave a different kind of energy to slaves. Hence, for hundreds of years the natives had driven harpoons into behemoth, then paddled as swiftly as they could to the shore. From there the hippo served as a pincushion for scores of spears. But every now and then an animal broke away, and like the elephant, he never forgot. In time he came to look on man as his worst enemy, to be attacked on sight.

Launching the Okovango expedition, 1934.

So with added respect for the river horse and a healthy distrust of deep water, we proceeded on our way, having been assured by Madomo that the headman would catch up with us before we passed Mathibe's Island. We had been told in Maun that three days' paddling would bring us to Tsubaora, at the top of the island near where the Bushmen were supposed to be. Truth to tell, we were not worried about Matseoakhumo since Madomo seemed a capable guide, although he had never been deeper into the swamp than about eighty miles. Never, we discovered, had there been a more optimistic estimate of a three days' journey. This is how I recorded what seemed like a never-ending struggle against weeds, currents, and monotony along the Santantadibe.

> So the hours passed from early dawn when we rolled out of our blankets on some palm-crowned islet, ate our rusks and drank our coffee, until five-thirty at night when it was time to seek a camping spot where we could cook our daily meal. Apparently all our crew's efforts brought us no results except another view of a turn in the stream, another reed-bed as thickset as before. The reeds, the brown water, the wooded islands slipped gradually by but we—and time—seemed to stand still.

Unfortunately, the edges of the swamp had been well hunted and the game had retreated, so that supplying meat for our paddlers

Members of the author's expedition camped in the vast Okovango swamps in Africa.

became a problem. Madomo told us there was limitless game farther on, where the islands were higher and the trees larger. He had been with a hunting party on Mathibe's Island, when a herd of buffalo had overrun their camp at night. His nephew had escaped with his life only by throwing himself headlong into a thornbush, from which he emerged like a human pincushion. This was about thirty miles farther on, and the place marked the limits of his penetration into the swamp.

Where the water spread out into *ledebas,* or small lakes, made, so we were told, by wallowing hippos, Madomo marked our channel by tying knots in the reeds to guide the chief, whom he was sure would follow us.

At the end of five days Knobel called Madomo to our fire.

"They told us in Maun," he said, "that we should reach Tsubaora in three days. Do not put me off with lies. When shall we reach this place?"

Madomo's reply was full of dignity.

"I am an old man," he answered, "why should I lie? The young may lie, for they have not yet made themselves known for what they are, but for a man whose life is all behind him, why should he lie? If we start at dawn and paddle all day, then the next day we should cross the big Ngoga river, and reach the end of the island. There is a shorter way, but the river is deep and full of angry hippos and crocodiles. If any harm comes to the white man, I shall be blamed."

So I decided to devote one more day to our quest. Already the streams were getting deeper and the islands higher, so next morning I promised to pay the men an extra shilling if they would raise the tempo of their efforts. One man in the bow, whom we called Hyena Cap because of his headdress, did not change his pace, so I leaned forward to touch him and cry, "urree, urree," the prelude to any sudden spurt. He laid down his paddle and held out his hands in mute explanation. Every finger on each hand was covered with raw blisters. The sight put me to shame for I had no wish to require both sweat *and* blood in furtherance of my project. I made no further demands for speed but tried to take the man's paddle to relieve him. There was more than a touch of pride in his refusal to accept any respite not shared in by his fellows.

That day the army of the reeds retreated, and we landed on a large island shaded by big trees. Wild game stood agog with curiosity at what was probably their first sight of humans, then wheeled in flight. Lechwe, light fawn antelopes, were in hundreds, so that the noise of their passage from island to island made a sound like thunder. There we had our first encounter with two buffaloes that charged as soon as they got our wind, but passed us by without seeing us. Here was a natural sanctuary, guarded only by tsetse flies that followed us far into midstream, preferring, however, to light on the backs and shoulders of our dark-skinned paddlers.

But of Bushmen there was no recent sign except some old frameworks of reed huts on the tip of an island, evidently unoccupied for several years. This was as far as Madomo had ever penetrated, and our campfire that night was built on the spot where two years before the herd of buffaloes had charged through his camp so close that the stock of his old gun had been broken by a buffalo's hoof. Late that afternoon we met a single Bushman paddling his makora downstream. To John's shouted enquiries, he said briefly that not a single Masarwa was left at Tsubaora.

That night I took counsel with myself, considering the question as to what justification a psychologist had to be wandering in this blackest niche of Africa. My friends, even though the interest of the trip had suddenly heightened, had had enough. Lechwe steaks had been our main diet for days since our stock of civilized provisions was about out. We agreed that eight days in the swamp were enough and it was time to turn back. After all, it seemed to me that I was merely playing at exploring, which was not my business.

Next day we had been paddled and poled some miles downstream when we suddenly met Matseoakhumo and his flotilla on their way to find us. His story was that important visitors at his kraal had prevented him from joining us earlier. He had ridden two days to a point on the Santantadibe where he expected to cut us off, but was too late. We had a fine reunion. We gave the Chief his new blanket and received in return roasted peanuts and a large bowl of mealie porridge and sour milk, a welcome change from lechwe meat.

Next day our party, now increased to 25, set off joyously for home. We swept downstream in fine style, until, meeting with new swarms of tsetse flies, the headman signalled for silence, telling Knobel quietly he could smell buffalo. Landing quickly, we passed through a fringe of motsweri trees, and in a sunny patch in the timber came across three huge buffalo bulls lying down. They had not yet got our wind so everyone dropped to the ground while the real hunters crept forward, rifles in hand. Mindful of our recent scare, I made for an anthill from which I hoped to film in safety any action that ensued. Suddenly a native ran up to the chief pointing excitedly at more buffalo moving through the timber to our right, while on our left I could see more activity. We were apparently right in the middle of a large scattered herd of buffalo.

With the crack of the rifles and the boom of the Chief's elephant gun, there was instantly mad commotion—natives climbing trees, buffalo galloping in front of us, a crash of underbrush and, suddenly, silence. We looked at each other in dismay, for with all the

The end of the buffalo hunt, 1934.

noise and shooting nothing remained except a distant thunder of game thrashing through a crossing. Then from about three hundred yards away came a deep lowing sound, sure sign of a mortally wounded buffalo. Everyone ran forward and we saw a bull alternately falling and struggling again to its feet. A couple of bullets finished it and there, not fifty yards away, lay another shot through the heart. It had enough vitality left to charge back again in our direction before dropping dead.

That night, thirty miles downstream, just where the reeds closed in tightly, we made our camp, with buffalo meat roasting at every fire. The headman reserved buffalo testicles for himself, but we gladly made no claims to such a supposedly potent tidbit. As for the rest, I have never in my life wrestled with such tough meat. Let no one tell you that buffalo is really fit for mastication. It has the resistance of a rubber heel.

Just at sunset we had been joined by two magnificently muscled Makubas, both over six foot two in height. I gave up on the buffalo meat, took the shotgun and brought down four doves, which Makumba, our special camp boy, cooked for me. Then we decided that the new arrivals, Kahu and Tembwe, who unlike our scratch crew, with the exception of Madomo, were real river men, should carry me down in their makora to Maun. Matseoakhumo assured me that being fresh, these two could make some short-cuts and cover the sixty-odd miles to Maun by nightfall, provided we were away by dawn. I would load our truck with supplies and drive back to meet the rest of the party at the Santantadibe. From there we would head north for Victoria Falls, making contact with Bushmen on the way. The headman would go with us fifty miles into the Mababe Flats, where as chief over the Masubeia tribe he would ensure that they would bring Masarwa to our camp. In my book *Primitive Intelligence and Environment* our Okovango excursion has been described. One or two minor incidents are worth mentioning here.

That evening while my new crew prepared their canoe for an early start, they found a young ten-foot python in the reeds. I later photographed it with one of them holding it up by the tail. I assumed it had been killed and left as extra food for the rest of the natives. On our journey next day, after hours of sitting with my legs stretched out on the floor of the makora, I shifted back a foot or so and suddenly found a comfortable cavity into which my behind fitted comfortably. It even allowed me to bend my knees a little. Some muscular movements I ascribed to the return of blood circulation following my cramped condition. When I felt these movements continuing, I lifted up a corner of my camp sheet to find that I was reclining in the midst of coils of a python, moribund, perhaps, but by no means dead. I moved hurriedly back to my former position, naturally preferring the discomfort of the makora's floor to any pythonic cushion.

When at last we reached the open stretches of the Thamalakane River, there was a brisk northwesterly breeze blowing down stream.

The partially-stunned ten-foot python on which the author sat for about fifty miles of his river journey.

I borrowed one of the men's assegais, fastened it so that it served as a mast, tied the corner of my camp sheet to its shaft, and used my arm as a yard arm; the result, a leg of mutton sail that speeded up our progress materially. The only difficulty was that sailing was an entirely new notion to the Makuba, so that pushing and recovering their long ten-foot poles brought about a swift change of pace. Moreover, the more the wind blew, the faster the men poled, so that it seemed to me that we fairly flew down the river. Possibly sitting carefully in the middle of the makora with no more than six inches of freeboard gave me an exaggerated sense of speed. Our sudden appearance round a bend sent a couple of crocodiles slithering off the river bank with more haste than dignity.

As we shot past Batawana river villages, excitement followed us. People shouted and screamed questions to my boatmen, groups of men and women ran along the banks, children fell into the water and were fished out of the reeds, until some tributary stopped all forward progress, and the next village took up the chase. Their excited queries received scant response, but that night I was assured

The *makora* in which the two boatmen paddled the author sixty miles in a single day along the Santantadibe and Thamalakane rivers to Maun in Africa.

in Maun that I would be henceforth known as "the man who rode the wind down the Thamalakane river."

Stirred by affection and animated by compassion for Bushmen, Laurens van der Post, South Africa's great writer, has given us in *The Lost World of the Kalahari*, a wonderfully moving account of his search for the little people of the veldt still living there, a journey that took him, not over the same ground, but over strictly contiguous areas visited by me 24 years previously.

We had different motivations. Mine was scientific curiosity, his a conscience-stricken regret for the cruel treatment meted out by his Boer ancestors to the merry-hearted Bushmen. His fond recollections went back to the faithful old Masarwa servitors on his grandmother's farm, where he spent his early boyhood.

Van der Post did everything in the reverse order to mine. He entered the Okovango swamps from the northwest, I from the east. He travelled by makora and motor launch. He, like myself, felt

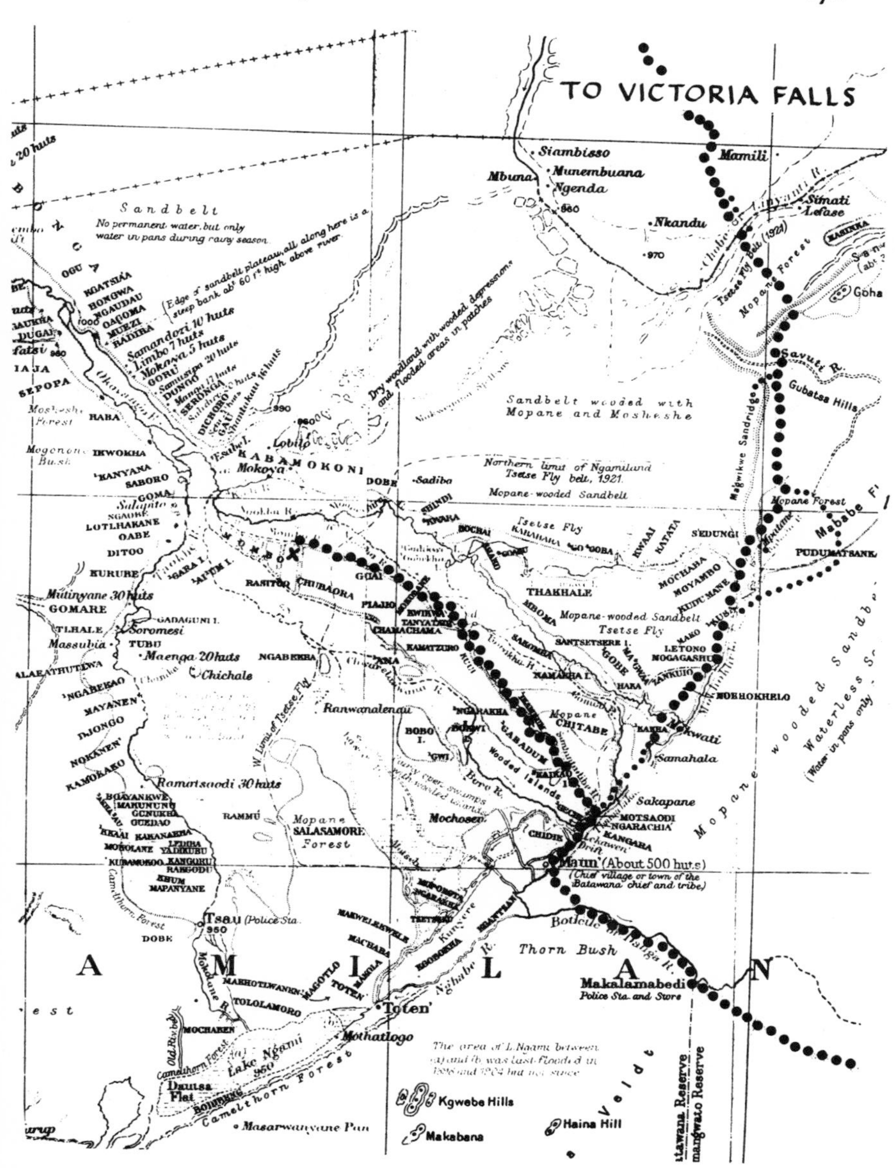

The broken line traces the author's route from the Haina Veldt along the Botletle or Dauga River to Maun and up the Thamalakane and Santantadibe rivers into the Okovango swamps. He returned to Maun and then traveled up to Victoria Falls.

the weight of mystery and monotony that the choking reeds imposed on man's spirit. He also saw, for all his travel and travail, only a couple of Masarwa. He, too, turned back just about at the spot where we turned around on our homeward journey. Adding together our itineraries, we spanned the ten thousand square mile morass area. He also took moving pictures, which I have not yet seen.

From there on I was done with monotony and was caught again in the need for hurry. At Mababe and Kachikau, I made up my testing quota to 25 subjects, of whom no more than 15 seemed to be, physically speaking, authentic Bushmen. But they themselves and other people called them "Masarwa" because they lived as the Bushmen lived, the men hunting and the women collecting "veldt kos," owing lip-service only to the surrounding Bantu tribes. They belonged in the desert, inheriting all that it imposed in the way of challenge to human adjustment.

CHAPTER 12

Mental Jungle Explorations at Home

THE YEARS of the early thirties were marked for me by several happenings of note. By 1931, the book setting forth the results of my work in Northwest and Central Australia was published in England by Edward Arnold and Co., and in America by Longmans Green and Co. I felt highly honored by its selection by the Scientific Book Club. I was recently made happy to note that, owing to a recent revival of interest among Australian psychologists in the question of aboriginal mentality, it still commands some attention. In the citation announcing my election as one of five chosen as the first honorary fellows of the newly organized Australian Psychological Association, it referred to "the famous testing expedition to the Kimberleys and Central Australia of 1929." Otherwise, it might as well have been termed *forgotten* instead of *famous*. Meanwhile, *The Matrix of the Mind,* by Wood Jones and myself, continued to receive very favorable reviews around the world. Also in 1933, I decided that, psychologists having had unrestricted use of the Maze Test for eighteen years, I would proceed to copyright the early form, known as the Vineland Revision.

Probably because of this wide attention, President David Crawford of the University of Hawaii informed me that for purely scientific achievements the Board of Regents had decided that I had earned the degree of doctor of science, conferred under similar circumstances by universities outside America. The citation referred specifically to the fact that the Berry-Porteus study of brain capacity, involving over ten thousand cases, was one of the largest ever undertaken, that my work with Australian aborigines represented a pioneering psychological effort, and that the Porteus Maze had been adopted for use around the world—in short, this D.Sc. degree had been really earned much more adequately than the conventional Ph.D. Later on a Phi Beta Kappa award for distinguished scientific work and high attainments in liberal scholarship was conferred, marking the first time that father and son had been simultaneously inducted. Sigma Xi election followed still later.

Considering the fact that for 27 years I was director of the Psychological and Psychopathic Clinic of the University of Hawaii, I do not wish to brush over too lightly this experience as if it were of minor importance. It earned me my daily bread even if my more interesting experiences provided the butter. At the outset of this prosaic accounting, it should be made quite clear that wandering over the face of the earth, doing what appealed to me most, would not have been possible without a steady job and extremely competent assistants.

Outstanding among these was Dr. Marjorie Babcock Robertson, who for months at a time held the clinic together while its director was rattling around sandy or rocky terrain in the interior of Australia or chasing the elusive Bushmen in the wilds of Africa. At one time or another the list of the clinic staff included some later well-known personages, such as Bernreuter, Leiter, Louttit, Peters, while Drs. Mendenhall, Chidester, Arkoff, Honzik, and Herrick (assistant director) carried on nobly. During one of my absences in Vineland, Dr. Stevenson Smith, of the University of Seattle, undertook the temporary direction of the Clinic.

As for field work, the late Dr. Kilton Stewart worked in various countries of Southeast Asia, while more recently Dr. James Gregor did yeoman service collecting data in Central Australia. My wife shared some of the hardships of trekking in South Africa and put in weeks of effort examining members of Bantu tribes assembled in a mine compound in Johannesburg prior to their being drafted to various mines. She thus saw a cross section of South African natives, becoming familiar with Basuto, Bapedi, Makalanga, Shangaans, and Mchopis, but remaining an object of ceaseless curiosity to them. Many of them had never seen a white woman at such close quarters before.

She therefore found it advisable to allow a new subject at least ten minutes to gaze his fill before settling him to work on a test. Occasionally the proximity of a raw native clad in a blanket was a little too much for her sensitivities. She still likes to tell about asking our Zulu assistant at the end of a long string of Mchopi subjects whether he could not find a clean one for her.

"Madame," he replied with extreme dignity, "that nation is all dirty." Possibly some of my loyal assistants in Hawaii would have willingly exchanged some of their feebleminded subjects for a group of more varied Africans or Australids.

In dealing with the history of the Psychological Clinic in Hawaii, I recognize that of necessity the treatment must be anecdotal, dealing with unusual experiences rather than with those familiar to any clinical psychologist.

However, from 1919 to 1948 was a period when psychological clinics were in themselves unusual. Probably because of this, the University Clinic had many strange jobs thrust upon it. It must be remembered that very little other professional assistance was available, yet Hawaii had a rather full list of institutions or organizations where such help was needed, including courts, homes for defectives, schools, hospitals, institutions for delinquent boys or wayward girls, social service agencies, prisons. In short, these organizations accumulated problems that they were only too glad to dump into the lap of a University department. In the course of years there was no public or department service facility that had not occasion to consult us, including even the Governor and the military. Perhaps our range of activities could best be illustrated by a few specific instances.

There was, for example, a famous kidnapping and murder case that shocked the whole community. A young Japanese man appeared at a classroom in Honolulu's best-known preparatory school, Punahou, stating that he had brought a taxi to take an eleven-year-old boy to the hospital to see his mother, who had been involved in an accident. In such an emergency, the teacher did not hesitate to release the child, the son of a well-known business executive in the city.

Later, she phoned the hospital to enquire how the lady was and was amazed at being told that there was no record of any such accident or patient. A check of other possibilities, such as medical clinics, etc., revealed no such occurrence. The mother herself was finally located and she promptly called the police.

Then ensued a frenzied boy-hunt. Friends and neighbors volunteered as searchers. With the arrival of a note signed "The Three Kings," demanding ten thousand dollars as ransom, every likely hide-out in the city or in rural districts was combed without result. The almost demented father, following instructions, obtained the money in marked 100-dollar bills and took it to a rendezvous. There he tried to seize a masked man, who broke away and fled into the darkness.

The police checked the destination of the taxi used in the abduction and found it to be the Moana Hotel at Waikiki. The driver, when located, said the boy appeared to be very upset emotionally, and that his Japanese companion seemed to be trying to comfort him. Then someone thought to search the immediate neighborhood of the hotel. Across the street in a vacant lot lay the body of the boy, who had been stunned by a blow from a heavy chisel and then killed. Beside him had been laid three kings from a pack of playing cards. Among the flowers sent to the funeral was a large wreath and a note of sympathy signed "The Three Kings." This apparent heartlessness was another shock to the community and confirmed the belief that the murder was the work of a vicious gang from the mainland. We had no such major crimes in Hawaii.

After the arrest for questioning of a former employee of the boy's father, I was asked to interview the suspect whom a handwriting expert (so-called) had identified as the writer of the ransom note. The suspect's very dubious alibi was that he had spent the whole day of the murder playing a very simple card game with a companion. I decided to recheck the handwriting of the suspect and dictated to him a statement in which I included some key words. It was at once apparent that the letter forms upon which the expert had relied for his judgment were entirely different from those in the ransom note. Questioned by me, the suspect told me that he had been given the ransom note *and told to copy it,* which he did to the best of his ability. I helped his alibi by telling the police that white ladies of my acquaintance often spent hours playing similarly simple card games.

There had never been a lynching in Hawaii, and this was the first time one had even been talked about. My uncertainty about the suspect's writing helped to calm public resentment, and the police withdrew the charges against the suspect. Next day came the electrifying news that a young Japanese had been arrested while trying to pass one of the marked ransom bills at a rural filling station, and had promptly confessed.

Anti-Japanese feeling ran high. In reply editorials in Japanese-language newspapers suggested that the youth had been "framed" because of his race. As commonly happens in all universities, a radical staff member, eager to lead an unpopular cause, was at hand to support this view. I received a call from the professor of Japanese, Dr. Harada, who brought with him two editors of Japanese-language papers who told me that their community was much disturbed. Having heard that I had interviewed the accused, they were willing to follow any counsel I might wish to give them as to editorial policy. Incidentally, the Japanese apparently had never resented my criticisms of their group as set forth in our book *Temperament and Race.*

The life story of the murderer as he told it to me was an almost incredible example of a tragedy in ethnic maladjustment. As far as I can remember, the youth was an only son, who with his parents lived in close touch with their white employers. He grew up with an intense wish to identify himself with what he thought to be the superior white race. Consequently, he had as little as possible to do with Japanese and came to be very ashamed of his own parents. He would not invite any white children to his home for fear they would remind him of his inferior status. He went to work at Queen's Hospital as a wardsman because that brought him into more intimate relations with white patients and the staff.

When he finally realized that an apparently insuperable barrier stood in the way of his attaining equal status, he determined to achieve attention even though it entailed commission of a major crime. He did not know the family of his victim, but selected the vice-president of a leading commercial organization listed in the telephone book. His action in sending a note with flowers to the family was not the callous outrage it appeared to be. He said he was really feeling very sorry for what he had done and thought that he was proffering his sympathy in the correct *haole* (white) fashion. He intended to use the ransom money to send his parents to visit Japan, an action that would, he hoped, assuage his sense of guilt for having rejected them. The fact that all his life had been spent in building up a wall separating him from his own people was well understood by my Japanese callers, who decided that capital punishment would fittingly conclude the whole affair. I was greatly disturbed but could not conscientiously declare the youth insane. He was the victim of tragic circumstances, and had no further wish to live. If guilt there was, it belonged with the whole course of events in Hawaii and could not be expiated. His execution was one of the few capital punishments that took place here.

This cooperation with the Police Department led to further work until quite a large proportion of the Clinic's work was concerned with criminal investigation. This spread to the military services. One particularly interesting case was rare in my experience. It was an authentic instance of a crime actually committed during a period of total amnesia, during which time the murderer was bereft of all sense of responsibility. The defense I was able to establish was that the prisoner at the bar was not the same person who committed the crime, but another with whom for the time being he had exchanged identities, and whose actions he had completely forgotten. In effect the defense was one of mistaken identity, which differed from that extremely common plea in that the mistake in identity was his own. In brief, at the time of crime, he really believed he was someone else.

As indicated, this is a defense extremely familiar to all who have any experience with criminal cases. The difficulty was to make it stick with a hard-boiled collection of high naval officers, serving as a court martial. The accused was a junior officer who had been under considerable mental strain following an almost incredible personal error in carrying out steering orders, which nearly brought about the ramming of one of our few remaining aircraft carriers when leaving Pearl Harbor. For this error he had been at once relieved as officer of the deck by the Admiral, who had personally witnessed the event.

On his next liberty, he was arrested outside the Moana Hotel after midnight. He then claimed to be the first mate of a freighter, then in harbor. But this story did not jibe with his possession of a naval officer's identification card, so he was taken down to the police station in Honolulu, then occupied by the Navy. As it was after midnight, a commissioned officer had to be sent for, and pending his arrival, the chief petty officer in charge left the room to get a blanket for an army cot on which the prisoner could rest. As he returned to the room, he was confronted by the prisoner, who had armed himself with a pistol left hanging on a hat-tree.

The gun hammer clicked on the first empty chamber, and the chief, knowing that the next was loaded, threw the blanket at the man and ran for his life. The officer pursued him as he dodged around the building, and then, thinking he had fled to the basement, ran on, saw a military prisoner sweeping the floor, and shot him through the head. On the street he also shot and wounded a military policeman in the side. By this time the alarm had spread and the officer was surrounded, wounded twice, and then overpowered and disarmed while lying on the pavement. Taken to the hospital, he stated that he was a naval aide attached to the staff of Admiral Cunningham in command of the British Mediterranean Fleet, and claimed he had been sent to Hawaii on a very secret mission.

Before his trial I had received letters from the officer's mother, giving an account of two previous amnesic incidents, one of which lasted about twenty-four hours. Owing undoubtedly to pressure of wartime activities, the Navy psychiatrists could not find time to see the accused for two months after the actual killing, but they agreed in the opinion that he was intoxicated at the time. There was, however, very little support for this conclusion from the evidence tendered at the initial inquiry.

My review of the records, which I then knew by heart, received careful attention, and its reception became cordial when the prosecutor's questioning elicited the fact that I was not being paid any fee at all for my professional services. I explained that I was employed by the University, was frequently called on by all kinds of governmental agencies for assistance, and that I regarded this whole affair merely as an extension of my official duties, adding that I had never accepted fees of any kind, either from individuals or organizations. The court seemed to think this rather unique, especially as the private psychiatrist called also for the defense spent one hour in an examination of the accused and charged $500.

In any case, the court was cleared after my formal testimony, and I was invited to go into a huddle with the officers of the court martial. This gave me the opportunity to give quite a lecture on the queer and sometimes tragic quirks of human behavior. The result was that they brought in a judgment with recommendations following exactly what I had suggested.

After two years in a famous mental hospital, the man was discharged as sane. I had hoped for a longer period of psychiatric observation. For more than 20 years I have kept my fingers crossed lest another amnesic episode with tragic consequences occur. The last I heard was that the one-time naval officer was head of a large business firm, was married, had several children, and, I hope, will be happy ever after. He, too, accepted my theory of temporary complete amnesia, and probably my advice to seek continued psychiatric counsel was helpful. It is my belief that the Court was glad of a "way out," as a verdict of guilty in wartime could have meant execution. I claim no special insight with regard to this case other than the realization that abnormal human behavior is often quite unpredictable. One does not need psychiatric training to know that.

Earlier, I had unwittingly found myself put in a very embarrassing situation on account of my official position in the Territory of Hawaii. The famous Massie case, which involved charges of sex assault on a Navy wife and the subsequent shooting of an Hawaiian suspect led to a charge of conspiracy to murder against the husband, Massie, a naval officer at Pearl Harbor, and the victim's mother. I was retained to watch the case on behalf of the government and, if needed, act as consultant to the prosecution.

There was considerable doubt as to the veracity of the wife's account of the alleged rape, although she had undoubtedly been severely beaten. A federal investigator, acting on behalf of the government, came to Hawaii to report. Mainland writers, especially in the Hearst press, had field days writing editorials on the lurking perils of Island jungles, and the extraordinary laxity of our local law enforcement officers. Our whole local community took sides, for or against the military, lines being drawn occasionally with relationship to race. Our civilian population was so disturbed that long-time friendships were sadly interrupted.

I watched the court proceedings and formed certain definite conclusions, but no one asked me what they were. The government prosecutor, suddenly catapulted into fame, decided to play his part untrammelled by advice from anyone, especially a psychologist, even though the request for my cooperation came directly from the Governor of the Territory.

Quite unknown to me, the prosecutor had learned that the supposed victim of the sex assault had at one time attended a class conducted by a faculty member of the Psychology Department, which was quite distinct from the Clinic I directed. The woman complainant had filled out a questionnaire that involved at some minor points her relationship with her naval officer husband. The prosecutor was informed that if this paper were produced in court it would have a very upsetting effect on defense strategy. He threatened to subpoena the University class records unless he was allowed access to the questionnaire. The faculty member being absent on one of the other islands, the University president allowed the prosecutor possession of the file.

Next day the prosecutor dramatically confronted the lady, who had taken the witness stand, with the questionnaire, asking if she recognized it. Quite properly, I believe, she said it was her private property, then tore it into shreds, threw them on the floor, and promptly went into hysterics. I had no knowledge of the paper and was not present in court at the time of its production.

Learning only that a psychologist had applied the questionnaire, a leading New York newspaper, in the belief that there was only one psychologist in the Islands, came out with a news story stating that I had supplied the document. Next day it printed a correction of the statement, but, as is usual, the same people who read the story do not always read its denial. For years after there were hot arguments in mainland departments of psychology as to whether Porteus did the right thing in producing what was certainly a confidential document. Since no one of the disputants knew the contents and I was ignorant even of its existence, the argument was truly academic, but raged none the less bitterly because of that.

Nor does the outcome of the trial matter very much any more; yet it might be worth stating. The husband of the victim and his mother-in-law were held to be guilty of murder, sentenced to a day in prison, and an hour later were pardoned by the Governor. Personally, while both were accessories, my belief was that neither of them fired the fatal shot. This was based on my observation that the only emotion shown by one of the two enlisted men also on trial was while the doctor described in detail the murdered man's wounds. Among the witnesses appearing for Massie's defense were two mainland psychiatrists, one of whom declared that Lieutenant Massie was suffering from "ambulatory amnesia," while the other testified that his trouble was "chemical insanity."

The original purpose in founding the Clinic was to ensure that legal commitment of mental defectives to Waimano Home should be on a sound diagnostic basis. The use of the Maze Test, which usually gives the scholastically dull, but not mentally defective individual a fair chance to achieve a normal score, was responsible for the fact that probably fewer borderline cases were institutionalized in Hawaii than in any other part of the United States.

One other case may be briefly cited wherein the director of the Clinic played a prominent, if inconclusive role. In this instance I was not instrumental in sheeting a crime home, but was helpful in turning the finger of suspicion away from a non-guilty person.

A woman's naked body had been found under a Honolulu

school, which like many similar structures of that day had been raised above ground about three feet on posts. She had evidently been knocked unconscious, and though not sexually molested, dragged under the building, and there bashed to death with a large lump of coral rock. Blood was splashed around everywhere except for one segment of a circle where the murderer had evidently knelt while striking his victim. His shirt was hung, partly washed, near a water tap beside the building. I suggested to the police that they concentrate on finding a pair of trousers with the front portion above the knees plentifully bespattered with blood.

With their usual thoroughness, they began a careful search of the neighborhood. Then I received a jubilant message that the crime was solved. A man's bloodstained trousers, marked as I had predicted, had been found rolled up and stuffed behind a locker in the nearby Salvation Army Shelter. The owner had been traced, arrested, and had signed a full confession. He had been previously convicted of attempted rape, and was a noted bad character, much feared by all his neighbors, none of whom wanted to talk about him to the police.

Naturally, I was pleased with myself, and the police were happy about the outcome. I began to fancy my detective abilities, and the Crime Commission was all ready to offer me official status as their criminal psychologist. I was very appreciative, although "criminal psychologist," like child psychologist, was a little bit ambiguous in its reference. In any event, I decided to spend a little more attention on this case.

There was one weak spot in the story. Here was a man with a previous record of a sexual crime, yet the medical examiner stated that in his opinion the victim had not been raped. I asked to see the accused again.

I took him over the story of his movements on the night of the crime. He told me that he had attended a *luau* at a little town about twelve miles away, and in fact had helped kill the pig for the feast. He said he had knelt on the ground holding the animal by the ears, while its owner cut its throat. The front of his trousers was well splashed in the process. Questioned about his confession, he explained that he was so drunk after the *luau* that he didn't remember where he went and could easily have assaulted someone. Besides, the detectives pestered him so much with questions, refusing even to give him a beer when he was dry and thirsty, that he thought the easiest thing he could do was to sign a confession.

My self-esteem was getting a little shaky at this point, so I called in the detectives and asked them to obtain an analysis of the bloodstains on the trousers. In two hours the verdict came back that they were not human and could easily be pig's blood.

Meanwhile, the husband of the woman, who might well have been the murderer, had had time to build up, with the help of friends, a nice alibi. He, too, was noted for having a savage temper, and none of his neighbors cared to refuse to support his story of his whereabouts elsewhere at the time of the crime. In addition, the police were by no means popular in this Puerto Rican neighborhood, the woman's reputation was unsavory, and the detectives realized they had no case. The crime remained unsolved, and I did not have to trouble myself as to what title I would assume.

At this point, I would like to inject a little psychological theory on this matter of false confessions. Criminal investigators in almost every noted murder are often plagued with them and spend valuable time disproving their validity. Why should anyone run the risk of conviction for a crime of which he is innocent?

Undoubtedly, in many cases the prime motive is to gain the spotlight of public attention, but the element of grave risk to the confessee is offset by his own consciousness of innocence. Willingness to make false confessions is, I believe, a tacit compliment to the ability of those whose business it is to unravel crime. The reasoning is: "I know I am innocent, and the detectives are smart people and will discover the fact. So, I may as well make the headlines without any real risk."

Notwithstanding this failure to locate the real criminal, the Clinic's services were much in demand, especially with regard to juvenile delinquents, and though the Maze Test did not show by its test age scores any marked differences between delinquents and non-delinquents, I found that giving the test afforded me a chance to observe closely the delinquent's general attitudes and personality. Gradually, all too gradually, it was borne in on my consciousness that the way in which delinquents behaved in carrying out this fifteen- to twenty-minute task was almost distinctive. The fact that some non-delinquents acted in the same style for a time discouraged me from trying to codify these characteristics into a scoring system. Twenty years previously I had noted that there were differences in the delinquent approach, but I had neither listed their frequency of appearance nor assigned to them different degrees of importance. What I wrote was this: "Observations of the test response may bring to light important temperamental differences which are not to be expressed in terms of mental or test age" (*Studies in Mental Deviations,* 1922).

Using this statement as a text, we may say that there is no better way of reaching behind the individual's social façade than to watch him at work. On the one hand he may reveal self-standards of neatness and care. He may betray his reactions toward success or failure, or any tendency to shift the blame from himself. Deep-felt resentments may come to the surface. His performance may be adversely affected by nervousness or anxiety, or distrust of his own capabilities. These last traits, it may be remarked, are not confined to delinquents. Under examination, many subjects, especially females, show a lack of self-confidence, which may help to account in part for sex differences in performance. Males often approach the task just as if it were a game or puzzle in which a perfect score is not required; females usually take the task much more seriously, feeling that errors reveal their disabilities either to their own eyes, or to those of the examiner.

Time and time again I have seen individuals put up an excellent record in what some term "tests of general intelligence," but make inexplicable errors in the Maze. From my point of view, there is no such thing as general intelligence, only specific intelligences —or if there is such a thing as global intelligence, I doubt whether there exists any numerical index of practical significance we can attach to it. What, for example, would be the use of attempting to assign an IQ to a Shakespeare or an Einstein? [1] What would one amount to without his verbal intelligence, or the other without his mathematical genius?

About 1940, I waked up to the fact that taking account only of the gross errors in planning meant that I was not getting full value out of the Maze Test. The style of performance could reveal what work standards the individual set up for himself, and the strength of his desire to do a good job. Had he the makings of a good craftsman, a fine artificer, or was he a careless bumbler, exerting only enough effort to get by? Faults of disposition and aptitude seemed to me characteristic of the delinquent.

Years ago Thomas Carlyle described human beings as if the clothes they wore became part of the man, and this was a very apt metaphor. His view of personality as a garment we fashion for our-

[1] Attempts have been made to estimate the IQ of various illustrious persons, but these amount to little more than guesswork.

selves for outward display is, I believe, as searching as any the social psychologists have achieved.

Freud, too, was right when he remarked on tendencies to bury unpleasant episodes under a mask of forgetfulness, which in some places becomes thick enough to be opaque. On the other hand, we tend to keep the memory of our personal triumphs and periods of happiness green. Thus the robes in which we adorn ourselves are gay and shining affairs, sewed lightly together with the threads of dignity and applause. And as for dignity, how little we have left when we take off our clothes!

One of my worst failures to follow an obvious lead concerned this qualitative scoring of the Maze. Though the performances of delinquents and non-delinquents tended to fall into contrasting patterns, we have already noted that the two categories of behavior are not mutually exclusive. In simple terms, 20 to 25 per cent of non-delinquents turned in performances similar to those of delinquents—and vice versa. Perhaps this is just as well. If any test scoring could unfailingly put the psychological finger on the delinquent personality, psychologists would have been armed with another weapon akin to the IQ, and subject to similar abuse. A Maze test qualitative score (*Q* score) might have been used to put the brand of mental defect on many a "low brow."

In short, the discovery that some normals appear to be slightly tarred with the same brush as some individuals in overt trouble with the law should have called for a more thorough analysis of deviant performers. It might have shifted emphasis from the average to the unusual individual. What I should have done was to have collected at least a thousand of such cases and made a thorough study of their personal, social, and family histories, in the hope of uncovering the clues to their unconventional behavior.

CHAPTER 13

Less Brains–More Social Efficiency

THIS CHAPTER of my postscript concerns a most bizarre experience, one that on appearance seems to be devoid almost completely of any debatable rationale. One can readily understand why, in a case of physical malformation, harmful growths, tumors, misplacement of organs, various malfunctions, the ill effects of which are known, the surgeon should step in and attempt to correct the condition with his scalpel. But when the situation is one of mental disease, deficiency, or anomalies of behavior, to use the surgical knife would seem like a most blatant malfeasance of medical practice.

When a mind becomes deranged, or a personality disturbed, when sensory perceptions are distorted, or reason upset, it seems senseless to expect any therapeutic result from a mutilation of brain substance and a severance of nerve connections within the central nervous system. To attempt to cure the woes of the psyche by a physical intervention seemed as illogical and extreme as the maladies themselves.

So, indeed, did it appear when the operation of lobotomy or leucotomy was first proposed for the relief or care of psychotic symptoms in human behavior. Psychoanalysts, steeped in Freudian beliefs, firmly held the conviction that psychotic and neurotic behavior had their genesis in the shocks or traumas of infantile experiences, including parental rejections and the like; to hold that the crude approach of lobotomy could correct mental disorder was heresy. If the stroke of the surgeon's knife could change the sick personality in what was almost the twinkling of an eye, what became of the psychogenetic theories of causation? This was a blow aimed at the heart of psychoanalysis, an assault on Freud himself.

Yet, the operation of cutting burr holes in convenient spots on each side of a patient's skull, inserting a blunt instrument called a leucotome, then by a downward and upward incision through the brain substance cutting from 60 to 85 per cent of the nerve connections of the frontal lobes with the rest of the brain, did bring about dramatic changes in behavior in many cases. Patients sunk in catatonic stupor, who had not spoken for months, moved about voluntarily and even answered questions. Hallucinations became less vivid and frequent, and sometimes disappeared. Delusions lost their disturbing force, violence was abated, hyperactive movements or uncontrolled verbosity were diminished, and even homicidal tendencies were checked. Nor was this therapy rare or spasmodic. About one-third of lobotomy patients were greatly improved, and half of all operated cases showed noticeable improvement, some to the point of being granted weekend paroles to visit their families, while others progressed to complete discharge. It was difficult, however, to predict the outcome of psychosurgery. However, the Maze Test did provide some indication. A low pre-operative score was a poor augury for improvement. It seemed as if planning ability, if gravely impaired before operation, could not readily be restored.

In the selection of cases for surgery to be undertaken by Dr. Ralph B. Cloward, noted neurosurgeon, I was fortunate enough to be closely associated with Dr. Richard Kepner, then Clinical Director at the Territorial (now State) Mental Hospital at Kaneohe, fifteen miles from Honolulu. From a monograph which we wrote in collaboration, I have picked one case to illustrate the effects, both negative and positive, of the operation. I will withhold the name of the patient, not to avoid an invasion of privacy, but as a concession to professional confidence. He will be designated only as C—.

C— was a Negro, about 58 years of age, who had been under observation at the Hospital for over a year, having been transferred there from Oahu Prison. He had a long record of stabbings and other serious assaults. His varied job experience, all at an unskilled level, had been interrupted by terms of imprisonment. He was born in Atlanta, where he reached the fifth grade in school by the age of 15 years. He then enlisted, and after being involved in a cutting affray, was sent to Fort Leavenworth. He later deserted the army and was dishonorably discharged. Sentenced to Iowa State Reformatory, he got into another stabbing affray and served four years in Fort Madison Penitentiary. While a parolee, he was implicated in a burglary in Illinois which brought him 33 months imprisonment in Joliet. A third stabbing followed in San Francisco, and after a year in prison he moved to Hilo.

There he got into a fight in which he inflicted over 40 superficial wounds on his opponent with a pocket knife. He told me that he had filed down the blade to 3 1/2 inches so that he could not be convicted of being armed with an offensive weapon, and also to diminish the likelihood of fatal results in any of his fights. His final offense in Hawaii took place at the local prison, and then he had been transferred to the mental hospital. In each of these incidents a reference to his color had at once prompted a murderous assault. I had been specially warned to steer clear of any reference to his being a Negro. I had no difficulty in remembering. As a graphic record of his career, I drew up what I called a prison time-line, which I had devised to give a quick summary of a criminal career in terms of major offenses and prison terms. This I found useful when serving as a member of the Parole Board. Of 35 years prior to 1941, C— had spent 20 years in prison, chiefly in mainland U.S.A.

Psychiatric reports from the Hospital showed that C— was quiet, orderly, and cooperative at most times, but irritable and aggressive at others. The staff, who were aware of his record, were fearfully expecting his next outbreak. He was hallucinatory at times, claimed to be a close friend of the Governor of the Territory, and wrote letters to President Roosevelt complaining of the food and his hospital treatment and demanding release. The diagnosis was dementia praecox, paranoid type. Evidently the psychiatrists were not going to make any mistake in regard to leniency, for a report added that all this was superimposed on a "psychopathic personality." That blanket indictment was wide enough to cover anything.

Dr. Honzik, Clinic psychologist, had examined him at the Oahu Prison a couple of years before. In spite of his unfavorable educational record, C— did surprisingly well in the Binet Scale, being credited with 14 years 7 months mentality. His rote memory span was uncommonly good; he could repeat 9 digits in order, about the level of college graduates. His IQ was 104, but the Maze quotient (TQ) was 79. His qualitative score was extremely poor. The average delinquent reaches an error score of 49, but C—'s performance was so impulsive and he earned so many penalties that his *Q* score was 81, or 32 points worse than the delinquent average. (The higher the score, the worse the performance.) Prefrontal lobotomy was recommended.

C— came through the operation satisfactorily. Post-operatively he was somewhat dazed and confused for a couple of weeks, had some urinary incontinence, undressed before nurses without any shame, and wandered about the ward in his underclothes. All his actions were retarded; he would take an hour or two to finish dressing and making his bed, though everything was done most meticulously.

Then for the first time he began to assume some ward duties, such as cleaning windows; but he would shine the same pane for an hour before going on with the next. Taking a shower took as long as two hours, and he seemed incapable of planning his next move. But five weeks after operation he was cheerful, helpful in small ways to other patients, but still aggressive, striking several of them for not keeping the ward tidy. He appeared more sociable, and even attended a dance. His irritability subsided and he was given the privilege of working outside the ward, and was finally made a member of a clean-up gang. Thirteen months after the operation he was recommended for discharge from the Hospital, but was returned to prison to complete his term. Three months later he was released and given a job as painter's helper at the Hospital where he had been an inmate. His success, however, was limited, since he was so lethargic. For example, he took a half-day to arrange his brushes and paints to his satisfaction.

Finally, a social agency arranged for his return to the mainland. He followed instructions and went down to the ship, but arrived at the dock minus his identification papers, his spare clothes, and other belongings. Except for the social worker's help he would have missed the ship. But by this time his aggressiveness had quite disappeared. "When anyone calls me a nigger," he told me, "I jus' tell 'em they oughta know better an' walk away. It don't disturb me no more."

But in his responses to testing, his mental impairment was very evident. Successive Binet examinations yielded post-operative scores of 11 years, 11 years 3 months, 11 years 9 months, and finally 12.6 years, still much lower than his pre-operative mental age of 14 years

7 months. His rote memory declined from a nine-digit span to six digits, while ability to repeat digits in reverse order seemed to have disappeared almost completely.

In the Maze Test, however, the deficits were extremely grave. Twelve weeks after operation he passed the five- and six-year designs on the first trial, but simply could not deal with the seven-year test. Five successive examinations determined his highest achievement to be only 7 years, showing almost complete inability to improve with practice. From his pre-operative level, his test age had declined four years, a loss of 20 TQ (test quotient) points. Despite his most deliberate and careful efforts, his planning ability remained that of a mental defective. He repeated the same errors, time after time, and showed little concern over his failures, even though he worked most carefully.

Interesting light was thrown on the question as to what specific deficits follow frontal lobe operations. Previously, C— had been a rather good checkers or draughts player. The necessity of looking ahead and considering alternatives certainly enters into success in this game as it does in solving a Maze. Though the patient's ability had declined in both respects, I was surprised to note that in at least one game I observed he worked out a combination of moves which won him the game. I remarked in my report that the type of perceptual planning needful in checker-playing was not seriously affected by the operation, although this was in marked contrast to his comparative failures in the Maze.

Possibly a different spread of attention is called for in a situation where the player is stimulated by the presence opposite him of a competitor. In the Maze situation he is "on his own," and this isolation may be conducive to bringing into play some factors that interfere with his ability to make decisions. I have already commented on his retardation, slowness of movement, and indecision. In the game of checkers the presence of a competitor may have resulted in some pressure to act promptly, and this extra stimulation may have helped. It is possible also that an experienced player may act automatically. We know very well how a sudden call to activity will stimulate some individuals to unwonted speed and achievement, much as the use of the spur drives the horse to temporary speed. Having too much time to think may act as a block to decision-making. If Billy Graham were to talk of the week rather than the hour of decision, the suggestion of longer consideration might cut his roll of conversions almost in half.

C—'s case has been discussed in detail, not because it can be called a typical case, but because it illustrates what may happen in lobotomy. One cannot insist enough on the immense variety of human responses. The emphasis on individual differences is to my mind the greatest contribution that has been made by modern psychology. Through the centuries statements have been built up which are true of common humanity, but are certainly not applicable to the uncommon man. It is true that exceptions prove the rule, but in human behavior there are such a lot of exceptions. Proverb-making represents a summary of a consensus of opinion, but the consensus is not necessarily correct.

If the reader has not already seen through psychological pretensions to unusual powers of insight into the human mind, then the time has arrived for a general admission of ignorance. Whether we claim to be psychologists, psychiatrists, or neurologists, how little any of us know about the foundation of all our professions, the matrix of the mind. In that respect we are all psychologists of sorts. To pinpoint this statement, we may cite the stubborn fact that no matter how careful the neurosurgeon may be to make lobotomy operations identical, he cannot achieve identical mental or physical effects. In short, he does not really know what he is operating upon. There is no positive uniformity of results. The psychologist can in most cases predict a change in personality, but whether that change will be beneficial and to what degree, he cannot say with any certainty. The social effectiveness of an operatee may be diminished, may improve, or may suffer no specific change, but which change will be effected no one can say.

All this is merely an expression of our fundamental ignorance. We do not know what life, mind, psyche, or soul really is, nor have we as yet any reliable means of measuring any of them, and until we have, how can we say how much they can be diminished or improved?

Then in the realm of psychiatry, how can we define such abnormalities as schizophrenia when we do not know what it is that upsets mental equilibrium? When in common speech we talk of a man losing his mind, we cannot tell what exactly he has lost. The term psychology presupposes that there is a science of mind, but so far only the initial pages have been opened to us.

When a man, who otherwise walks, talks, sleeps, wakes, and for the most part reasons as you and I, tells us that he hears voices or receives information or instructions from a non-existent source, or claims that he is the President of the United States, or produces other bizarre ideas such as that his friends, neighbors, or family are plotting his destruction, what has gone wrong? He may claim that he is in direct communication with spirits. If he announces that he has invented a machine with which he can destroy the world, we hasten to put him under restraint, unless, of course, he is a nuclear scientist. With the progress of science, so-called, many of man's achievements, once believed incredible, are now within his power. But as regards these accomplishments, the scientist can produce actual examples to substantiate his claims. The insane person has none. Physiologists can experimentally produce psychotic phenomena, but are still far from defining normality. What, in other words, has been changed?

Because of this lack of understanding, we subject our fellow-beings to remedies that are as bizarre and outlandish as their complaints. Lobotomy and other forms of psychosurgery were some of these strange but hopeful therapies. Psychoanalysis was also one, in process, I believe, of re-appraisal. At one time, in mental hospitals, once a rather uncertain psychiatric diagnostic label had been attached to the sufferers, psychiatrists proceeded to shock the daylights along with the delusions out of patients, or put them into comas so severe that they came out with only very imperfect memories of their former ideas. They had something else to worry about.

Nowadays, electric shock and insulin comas are no longer standard treatment in mental hospitals, while lobotomies (or leucotomies, as they call the operations in England) are, except in rare cases, things of the past. These drastic therapies have been displaced by the use of much milder treatments, particularly continued medication with tranquilizing drugs, which is in its turn superseding psychoanalysis. At extended intervals in the sixteen years between 1943 and 1959, I was interested in measuring the effects both of psychosurgery and the drugs, and this work, therefore, became an important part of my personal history.

To illustrate the changes in behavior that may result from brain operations, I have already given the history of a single patient, C—, in considerable detail. That experience became part of rather prolonged research. Unfortunately, as we shall see, psychologists in general neglected the opportunity to use operative results as one key to the meaning of mental tests. These measures were claimed to be brain tests. An obvious enquiry was—what happened to test scores when the frontal lobes suffered such drastic cerebral *insults,* designated together as psychosurgery?

My first excursion into this field was reported under the horrific title *Mental Changes After Bilateral, Prefrontal Lobotomy,* by Richard deM. Kepner, M.D., and myself, and this became a first step in an investigation of considerable significance. It is discussed here because it seems extremely unlikely that this experience can ever be repeated, since scrabbling people's brains has gone out of fashion. Uncovering infantile complexes is likely to be next among discarded procedures.

The monograph mentioned above reported results with 18 patients who had been operated upon by Dr. Ralph Cloward. They had been given pre-operative mental examinations. To summarize briefly, seven out of eighteen cases actually showed post-operative improvement in their Binet scores, ten lost ground, and one remained the same. The group's over-all change averaged 3 IQ points. But the picture was altered rather radically in their Maze Test scores. Thirteen cases lost post-operatively, three remained the same, and only one improved his score. The over-all Maze Test deficit was 14 test quotient points. This was in strong contrast to the inconclusive results obtained with the Binet scale, a surprising finding in view of the improvement in socialized behavior of some members of the group. The experiment was reported in 1944.

Dr. Henry Peters, of the staff of the Psychological Clinic, and I decided to continue the mental examinations with additional lobotomy cases, numbering in all 55, divided on the basis of social improvement. Seventeen of these patients (31%) were considered unimproved, 22 (40%) were improved, and 16 (29%) were so improved that they were recommended for extended parole or discharge from the Hospital. In round numbers, in almost 70 per cent of the cases the operation had been of benefit to patients.

We could not, even in the interests of so-called science, operate on criminals, but we could at least find 55 prison inmates who had been given a second Maze Test examination after an interval of time. We could use these as a control group to judge whether observable gains in test scores were due to the operation or merely reflected practise in repeating the test.

Though the average elapsed time between testings was 4 1/2 years for the unoperated prisoners, they made a practice gain of over 10 points on the average as compared with a mean loss of 14 points for the patients. This spread of 24 points was, of course, a very different deficit from the 3 points demonstrated by the Binet.

However, some explanation was still needed for the fact that an operation, which made individuals easier to live and work with, resulted in lower scores in a test supposed to be measuring, among other things, social adjustment. It seemed evident that lobotomy blunted affective reactions, impaired initiative, and reduced environmental sensitivity. Like C—, our first illustrative example, these patients were still aware of things that formerly annoyed or excited them, but they no longer "bothered them." C— still disliked people referring to his race, but it did not seem worth while to do anything about the matter. He had lost the initiative in aggression. His formula for indifference was, "They doan know no better." It became much easier for him to count 10 before an angry word, and if he counted to 100 before acting, his resentment had dissipated.

Similarly, patients who had undergone lobotomy for intractable pain acknowledged that they still felt the pain but were not as worried about it as formerly. In other words, a certain amount of passivity helps. This dulling of emotion may be reflected in the reaction to a test that puts emphasis on dynamic attitudes in social relationships.

The sudden increase of interest aroused by the experimental work done by Moniz in Portugal, which was followed by the introduction to America of lobotomy by Drs. Freeman and Watts, was responsible for the setting up of one large-scale, thorough investigation of psychosurgery in the United States. In spite of the apparent severity of the cerebral *insults* that made up psychosurgery, there did not seem to be as much risk and discomfort in lobotomy as there was with electric shock. Moreover, if anything between 50 and 70 per cent of patients showed improvement, the whole process seemed worth while, though it was still regarded by medical men as a last resort.

There had already been enough cases in America and elsewhere to disabuse people's minds of the idea that the brain was of such delicate texture that any injury to it would necessarily be fatal. Doctors, of course, were quite aware that the soul's frail dwelling place, as Shakespeare called it, might not be so fragile after all. For many years they had been familiar with the interesting case of Phineas Gage, railway foreman, who had suffered a purely accidental lobotomy. While tamping down a charge of dynamite, he managed to blow a small crowbar through the base of his skull, which emerged, covered with blood and grease, at the top of his cranium; nevertheless, he survived the accident and lived for over 12 years. It was recorded that he later held a variety of jobs, but none for very long. Though he had been a most efficient foreman, changes in temperament were so marked that his former employers could not retain his services. From our standpoint, the following characterization is most interesting. He was reported by Dr. Harlow, who followed the case for many years, to be "capricious and vacillating, devising many plans for future operation, which are no sooner arranged than they are abandoned in turn for others appearing more feasible. A child in his intellectual capacities, but with the general passions of a man."

He appeared so radically changed in his personality and reactions "that his friends and acquaintances said that he was no longer Gage." [1]

The description above reflects so well the behavior of an individual with low-level performance in the Maze that I would have expected of him, not only low test age, but a very sloppy *Q* score. It is a pity that at that time no tests of planning capacity or quality of test execution were available. But if nothing else, Phineas Gage proved that the human brain is of such tough fiber that it can withstand the rudest of physical shocks and still continue to function to some degree of social adequacy.

No account of investigation of lobotomy and its effects would be complete without reference to one of the most highly powered researches in the history of psychology—the Columbia-Greystone projects I and II, and the New York Brain Study. The list of Columbia-Greystone Associates fairly glittered with names of rare effulgence in neuroanatomy, neurology, psychiatry, psychology, and allied professions, to the number of 43. Their reports combined in three hefty volumes amounted to well over a thousand printed pages. Cleaning the Augean stables would be a small task compared with the job of tidying up and presenting all the accrued evidence as to the effects of psychosurgery. Some of the criticisms that ensued were very unfavorable.

One commentator went so far as to express his opinion that the mountain had labored and brought forth a mouse. This most prestigious array of talent, he suggested, spent a couple of years and probably half a million dollars to establish a single positive finding,

[1] Quoted in Freeman and Watts, *Psychosurgery* (1st ed.; Baltimore, Md.: Charles C Thomas, 1942), pp. 44, 45.

namely, that the Porteus Maze Test was the only standard mental measure that revealed any consistent psychological deficits following psychosurgery. This included not only lobotomy, but more localized brain damages, such as venous ligation, thalamotomy, thermocoagulation, and transorbital lobotomy. In lay terms, these surgical procedures consisted of tying off veins so as to interfere more or less seriously with blood circulation in the brain, partially cutting off communication with the thalamus, a most important way-station near the midbrain, destruction by electric heat of cell layers in the cortex, and a literal scrambling of brain matter by means of an instrument like an icepick rotated through a small bony aperture in the supraorbital region of the head. It seems to me that the deficits in Maze performance which follow these surgical *insults* are important enough to indicate that the frontal lobes do play a vital role in human adjustments. The unique sensitivity of the Maze Test may have diminished the significance of this finding in the eyes of psychologists who had failed to realize the relationship of planning and foresight to intelligence. Still, when so little was achieved, surely any result becomes significant enough to be closely examined and evaluated.

Naturally, considering how upsetting the final verdict was to psychoanalytic theorists, and even to biologists who regarded the frontal lobes as the culminating point of evolution, there were many unkind reactions. One objector suggested that improvement in some psychotic behavior could be achieved by cutting off the patients' hands and leaving their brains alone, the theory being that capacity for getting into mischief would be tremendously diminished. Castration also might make important changes in male temperament.

In any case, the deficits in the Maze were large, while those in other tests were small. Peters and I had noted a distinctive pattern of Maze responses in the more successful cases. This we called a *V* profile, apparent in successive testings before and after lobotomy, the low point of the *V* representing the post-operative fall, followed by successive Maze Test improvement in later examinations. In brief, what commonly happened in cases with a successful outcome was first of all a sharp fall in Maze Test score from the pre-operative level to the first post-operative record, followed, when the tests were repeated over a period of three months, by a fairly regular rise up to or above the pre-operative level. This was what the psychologists employed on the project (Drs. Carney Landis, Joseph Zubin, and H. E. King) called the "drop and rise" pattern. Their finding was:

> Inquiry into the pattern of performance over the four testing periods showed a marked relation between performance on this test and social improvement. . . . The answer is not long in forthcoming. Those individuals whose pattern of performance most resembled the pattern of group performance (drop and rise) were found to be the ones who had shown the greatest degree of social recovery.

Six patients were selected by the psychiatrists on the basis of this type of initial loss and subsequent test improvement. Five of them had been discharged and were at home or working. On an eight-point scale of social improvement they averaged 5.85, as compared with 1.0 for all other operatees. But—and this finding seemed important—these greatly improved cases did not differ from the other patients as regards age, amount of brain tissue removed, or change in Wechsler-Bellevue IQs. Moreover, according to the summary by Landis, most of their Rorschach scores were unchanged after the operation, surely a surprising insensitivity in a test so often relied upon as an index of personality.

The importance of such negative results lies in the fact that many of the mental measures shown to be unchanged after brain damage suffered no apparent loss in popularity among clinical psychologists. Most of them continued to rely heavily on Wechsler-Bellevue scores to indicate either impairment or arrest in intelligence, or on the Rorschach to provide a personality picture. Both verdicts badly need correction. Any person who has suffered lobotomy or extensive topectomy is, like Phineas Gage, a different kind of person. How does it come about that the tests, with the exception of the Porteus Maze, do not reflect these changes?

One flaw in the Columbia-Greystone research design was the repetition of the same form of the Maze several times. This resulted, in some cases, in a marked increase in score due to practice. Though Peters and I had shown this improvement in scores in our control group of 55 criminals, the conclusion reached by the Columbia-Greystone Associates was that the Maze deficits disappeared after an eight-month interval, and that therefore the operative effects were transitory.

In 1951 the U.S. Department of Health, Education and Welfare called a conference in New York of alleged experts on the effect of psychosurgery, to which I was invited. The list of members was besprinkled generously with names of note—Drs. Freeman, Ackerly, Eberhart, Grant, Heath, Hebb, Landis, Zubin, Mettler, Overholser, Solomon, Whitehorn, Wolfe, and the like.

But as regards what psychosurgery does and how it does it, it may be said that never did so many know so little. In the arguments "about it and about," I upheld the view that recovery in the Maze was not real, that it was only apparent, and was due very largely to practice gains. The dispute might have continued to this day except that Dr. Aaron Smith, at the suggestion of Landis and Kinder, re-examined all available hospital patients of the New York Brain Study eight years after the operation. As far as the Maze was concerned, the losses in score increased more than ever, indicating that they were anything but transitory. Smith's paper, "Changes in Porteus Maze Scores of Brain-operated Schizophrenics After an Eight-Year Interval," was published in the July, 1960 issue of *The Journal of Mental Science*. There has been little or no argument on the subject since.

This was not so much due to the conclusiveness of Smith's findings as to the permanent decline in brain efficiency as it was to the decline in popularity of the operation itself—popularity, that is, with the neurosurgeons. It was never exactly popular with the patients. The advent of the tranquilizing drugs, however, changed the picture completely. Taking pills did not involve any shedding of blood nor a lengthy stay in hospital plus surgical expenses, yet it seemed to bring about improvements similar to those following psychosurgery. One almost immediate effect was a change in the average period of initial stay in a mental hospital of newly admitted patients. This was reduced in most cases from 6 to 2½ months on the average, a result attained by no other therapy, psychoanalytic or otherwise. Insufficient credit has been accorded to the tranquilizers for this amelioration. Some would like to claim that it has resulted wholly from improved mental hospitalization and psychiatric care. If this were the case, the psychiatric benefits were unconscionably delayed.

Some of the behavioral effects were similar to those that commonly followed lobotomy. Patients on the drugs were less disturbed, more cooperative, less physically active, and more amenable to other methods such as group therapy. Under such circumstances, it seemed worth while to see what happened to their Maze score before and after the administration of the chlorpromazine, one of the most effective of the tranquilizers. Assisted by John Barclay, I instituted a research project on the subject. This involved first of all the setting up of a scale of ward behavior as an independent measure or criterion of social improvement.

After a period of initial practice and training with the scale, we asked psychiatric aides to rate all the inmates of two wards, occupied almost wholly by chronic patients. All those who could respond were then tested by the original Maze series, and after two months of routine administration of chlorpromazine (300 mg. daily), they were re-examined by means of the Extension series of the Maze, so as to avoid practice effects. Again, I was faced with the same question that appeared in psychosurgical cases—would the observed social improvement be reflected in higher test scores? The answer was the same as formerly. Instead of scores rising, they fell, whereas with the control group, for whom placebos were substituted for chlorpromazine, the scores in the two testings remained the same.

In other terms, the reactions of drug patients were slowed down and their planning ability and initiative diminished below their level before treatment. It had been suggested by other investigators that chlorpromazine depressed the action of the reticular formation in the midbrain, the normal function of which is to stimulate mental alertness and to keep people wide awake at a high level of attentiveness. Depressing reticular formation activities makes the patient drowsy, retarded in movement, and generally lethargic. These effects are particularly apparent in the initial stages of response to the drug. For explanation of this unexpected decline in Maze-tested ability I had to fall back on the theory that social reactions are of two types, dynamic and passive, and that social improvement of patients is due to the increased tendency toward passivity. In short, things in general do not matter as much to the chlorpromazine patients as they used to.

Though the findings of psychosurgical research were slow to affect the practice of clinical psychology, I believe they had an important personal effect, especially on psychologists' attitudes toward my work. To many, threading through a series of paper-and-pencil labyrinths seemed a rather childish procedure, and it was hard for them to accept the value of the tests. It seemed a more serious psychological undertaking to sit down with an individual and put him through an extremely varied series of trials of memory, range of vocabulary, completion of sentences, interpretation of fables, and other tricky tasks, capping the whole by expressing results in a measure no one but a psychologist could work out. People are impressed by the mysteries of science, and determining an IQ was certainly one.

The whole routine seemed to be more in keeping with what a

psychologist was supposed to do—a more serious procedure than to simply sit and watch his subject blundering through a whole series of what at first sight appeared to be paper-and-pencil puzzles. Only when realization came about that what the examinee did with these "puzzles" was probably the best indication of brain damage that the psychologist could lay his hands on, was he suitably impressed. That they also provided a key to practical abilities, thus dividing the scholastically dull from the industrially competent, was a more prosaic use. Another value was in the recognition of delinquent trends in behavior. They could also be employed to measure the progress of mental therapy of various kinds. As a consequence, I began to be regarded as something more than an individual obsessed with a single non-verbal measure of intelligence. Had any of this jury of accreditation been interested in cataloguing the mental traits that further the survival of primitive peoples in savage environments, this realization might have come sooner.

Somewhat jestingly, I have occasionally twitted psychologists with being slow learners, but this neglect of a potentially valuable tool probably has its root in predilections for the familiar, a fondness for doing our job in the manner in which we learned to do it, and with the tools that come most easily to hand.

The Binet, the Wechsler-Bellevue, and other verbal tests are indeed necessary, and when we say that they do measure scholastic potentialities, we are stating something of tremendous value in civilized life. Whether we are taught facts or discover them for ourselves, factual knowledge is essential to success.

When we consider that planning ability, or what I have called prehearsal, enters into almost all our mentally directed activities, from adaptive movements up to arithmetical calculations, social relations, writing, logical reasoning, right through the gamut of skilled operations, then to neglect a method that offers a measure or even an estimate of such a fundamental accomplishment is certainly unintelligent.

That the Maze Test is an imperfect tool is undeniable, but in its class it is the best we have. This statement does not down-grade general intelligence measures such as the Wechsler-Bellevue. Any psychological approach that leaves the Maze verdict entirely out of consideration is one-sided and inadequate. What is needed is more effort directed to an improved method of measuring foresight, but this will not be achieved by merely doing our best to get along without it.

CHAPTER 14

Beauty, Peace, and Indolence

STRANGELY enough, the fact that I embarked upon a six-year phase of writing for profit came about through my interest in psychosurgery. By 1945 I had stored away at the back of my mind (a most untidy place) two very vague projects. The first was to write a book about Hawaii, a job that at least 150 other people had attempted with mixed success; the second was to produce a novel, mainly to settle my wonderings as to whether, if Fate had dealt the cards differently, I had it in me to make any kind of mark in writing fiction.

But in early 1945, the prospects of doing either were indeed slight. In common with almost all men grown too old to fight, I felt the strongest urge to get as near as I could to the front lines of the war in the Pacific. Pearl Harbor had happened just as I had finished my longest book, *The Practice of Clinical Psychology*. I like to comfort myself with the belief that its appearance when the nation was in the throes of a life-and-death struggle provided an adequate reason for its almost complete neglect by my professional colleagues. I have the notion that it was not such a very inferior effort.

At that time, to use the Churchillian phrase, we were nationally near the end of the beginning of the war, but still some way from the beginning of the end. Any work or project that promised an advance toward national improvement seemed very worth while.

My second son, J. R. Porteus, had risen to the rank of major in the intelligence division, and was by this time in the Philippines with the Sixth Army, scheduled, if ever events justified the attempt, to be in the first waves of invasion of the Japanese homeland.[1] Already hundreds of thousands of young men, the flower of the American people, had lost their lives in the struggle, and it looked as if invasion would be the only way of ending the deadly conflict.

Looking ahead, it seemed to me that the new brain operations promised to lighten the burden of mental disorder and disease that imperilled our national future. Hawaii's situation in the Pacific brought the war very close to us. Thousands of men in uniform, lines of warships protecting great convoys, and news of battles and naval strikes against enemy concentrations all helped to strengthen resolution. Even in the rear echelons there was a sober sense that work was to be done.

There were personal as well as patriotic reasons for activity. No one could describe our civilian population as war-weary, but we were certainly weary of monotony, the role of lookers-on. Anything that took our minds off the slaughter in Europe, Africa, and the Pacific was helpful to our mental health. Men digging bomb shelters that were never occupied, and women making thousands of bandages that they never saw used began to feel that their efforts were humdrum and futile. This was a young man's war, and all we older people could contribute were fringe services.

From the first daylight hours of the Pearl Harbor attack, the State hospital at Kaneohe, situated barely three miles from the first Japanese point of attack, the Kaneohe Naval Base, was in action. Following the first alarm, Dr. Ralph Cloward, aided by the hospital staff, had taken over the treatment of men who had suffered head wounds at the Naval Base. Psychotic patients were removed from the surgery and their places taken by these military casualties. In a couple of days of continuous work at Tripler, Aiea, Kaneohe, and the Leeward hospitals, Dr. Cloward operated on over a score of serious brain injury cases and lost only three. Because of the potential value of the Kaneohe Mental Hospital, the military at once took it under their command.

I have already mentioned that reports on the psychosurgical

[1] My elder son, D. H. Porteus, graduated from Harvard Law School, entered politics before World War II and has served continuously in the Legislature, first in the House of Representatives and for the past ten years as a Senator. Two of my grandchildren hold Ph. D. degrees, one from Case, the other from Stanford.

work done at the Hospital had been published in 1944 and 1947, some years prior to the Columbia-Greystone Associates' account of their projects. Since these confirmed our own findings on almost all points, they naturally attracted widespread attention. The main difference in approach was that in the second of our monographs (Porteus and Peters), we had raised the question as to whether practise effects in the test might easily serve to mask the mental deficits occasioned by the operation.

At the research conference on psychosurgery held in New York in 1951, I met Dr. Walter Freeman, who with Dr. James A. Watts had introduced lobotomy to America. There we began a discussion of the effects of practise in Maze scores which we continued in later correspondence. Even though Dr. Freeman realized that my demonstration of patients' impairment in planning and foresight told against the therapeutic benefits of the operation, he urged me to continue my research.

Freeman was instrumental in setting up a plan whereby I was to obtain a year's leave of absence from the University of Hawaii which I would spend at St. Elizabeth's Hospital in Bethesda, Maryland organizing their work on the mental effects of lobotomy. This plan was to be financed by a grant from the John and Mary Markle Foundation, set up to support medical research. The Board of Regents of the University of Hawaii gave me the necessary leave, with the understanding that Dr. Colin Herrick, my chief assistant, would carry on the work of the Psychological Clinic during my absence. Dr. Overholser, superintendent of St. Elizabeth's Hospital, appeared enthusiastic over the project.

I was about ready to depart for my new assignment when news came that the vice-president of the Foundation had been killed in an automobile accident in California. His successor, who knew little about the plan, asked that it be postponed for a year. As an alternative, Dr. Overholser suggested that he would arrange a temporary civil service appointment for me, which would give me a free hand as regards research.

Everything seemed very satisfactory except that I would need a first-class priority so that I could be assured of my return to Hawaii when my year was up. Here was where I made the fatal mistake of trying to work through an admiral when a lieutenant commander would have done better—a case of sending a man on a boy's errand. My friend Admiral Bloch (formerly C.-in-C. Pacific), before whom I laid my problem, was so obliging that he took the matter right to the top man, Admiral King, Chief of Naval Operations. He, of course, took the only course open to him—a rigidly official position.

"Tell your friend," he told Claude Bloch, "that in a year's time we expect to be carrying out such important maneuvers that all civilian travel in the Pacific will be absolutely forbidden." We did not need to guess what those maneuvers would be.

A lieutenant commander, or even a lieutenant, would not have known much of over-all naval plans and would probably have assigned me a good priority without question. But now, in legal language, I was estopped, which sounds terriby final. I stayed home.

But I had my year's leave, my deputy director had been approved, and most unusual of all circumstances, my desk cleared. All these preparations could not be wasted. I decided to take my leave of absence and write a book. After all the uncertainty and piles of correspondence, I felt I was just in the mood for some light-hearted writing, as far removed as possible from bilateral prefrontal lobotomy as I could get.

There was, I believed, something left to write about Hawaii. The early explorers, Captain Cook, Vancouver, and the like, had had their innings. Cook himself was somewhat overcome by the importance of his own discoveries and had little time to study or understand the natives before they struck him down with club and dagger in the surf of Kealakekua Bay. His fatal error was the psychological one of underestimating the loyalty and affection these Polynesians had for their king, who had been seized by Cook as a hostage for the return of a ship's cutter stolen for its iron nails, which the natives valued highly. Later, Vancouver was too busy trying to bring the islands under the British crown to pay much attention to the human factors in the situation.

Next came the missionaries, so obsessed with saving the idolaters' souls that they took little notice of their bodies or material welfare. Except for a thin sprinkling of medical missionaries, they were content to leave such problems to local medicine men, or Nature. As for themselves and their families, life in the Sandwich Islands demanded more than its quota of sacrifice and endurance. Their efforts to improve the moral character of the Hawaiians were unceasing, but the people themselves did not enjoy such unwilling elevation, and took every opportunity to return to earth. It was difficult indeed to enable a whole nation to lift itself by its own moral bootstraps, but impossible when they wore no boots. The great frustration that missionaries experienced was the inconstancy of conversion. The Hawaiians were quite comfortable as they were. It was rather too much to expect the heathen, who had just been informed that he possessed an immortal soul, to begin worrying about it.

Following the missionaries came a host of world travellers, Robert Louis Stevenson, Mark Twain, Isabella Bird—with the woman making the best job of her descriptive efforts. And after them came the debunkers, who found much to be caustic about. The missionary descendants, who had taken no vows of poverty in their own or their fathers' names, were diligent dividend-seekers, and made excellent targets for criticism. Attempted rebuttals made on their behalf were stodgy. Considering the generally sad outlook for the world, I decided to deal with our local problems as good-humoredly as possible. The very fact that the Hawaiian monarchy and way of life had survived amid such a pack of international wolves of world diplomacy spoke well for our good luck and good management. It seemed to me that Hawaii was about the only place in the world where if you forgot your troubles, they did tend to go away.

Parts of the book, which was entitled *Calabashes and Kings,* were devoted to the contrary thesis that Hawaii was certainly no earthly paradise, that we had the same social problems here as were to be found anywhere, and that our political pupation was still in the emerging stage. Some of my chapter headings were intended to reflect those facts. Among these were Myths and Missionaries, Of Sugar and Shekels, Perplexities in Paradise. The last-named I have just re-read and find that our military vulnerability, statehood, our political future, racial differences, Japanese legislative dominance, education and language handicaps, tolerance and good humor—all part of our Polynesian inheritance—are the topics that include our problems today. This chapter demonstrates both the common nature of our perplexities and our uncommon attitude of indifference to them. It also maintained that we can claim little credit for getting along with our neighbors, or for the Aloha spirit which we extend to our customers. How can we pride ourselves on the fact that we have in these islands no instance of oppression of a minority by a majority, when we have no majorities or minorities either?

To my mind, government by consensus is a most intellectually deadening thing. Differences of opinion not only make horse races, but provide a very healthy mental state. Majorities, as far as human history goes, have been rather generally wrong. This applies to religious ideas, human rights, and, I'm afraid, educational methods.

But I have no wish to rewrite *Calabashes and Kings,* dated as it undoubtedly is by its discussion of problems that somehow or another have been or are on their way to settlement. It is not only the British who have the habit of muddling through. What amazed me at the time was the book's instant success. It ran into four large printings, has rather miraculously escaped serious criticism, and every now and then someone even now compliments me upon it. My usual unthinking reaction is to ask—who wrote that?

Its publication history was peculiar. The editors of the University of Minnesota Press approved it, but like Stanford University Press, found they had about exhausted their war-time quota of printing paper. It looked very much as if my left-handed brainchild would be stillborn, but after all, I had had fun in writing and it represented a welcome diversion of interest from lobotomy to light literature.

Then came an unexpected letter from Stanley Croonquist, Stanford University Press managing editor, who had read the manuscript. He had been thinking of resigning his job and launching himself into the publishing business. *Calabashes* seemed to him to be just what he needed to start the venture. Incidentally, if he set up a new firm, he could obtain from the government a new quota of paper stock.

Croonquist did an excellent job, both with the printing, the Hawaiian *motif* on the cover, and the photographs of the Islands. The chapters on Sugar and Shekels and on Myths and Missionaries helped to lay a couple of ghosts, or at least silenced the rattling of mouldy skeletons reputed to be hidden in some of our best families' cupboards. I also noted some anti-paradisiac features, as I called them, of living in the Islands. For these and other reasons, *kamaainas,* or old-time residents, approved the book and one of the Big Five companies gave it a healthy sales boost by purchasing a thousand copies.[2]

Someone has observed that an athlete is on the downward path when he begins to believe his own press notices. Seeing that I left the track in 1951 and have had no literary yearnings to return to popular writing, it seems allowable to dip a toe again into the

[2] The five organizations which together dominated the commercial outlook in the Islands were commonly known—and abused—as "The Big Five." Hawaiian arithmetic was not very exact; the Dillingham Corporation was equally important in local politics and business and everybody could count at least to five.

stream of generous criticism that these essays evoked. But first I would like to remark that scientific and non-scientific reviewers work from a different basis. For the first named, their sole consideration should be, and usually is, the validity of the author's statements or results, though they may disagree with his methods of collecting data and his analysis of the same. But non-scientific books are descriptive rather than experimental, and are based on viewpoints instead of conclusions. Their reviewers are concerned with such matters as literary style, in which their own personal attitudes or preferences are involved. One could wish that scientific reviewers could be at times a little less objective and the other class of critics a bit more factual.

Perhaps there is another difference. Reviewing general literature has become a profession in itself. The literary shark has its pilot fish, and it is often an interesting question as to who is leading whom. But far be it from me to appear to discredit reviewers. I owe them too much.

Here are a few comments on my first non-scientific effort, beginning with some local critics who ought to know their own territory. The Honolulu *Advertiser* found in the book "kindly humor, sharp as a scalpel, which lends appropriate emphasis to Dr. Porteus' discerning view of the peoples of many races and conditions who play the roles in Hawaii's drama." I had twitted the friends of missionary Bingham for his description and observation of the natives who met his ship as being "shrouded in deep gloom" by saying that I had never seen a Polynesian, shrouded or unshrouded, in anything like gloom; on the other hand a New England reader quoted with approval my summation of the gifts the missionaries carried with them:

"Along with night-blooming righteousness, the missionaries brought for transplantation a goodly stock of the hardy perennials of education, temperance, social decency, sanitation, health—benefits less showy than religious conversion, but more lasting in their effects."

As to jealously guarded family secrets, I had remarked that "there is too much mystery, and more people sensitive about their grandfathers' reputations here than anywhere else."

Another publication credited me with "the rare knack of translating arid fact into the realm of exciting, amusing adventure, without marring the verity of what he has to report."

One other quotation from the book embarrassed me somewhat

because I feared it was a sample of purplish prose to which I occasionally gave way:

> Some things are plainly here for anyone to see—bits of history when this place was not a cross-roads but a one-way street to happy adventure in the South Seas; a background of the Polynesian sort, so easy-going and laughter provoking on the surface, so tragic in its end; green valleys barred with rainbows; windswept palis, unscaleable but never grim; little quiet beaches with flashes of bright beauty around each headland; strange rumblings and volcanic fires, with fern and forest hastening to cover up the scars; a welter of all the world's human problems thrown carelessly down and left to time, tolerance, and good humor for solution—all these should appear in the *palapala,* the writing of the book.

A university professor's audacity in venturing into the field of public entertainment did not, of course, escape attention. The *Saturday Review of Literature* remarked that "the book is distinctive, not for psychological profundity, but for the light touch and the occasional quip, only the least bit professorial, with which he treats everything from scenery to politics."

The *Pacific Northwest Quarterly,* though it termed it "this delightful book," felt it to be "a pity that in a book of such general excellence more care was not taken to iron out some awkward sentences that jar the more because they are few." But one critic was undoubtedly right when he implied that the book was joyously rather than carefully written.

Ellsworth Huntington, well-known author and geographer of Yale, wrote in the *Geographic Review: "Calabashes and Kings* may not be the best book on Hawaii, but as a combination of good writing, friendly humor, sound judgment, and scientific acumen, it is hard to surpass."

Knoles of Stanford also gave it a professional pat on the back in the *Pacific Historical Review* by saying that the book "made no pretense of historical scholarship as the profession practices that art, but the author at no point has wandered far afield, either in judgment of fact or opinion." That was probably as far as any historian could be expected to go, and he was quite right in declaring that "a more thorough and systematic survey of the extensive literature on the subject would have added distinction to the volume." However, I never had the slightest expectation of being a distinguished historian.

After *Calabashes* had run through four printings, the London publishers, Harrap & Co., decided to bring out a British edition. It is well known that anything in the way of books that crosses the Atlantic either way suffers a sea change. The spirit of the old query —can any good come out of Nazareth?—is not yet dead. No one on either side of the ocean had any difficulty in restraining his enthusiasm. So *Calabashes and Kings* met with some cross-Atlantic criticisms that, for the diminution of my own self-esteem, might be cited.

Quite typically British was the comment of the *Manchester Guardian,* which found that "the book has excellent photographs and a few fascinating stories." However, it went on, these "are scattered over an unindexed waste of facetiousness, more or less relevant quotations, and the glossy descriptions of an American travelogue." The reviewer confessed that he would have liked to have heard a great deal more about the eighteenth- and nineteenth-century royal courts. (The reader may remember that they have such things in England.) Another complaint was that I should have concentrated, not on what makes Hawaiians different from Americans, but on their similarities. This may have been a reasonable objection, but I still cannot understand why facetiousness, whether wasted or unwasted, could be improved by indexing.

Dr. Kathleen Freeman, in the *Cardiff Western Mail,* listed it among four excellent books, this one written, however, "in vivid American English." The *Yorkshire Post* termed it "gentle lotus-eating descriptions, to which only George Bernard Shaw was impervious." The reviewer quotes me to the effect that G.B.S. stayed in Honolulu a day and a night, "and was irascible only once; true, it was for all day, but as far as I knew, the night was peaceful." Incidentally, I had lunch with the bearded "matriarch," but he would talk only about music, of which I knew nothing. He had expressed a wish to discuss Australian aborigines with me, but in the course of careful, not to say meticulous, mastication forgot all about them. Rarely, I am sure, did he have such a silent luncheon companion. I couldn't get a boomerang in edgewise.

The London *Times Literary Supplement* recorded that "Mr. Porteus has lived for some time in Hawaii and writes with vigour and insight and a wealth of metaphor that is sometimes disconcerting." However, the reviewer did admit that though my pages were discursive, the author was "careful not to over-sentimentalize."

Not all English reviewers were so chary in their praise. Trevor Allen, in *John o' London's Weekly,* called it "the most comprehensive account of these islands that I have read. In knowledge, range, style, it is a model of what a book of its kind should be," though he does point out that I misquoted Stevenson on my first page.

Alas, the reviewer was correct on this point. I made an inexcusable mistake in the epitaph which Stevenson suggested for his grave. My quotation was: "Home is the sailor, home from the sea;" whereas, I should have written "home from sea," a real disarticulation. Like the other strictures that appeared, they were richly deserved.

In any case, my purpose had been fulfilled. I had at least proved, to my own satisfaction, that had circumstances been different, I probably could have made for myself an entirely different kind of living. I was encouraged enough to go on in the same way for the next five years before returning to the ways of respectable, if unconventional, psychology.

CHAPTER 15

The Ineffaceable Seventh

No matter what a man's profession was, the fact that he was sitting at home within seven miles of Pearl Harbor on December 7, 1941 would surely be recorded as the high point of crisis in his life. He came within an ace of witnessing what was nearly the most decisive military disaster in human history.

That Sunday, shortly to be known as "the day of infamy," dawned as it usually does in Hawaii, with the quick extinction of the night lights that sprinkle the heights above the city. As they disappear, they are displaced by sunrise glowing on a curtain of clouds hanging over the backdrop of mountains. Lazy trades ripple the sea off shore, carrying with them the faintly floral odors of this semi-tropical land. Drawn up in perfect order alongside their moorings were the ships of the United States Pacific fleet, surely one of the most powerful ever assembled. Heigh-ho, thought many of the men on board, we are the unlucky ones, who have drawn ships' duties on such a perfect Sabbath morning; how unlucky they little knew. For this was the last time for thousands that the scents of the garden, the savor of life itself, would linger in their nostrils, soon to be eclipsed by the acrid, suffocating fumes of death.

On the previous day, the Japanese fleet, each ship with a smoke plume from its funnels and "a bone in its teeth," had steamed until midnight, so that by dawn it was within 200 miles of the small pineapple island of Lanai, just about fifty miles from

Honolulu. The seas and skies between were empty, for the watch had been withdrawn. Then throughout that great flotilla, one of the largest assembled since the Spanish Armada, bells clanged and whistles sounded, the fast carriers swung around, each curving through its low streaming smoke cloud. At 3 A.M. the first planes lifted into the air. They were lined up in two main assault formations, 81 fighters, 145 dive bombers, 104 horizontal attack planes, and 40 torpedo bombers. Thirty-nine fighters circled aloft to repel the desperate counter-attack that everyone on board anticipated. The rest homed in on Honolulu's Sunday morning radio broadcasts and were on their way. Off shore they would finally divide into three waves of attack, the first to strike hard on the Kaneohe Naval Base and immobilize its secondary airfield; the second to smother Hickam Field; the third to sweep around the Koolau mountains, blot out the Army airplane concentrations at Wheeler Field in Schofield. Then the three would converge in one terrific attack on the fleet in Pearl Harbor.

To the men on shipboard, blind without radar communications, came a drone of airplanes, a sound so common in Honolulu those days that probably not one man in twenty looked aloft to the skies. Suddenly there was a roaring crescendo of diving aircraft, the whistle and gigantic *hrumphs* of bombs, answered by a thin rattle of machine guns. A couple of minutes of near-paralysis followed, then shouts, screams, and hysterical orders. From the ship's decks the crackle of machine guns grew and grew until it was extinguished by a continuous roar from the fleet's heavier armament, punctuated by the shock of giant explosions. At first there were mere swirls of smoke, then billows upon billows of it, and close at hand the spatter of blood, or fragments of flesh falling on the decks beneath. Several of the torpedo bombs sped home. Two warships, shuddering from the impact, capsized, imprisoning many hundreds of men below. To hundreds more came the sledge-hammer blows to consciousness, the searing flash that ushered in the eternal dark.

This is, of course, a personal account, not a general history, and I am quoting in part from my own book, because emotional effect is in inverse relation to the distance in time and space that separates us from actual tragedy. Perhaps it is well to remind ourselves of what war really means in terms of human shock and horror. On the fringes of catastrophe there was at once a vast confusion, a multitude of flying rumors, and even tragic errors. When, by nightfall, we had at last got our mobile anti-aircraft batteries in position, they promptly shot down some of the inadequately briefed planes being flown in from California to our rescue.

For all of this, it is my belief that as far as the civilian population was concerned, we were not nearly as alarmed as we should have been. In the first hours after the catastrophe, we were all looking for miracles in the form of counter-attack, which never came. It took us some time to realize that all sense of easy security was gone and that it would take years to be rebuilt. We all of us had Japanese friends and thought they would fight a civilized war.

Early in October, 1941, my second son Jack and I had agreed that America's involvement in the great conflict was inevitable. He then decided he would not wait for conscription, but would enter the armed forces, in which, on account of his R.O.T.C. training at the University, he would hold the rank of second lieutenant, with prospects of early promotion.

On the morning of the fateful seventh, we were sitting at breakfast in Manoa Valley where we lived, scarcely seven miles from the Pearl Harbor lochs, listening to a radio broadcast by the Mormon Tabernacle choir in Salt Lake City. It was about five to eight and they had just begun one of their favorite hymns, with its closing phrase "All is well, all is well."

Attracted by the unusual volume of sound, I stepped outside into our front garden and saw over the shoulder of the mountain buttress that forms the lower boundary of our Manoa Valley a number of bursts of anti-aircraft fire, globular in shape, grey in color. When I remarked on the unusual activity, my son quieted my curiosity by saying:

"Just another practice maneuver, I suppose." As he was an intelligence officer, I thought that he should surely know if anything were really wrong. Just at that moment he was called to the phone, then grabbed his military cap, and drove away with the rather nonchalant comment:

"If they want to start a war, I wish they didn't pick my day off." We were to see little of Jack for the next five years, while his duties took him all over the Pacific. Then my neighbor called to me to say that through his binoculars he could see four strange-looking planes high over Waikiki.

"They seem to have red crosses under their wings," he observed. The markings were, of course, symbols of the rising sun; but even then we were not unduly concerned, being still obsessed with the idea that unusually realistic maneuvers were in progress.

I turned the radio on again. The choir was still singing "All is well," but suddenly the music was interrupted by the shakiest voice I've ever heard.

"Oahu is under attack. Please keep calm, and stay off the streets. Don't telephone. This is not a practice alert—we are at war. This is the real McCoy. Keep calm." And then the choir resumed; the words are worth repeating for their strange significance.

> "Why should we think to earn a great reward
> If we now shun the fight.
> Gird up your loins, fresh courage take,
> Our God will never us forsake.
> And soon we'll have this truth to tell—
> All is well, all is well!"

When this hymn was recorded in Salt Lake City, little did the singers know under what dread circumstances it would be heard in Honolulu.

Fortunately, we were only on the fringes of battle. As we sat listening to all kinds of confused and excited instructions coming over the radio, a large shell burst about 200 yards away on the side of a hill at the edge of Manoa Valley. When I sneaked across some vacant lots to reach my elder son's house,—he was enrolled for special police duty—I found that my daughter-in-law had made a bed for the baby in the partial shelter of the stone wall of their garage. She handed me a still warm fragment of the shell which she had picked up near her house. My son was deputed to guard the roof of one of our radio stations from sabotage or attack.

Radio reports were confusing and confused. They first announced, then denied, that the enemy—for the first time identified as the Japanese—had landed on the other side of the island; also that hundreds of civilians had been killed by bombs downtown. Waikiki had been shelled, and the water in the reservoirs was suspected to have been poisoned, though this was also denied. Actually no enemy bombs fell in the city; the damage had been done by our own shells exploding on impact. In the meantime, martial law had been proclaimed and we were again warned to keep off the streets and not to use the telephone. When I hurried back home, I found our Japanese maid weeping in the garden. When I tried to calm her, she told me that in case of a successful invasion, Japanese who worked for *haoles* (whites) would be the first ones to be lined up and shot. In the late evening a policeman arrived in an official car to take her back to her parents' home. At that time I had no intention of writing about our experiences, and thus kept no notes. After nightfall Jack arrived with a pistol. "Don't open the door to anyone," he advised, "and if you shoot, shoot to kill."

Within a few weeks there was a frantic official scurry to try and fix the blame for the disaster. There was a flood of investigators, congressional and otherwise, all united in a tremendous urge to discover a scapegoat. Everyone knew that heads must fall, and the initial victims were Admiral Kimmel and General Short, our top military commanders. No one seemed to realize that it was not individuals but the American people who were also on trial for our overweening national self-confidence, leading to a sense of false security and isolationism, expressed in the "it can't happen here" philosophy. The forthcoming war, we all understood, was on someone's doorstep, but assuredly not on ours. President Roosevelt added to the confusion by making a short visit to Hawaii, after which he heartened, and deluded, the nation by the statement that only five warships had been sunk. All Honolulu, including even the feebleminded who lived at Waimano overlooking Pearl Harbor, providing they could count, knew that at least 15 vessels lay stranded around the harbor foreshores.

But in the generals' rush to shift the blame and to justify their actions before congressional investigators, some of them went much too far. One of them, desperately seeking an alibi for not having anti-aircraft batteries in position, claimed that the sugar plantation managers had refused to allow the Army access to their private property when the commanders wished to establish batteries in proper positions to defend Pearl Harbor. This charge was so absolutely contrary to the facts of the situation that the Hawaiian Sugar Planters' Association decided that they must publicly refute it. To make this exposure effective, they thought that it should be left in the hands of a competent writer, and with the success of *Calabashes and Kings* in mind, they asked me to undertake the job.

They produced all their correspondence with the military on the subject for my inspection, proving to my complete satisfaction that the facts were just the reverse of what the Army spokesman alleged. The letters showed that the plantation authorities had not only granted free access to their land, but had put all their facilities —roads, bridges, electricity, water—at the Army's disposition, assistance which had been gladly acknowledged by the highest military authorities. The lies were not only vain, but clumsy and stupid. Since the civilian record was unmistakably clear, I was glad to accept the H.S.P.A. proposal, and after a thorough review of all the correspondence, I arranged to visit each of the other islands so as to judge for myself the extent of civilian cooperation with the over-all defence plans. This was, of course, most important, for from the economic point of view, the Hawaiian Islands were in a most vulnerable position. Any hint, not of disloyalty, but merely of insensitivity on our part to the realities of national peril could influence Congress against us, and politically we were hamstrung. Any reduction of our local sugar production quota in favor of Cuba or the Philippines would cripple us financially. As to domestic competition, both the Midwest beet sugar people and the Louisiana sugar cane-growers could quite naturally command much heavier support in Congress than a single voteless delegate from Hawaii could. Were we admitted as a state into the Union, our situation in the legislative halls of the nation would change tremendously.

Now, just when the reasonableness of Hawaii's claims for statehood was gaining widespread recognition, here were not only allegations of lukewarm patriotism, but worse still, of overt interference with military plans for national defence. Only ten years had elapsed since the Massie case, when the Islands had been described in the mainland press as a jungle in which white women were unsafe. Navy and Army personnel had been at that time our worst critics, and there had been serious proposals of government by military commission. Now, with current accusations of obstructionism, or at least rank indifference, the goal of statehood seemed farther off than ever. The Hawaiian Sugar Planters' Association knew that they had much to lose through any imputations of unfitness for self-government, and felt that a book that would improve the climate of public opinion was worthy of generous support.

It seemed to me that the best thing to do was to carry the fight into adverse territory, rather than to adopt a defensive attitude, as if we really had something to hide or excuse. The obvious strategy was to attack, not the military personalities involved in the disaster, but rather the "it can't happen here" smokescreen which everybody, military or civilian, had adopted. But I could not avoid placing the immediate responsibility where it plainly belonged.

So I chose for the book's title a phrase from Ezekiel, who in a similar situation had set forth where and how the blame for failure in mental alertness should be apportioned. Ezekiel's verdict was:

". . . if the people of the land take a man of their coasts and set him for their watchman. . . . but if the watchman see the sword come, and blow not the trumpet, and the people be not warned; if the sword come, and take any person from among them. . . . his blood I will require at the watchman's hand."

Apparently, Admiral Kimmel had been picked for the watchman's role and had suffered his punishment, whether with entire justice, I could not determine. To those who had read our 1926 book, *Temperament and Race*, it should have been apparent that the American nation in its misapprehension of Japanese character, ability, and world intentions was also to blame. There were many who believed that Roosevelt himself deliberately baited the Pearl Harbor trap with the U.S. Pacific fleet, and caught far more than he bargained for.

Much as the President wished for our country's entrance into the war on the side of the Allies, surely not even the most purblind Republican could seriously believe that he would knowingly have sacrificed the American navy and brought the whole nation to the brink of final disaster to achieve such a purpose. I believe that Roosevelt, like everyone else, thought that Japan would attack the East Indies, and that eventually America must intervene, in which case the war would be fought best from our base in Hawaii. But he misjudged entirely Japanese ability to fight an all-out war so far from their own country.

Diplomatically speaking, Pearl Harbor was an unforgettable lesson in the practice of international deceit, which merely means that the enemy were much better liars than we ourselves were. But taking the long-term strategical view, Japan made her own fatal mistakes. The first was that in the attack they failed to knock out completely all of Honolulu's utilities, without which the fleet would have been forced to remove its fighting base two thousand miles to the East. To have destroyed or put out of commission our electric installations, our water supply system, a couple of bridges, and other essential facilities would have been worth a dozen battleships, especially if, as happened, our air force had been effectually blanketed.

The second fatal error was for the Japanese to have made their attack when their navy had stated its unwillingness to support an invasion of Hawaii, which their army wished to institute simultaneously with the assault on the American fleet. These facts were established by reference to Japanese official papers after their surrender.

My immediate purpose in writing the book was merely to see that no shadow of unjust blame could be attached to our sugar plantation administrators. A very little investigation revealed another strange anomaly. The civilians in the Islands generally were excellently organized for war, and this had been brought about at the urgent solicitation and direct instructions from the military. Within a couple of hours of the initial attack, teams of civilian doctors were operating on the wounded at various hospitals, the Red Cross went into action, and even the Blood Bank was efficiently mobilized. By the end of the day, and even under menace of another attack, trucks and workmen were converging on Pearl Harbor, and repair and maintenance measures were well under way.

In the succeeding weeks and months, homes on every island were being opened to soldiers, sailors, marines, and airmen. It was then that the slogan of Hawaiian hospitality was revived from the old sailing vessel days. Undoubtedly some of that hospitality was of the same type as formerly. We could not have experienced a sudden irruption of a million lusty young men on our shores without somebody's eggs being scrambled.

Even the effect on children of being at war was noticeable. Games of cops and robbers suddenly went out of style. The attitudes of the local Japanese children were interesting. In their games they assumed the role of the patriot defenders, the Nipponese being the enemy. I can illustrate the situation with a single story. In the course of gathering material for my book, I was staying with old and close friends—a plantation manager, his wife, and their five-year-old son.

Their back lawn had been converted by the children into a battlefield with trenches and coconut palm bomb shelters, the weapons being mangoes, squashy guavas, and for heavy artillery large, over-ripe papayas. A juicy papaya hurled from a dozen feet made a most effective impact and the kids were all good baseball players.

Then in came their own little son crying bitterly to his parents.

"Mother," he complained through his tears, "I'm sick of the war. Sakai and Tomatsu [the yardman's somewhat older offspring] won't let me be the marines. I always have to be a Jap and stay in the trenches. They're giving me one heck of a guava and papaya bombing. Can't you do something about making them give me a turn at being a marine?"

How successful *And Blow Not the Trumpet* was in changing the popular image of Hawaii on the mainland, I do not know for certain. At least every member of Congress was sent a presentation copy and about a third of the number acknowledged its receipt, almost half of them stating that they hoped to read the book. It may even have advanced the cause of statehood. According to the reviews, it had not done a bad job. It also won the award for the best book published in Hawaii for the year 1947.

I will not burden the reader with lengthy reviews, but the following excerpts may give some idea of the book's reception. The *Saturday Review of Literature* said that I supplied "a footnote to history that in justice needed to be told. He does so in a style often sharp and amusing, light in manner, yet well weighted with facts. . . . Yet why and how civilian Hawaii was prepared for war, and the armed services were not, is a thing worth knowing. In these times, when we lean more and more upon men of military experience, it may be a matter of vital importance." I have already suggested answers to the questions implied by the reviewer—particularly our tendency to pack up our troubles in the other fellow's kit bag, and, second, that the reason for the military's prodding of the civilian population to organize for defence was probably the belief that if any crisis occurs, it is an excellent idea to keep everybody busy, a fine antidote to mass hysteria.

The *San Francisco Chronicle* declared the book to be "a good clinical study of what happens in an American community in total war" (provided, of course, it is prepared for it). Dr. Kirtley Mather also reviewed it for the Non-fiction Book Club of New York and wrote:

"His personal record of the first 48 hours of American participation in World War II occupies only seven pages of the book, but it is the most effective account I have read. Rarely do information and enlightenment come in such palatable portions."

In the book itself, I did attempt to suggest a more directly psychological reason for that extraordinary lapse from vigilance that formed the prelude to disaster, that inexplicable letting down of our military guard that still keeps us wondering—what happened to the watchman?

I believe that I discovered a parallel to this somnolence in something that happened in Pavlov's famous experiments. After the dogs had been conditioned by the sound of the bell to salivate in expectation of food, a strange thing happened if a relatively lengthy period of time was allowed to intervene between signal and feeding. In the interim the animals went to sleep.

The idea I put forward was that the alert had sounded so many times already—but nothing of note had ever happened. It was as if the cry of "wolf" had been uttered so often that the watchman had become deaf to that specific warning. He had been looking and listening for the Japanese too long. In addition, our ears had been muffled by what seemed like a blanket of strategical common sense. What nation in its senses would dream of starting and supporting an attack across 4,000 miles of ocean, guarded by a tremendously powerful naval and air force? After the war we learned, as was previously mentioned, that the Japanese army wanted to invade Hawaii but their navy refused to guarantee support. Given an inner assurance of safety, the psychological effects of delay imposed between stimulus and opportunity to respond could not be avoided. We were warned, but nothing happened. Again we were warned—and we went to sleep!

Our national leaders might still listen and learn this lesson. The warning stimulus, in order to be effective, should be varied, and false alarms, provided we do not become inured to them, are certainly better than no alarm at all.

Some of the reviewers of *And Blow Not the Trumpet* picked up this point. Bradford Smith, for example, wrote in the *Saturday Review of Literature*:

> As a psychologist he advances a theory of some merit—since no other theory, excuse, or explanation has held up—to explain why the military could warn themselves of the very danger which materialized and yet be asleep when it happened. Everyone knows the Pavlov experiment with dogs whereby saliva was caused to flow when a bell rang. The sequel is not so well known—that when withholding the food for sixty seconds instead of ten after ringing the bell, the hungriest dogs went to sleep. A similar lassitude appears to have overcome admirals and generals at Pearl Harbor, who had been on the alert for several years.

I would agree completely with the reviewer if with the admirals and generals who were lulled into a sense of false security he had included the whole nation. Possibly, one of the values of books such as the present volume may be that passing national preparedness activities in review may serve to bring to prominence our former blunders. I still maintain that our present learning achievement is far exceeded by what we have unfortunately forgotten.

CHAPTER 16

Literary Excursions

NEITHER *Calabashes and Kings* nor *And Blow Not the Trumpet*, my first two ventures into general writing, had answered the question I had posed for myself. Could I have made any success in the field of fiction?

In 1948, I retired from the University with the title of emeritus professor of clinical psychology. The direction of the Clinic passed into the hands of the assistant director, Dr. Colin Herrick. My wife and I then decided to spend a full year in Australia. One of my purposes was to visit the city of Hobart, capital of the Commonwealth state of Tasmania, with a subsequent stay in New Zealand. I also had two professional interests.

The Australian branch of the British Association for the Advancement of Science was to hold its annual meeting in Hobart, where I was to deliver a paper, my second in 34 years in this organization. The Pan-Pacific Science Congress was also meeting at the University of Auckland, with a second session two weeks later at the University of Christchurch in the South Island. The time before and after these meetings was provided for most generously by the New Zealand government. It chartered a number of busses to carry all the overseas delegates on a two-week sightseeing trip through both islands, South and North.

Sir Peter Buck and I had been appointed to represent the University of Hawaii at the Congress. I was too late to be assigned on our arrival to the Anthropology bus, so my wife and I were put into a mixed group of delegates, whose subjects were thinly represented at the Congress. The result was a very interesting mixed grill of geographers, sociologists, psychiatrists, a single ornithologist, one psychologist (myself), and other odd characters. The result was that there were never enough of the same brand of scientists to talk "shop," and we all had a very congenial time. There were so few land birds to be seen that the ornithologist requested the driver to stop the bus every time we met a flock of sheep so that he could at least photograph "mutton birds." The rest of us cheered his efforts and stretched our legs at the halts, which were frequent.

Hobart was a most interesting and beautiful city, where the inhabitants seemed to think more of their convict mementos and history than of their excellent scenery. It is strange how people cling to their past even if it is not wholly savory. I could not find the place where my grandparents were buried. The cemetery was quite near the center of the city, and its urban council, quite wisely I thought, had turned it into a beautiful green park and had lined its walls with the transplanted grave stones. It would have taken a day to decipher all the inscriptions which went back 150 years, and I could not spare the time. We may have sat and eaten our lunch on my grandparents' graves, but if so, I didn't know it. The Tasmanian Tourist Bureau was too concerned with exhibiting all the showplaces of convict days to allow of more careful sepulchral research. I was quite content in the knowledge that my own relatives had made their first trip between England and Tasmania quite unassisted, and liked the place well enough to return.

The government was not assisting us either in our travel expenses, which were being met under rather peculiar circumstances. When I became 65 years of age, having left most of the actuaries behind in the life-race, my two Australian life insurance policies came due. My understanding was that funds could not be taken out of the country, so my wife and I had the joint bright idea that we would spend a year "down under" at the insurance company's expense. During that time I planned to finish one book, and begin gathering material for another. This project we proceeded to follow, and spent our money like drunken tourists. In our case, drink had nothing to do with it, in spite of one occasion when I created quite a false impression as to my sobriety. Having just boarded the steamer for New Zealand, and merely to make conversation with our fellow passengers, I enquired pleasantly from a group at the dining table whether anyone knew what time the bar opened in the morning. My wife's expression was worth the social effort, and it took her several days to convince our shipmates that I was not a confirmed inebriate, but a very mild near-teetotaller. My friends had always said that I looked like an elderly curate who had been thrown out of the church for drunkenness, but I really belied my looks.

To continue with my autobiographical postscript, I should explain that early in 1948 I had just sent to the publishers my first essay into fiction, the manuscript of *The Restless Voyage*. As a matter of fact, the skeleton of this story had already been provided for me in the form of a personal narrative written nearly 150 years ago. All I had to do was to put the flesh and blood on the bones. A leading moving picture producer had corresponded with me, proposing that I write the story of Hawaii's King Kamehameha I, in the hope that he might get a full-length picture out of it. In searching the historical records, I came across the story of a minor personage, who, for dramatic adventure, put the Hawaiian king's story entirely in the shade. The man was Archibald Campbell, a seaman, who had published an account of his own life in a little book, *Voyage Round the World from 1806 to 1812*, which appeared in Edinburgh in 1816 under the editorship of John Smith of Glasgow. It is only lately that I learned that Smith himself was subsequently interested in the Sandwich Islands from a botanist's standpoint.

Campbell's own story really begins with the wreck of the ship *Eclipse* on Sannack Island in Alaska. Of the crew of 28, only Campbell and 6 others survived. Their struggle through freezing seas to reach the land and their efforts to keep themselves alive until the arrival of some Indians was to me a most interesting tale, after the style of Robinson Crusoe's adventure.

After repairing the ship's longboat and gathering all salvageable articles that had washed ashore, the survivors decided to build a larger boat, capable, they hoped, of carrying them to the Sandwich Islands. Their position was much improved by the arrival of Mr. Bander, Russian commandant of Oonalaska, who advised the men to outfit the longboat and proceed to Kodiak, where they were assured of carpenters' assistance in building a larger vessel. From Alexandria, the capital of Kodiak Island, they attempted, with Governor Baranoff's approval, to return to the island of Sannack where they had first landed. Their boat was wrecked, and in an attempt to travel overland, both of Campbell's feet were frozen. When Campbell arrived back at Alexandria after fearful sufferings, the Russian surgeon partially amputated both feet, leaving only the stumps in the hope that Campbell would find them helpful in attempting to walk. In December 1808, the captain of the Russian ship *Neva* offered him a passage to the Sandwich Islands which he gladly accepted.

The history of his ten months' stay on Oahu, where Kamehameha's queen befriended him, forms part of his own book, which also includes his account of his return to Scotland via Rio de Janeiro, his further ineffectual medical treatment in Edinburgh, and his emigration to America, where his legs were amputated below the knees. He was able to use his carpentering skill to fashion a pair of artificial limbs. The story of these adventures had been set down simply and plainly in Archibald Campbell's narrative. How it came to be published is in itself an extraordinary story of Scottish pluck and persistence in the face of difficulties that could hardly be realized.[1] Campbell's book ended with his arrival in the Clyde on the 21st of April, 1810, after an absence of nearly six years.

The rest of the story of his life as told in *The Restless Voyage* was largely fictional, but factually supported by bits and pieces gleaned by the present writer from the editor's preface, from articles in the *Edinburgh Review,* and records of the school established in Connecticut to aid in the training of missionary volunteers for work in the Sandwich Islands. This school was attended for a time by Campbell and his wife Isabelle, whom he had married after his return to Scotland. Apparently the school authorities found the pair rather unsuitable for the mission field: Isabelle's light-minded behavior was signified by her possession of a canary in a cage, and a gaily colored Paisley shawl, colorful vanities ill-becoming to missionary sobriety. Campbell himself displayed a pack of playing cards, obviously the invention of the devil. But for these rather mild misdoings, Campbell might have been in charge of the first missionary excursion to Hawaii. As we all know, this devout undertaking was left in other more responsible hands, the outcome being the arrival of the first missionary company in 1820, some six years later. That story has been told and retold many times and by many writers, missionary and otherwise.

[1] Campbell had no funds and gained a bare living by travelling up and down the Clyde on a small vessel "The Comet," entertaining passengers with a metrical version of his life story, which attracted the attention of John Smith, a Glasgow publisher, who issued the first edition in 1816.

Like my friend Michener and his book *Hawaii*, I never claimed that *The Restless Voyage* was not in large part fiction, with, however, a solid basis of fact underlying many of the events therein recorded. I was fortunate indeed in having Campbell's book as a foundation on which to build an imaginative superstructure. I am obviously greatly indebted to him. After I had discarded the idea of making Kamehameha the central figure of a story that could be used in a moving picture, I proceeded with *The Restless Voyage*. By the time I had left for Australia at the end of 1948 it had been accepted for publication by Prentice-Hall. It drew some excellent reviews in America, but owed its British success to the London firm of Harrap & Co. Mr. Walter Harrap, in search of American books that promised well for republication in England, read the book—or its manuscript—and approved it wholeheartedly. The overseas edition was indeed most surprisingly successful. This was due to an enthusiastic review by John Keir Cross, which came over the Scottish division of the B.B.C. This resulted in the exhaustion of the first printing in about five weeks' time.

With the idea of giving Campbell all possible credit for his literary achievements, I was responsible for the appearance on the dust-cover of the book the statement that it represented the original author's account of his wanderings in five oceans from 1806 to 1812, *supplemented and re-indited by Stanley Porteus*. This matter of "re-inditing" apparently caused indignation among certain reviewers, who appeared to think it was an attempt to coast into the literary realm on Archie's credit and coattails.

The *Scotsman* (Edinburgh) apparently cast the first stone, which was, however, carefully wrapped in good soft Scottish flannelette. The review said in part:

"Certainly, the style in which Dr. Porteus has re-written the narrative is not like that of a seaman; it would do credit to a novelist or man of letters. . . . Campbell is made to talk a variety of Scots that has hardly an authentic ring."

The *Times Literary Supplement* went a little further in describing the seaman's idiom. "It is Californian-Scotch with here and there a Cockney talking in a way that was heard in Flanders in 1916. There is also a startling suggestion of Hollywood glamour and sentiment."

I was naturally quite doubtful of my ability to reproduce the speech of the present-day Scotsman, no matter when or where he lived, in California or on the high seas. To imitate the language of a hundred and fifty years back was, of course, still more difficult. Since I have never lived in California, it was a mystery how I could have seasoned Archie's speech with a Far Western ingredient. The London critic would have cut much closer to the bone had he detected an Australian flavor. I happen to know the Scottish breed of men quite well, and that is how I have heard them talk. Perhaps they had picked up more than a trace of Cockney speech, but it could not have been more than a faint echo. As far as I can tell, the Scotsman, whether in the wilds of Australia or in Hamakua on what is known as "The Scotch coast" in Hawaii, in Flanders fields, or in California, is singularly resistant to any local changes in speech, pronunciations, or idioms. It takes more than a generation to get rid of a Scottish burr. He hangs on to his burr about as tightly as he does to his bawbees, or small change. But it is quite possible that a Londoner is more sensitive to vocal overtones than I am.

Another Englishman, Daniel George, in the *London Daily Express* was seriously annoyed with my whole performance. He found the book to be "a seething broth of anachronisms, Americanisms, Scotticisms, and other solecisms that will set the strongest teeth on edge." Mr. George seems to have a very wide collection of dislikes, including even Scotticisms in a book about a Scot, and when his strong teeth were on edge, he had a formidable bite. A *San Francisco News* reviewer was not quite as explicit. To him the book was "only fair," being "marked with some fantastically stilted writing and characterization." I cannot say, of course, whether blame for this stilticism belonged with me or Campbell. If the fault were mine, then the resentment might properly be directed against a college professor's intrusion into the field of fiction.

Unlike scientific writing where matters of style are secondary, and validity and accuracy are essential, fiction has other standards. What I am attempting to say is that fiction writing has an entirely different set of criteria, and it may well be that the professor was indeed a fish out of water. To make any kind of judgment on this point, it seems necessary to quote what other people thought about the book.

But before doing so, it seems most desirable to settle the ethical question which was raised by several reviewers. One reviewer was evidently very exercised about the propriety of the whole project, if it indeed were merely a job of rewriting. He exclaimed: "Re-indited and supplemented! What a happy prospect is thus opened for literary aspirants, with all the world's non-copyright books for them to improve upon!"

More concisely, Philip Hewitt-Myring raises and answers the same question in the *New York Times.*

> The central problem presented by *The Restless Voyage* is that of who, precisely, wrote the book—one wonders how much of its often excellent prose should be ascribed to Campbell and how much to Dr. Porteus.
>
> A critic who feels he ought to know whom exactly he is praising or blaming when he is reviewing a book, can only in this instance secure a copy of Campbell's original text and find out—which done, he is in a position to say that the palm should go to Dr. Porteus. Campbell's own account of adventure in China, shipwreck in the Aleutians, and life in the Sandwich Islands, thirty years after Captain Cook was murdered there, is an honest piece of work, but it is far from being an exciting one. *The Restless Voyage,* on the other hand, is never dull, and it contains many really stirring pages.

The Irish took a very appreciative standpoint. In a radio review, a critic called Campbell's book "a masterpiece, which has been lying in dusty oblivion for over a century." He believed that as the author of *The Restless Voyage,* I "deserved great credit for issuing this book, and it can be read and re-read many times with pleasure." That would seem to dispose of any imputation of plagiarism.

One could expect a story that began in Paisley to excite some interest in southern Scotland. Harold Stewart, writing in the *Glasgow Record,* declared *The Restless Voyage* to be "a brisk, vivid and moving story, if at times the literary style is more that of Professor Porteus than Archie Campbell, with flavorings of Defoe, Conrad and Stevenson. . . ." Soon it became quite the fashion to discover in the narration reminiscences of other much more famous writers. Four different reviewers found a "flavor" of Stevenson, a couple of others of Smollett, Marryat, or Kenneth Roberts, while still others found something to remind them of Dana, Van Wyck Mason, Masefield, Ballantyne, Melville, Fenimore Cooper, Nordhoff and Hall, and even Swiss Family Robinson.

I believe there is a good reason for this nostalgic effect. Enjoyment of the tale or, conversely, a sharp exasperation with it, clearly dates the reader as it does the author. In short, it belonged with a day and age that was past, but is in some quarters still cherished. It appealed to many who would not have had patience to read again their boyish favorites, but were glad to be reminded of them. Modern youth, thoroughly conditioned to the swift pace and crowded crises of television, would not be bothered with *The Restless Voyage*. Half an hour spent looking at the screen would yield more thrills than fifty pages of Archie Campbell. The latter's story did not fall between two stools as much as it did between two chronological periods. And here is some evidence.

Alistair Macrae, writing in the *Glasgow Record* (August 17, 1949), reveals his literary age. "I give the credit," he says, "to the pen of Stanley Porteus, whose novel *The Restless Voyage* has filled me, body and soul, with all the old 'Marryat' music—the wind in the rigging, the sails flapping, the creaking of lines, and the voices of men who speak the language of the sea. . . . Thank you, Mr. Porteus, for restoring to me the real meaning of the word 'thrilling.'"

Across the Atlantic, Kensil Bell (*Philadelphia Inquirer*) was similarly reminded of far-off things when he wrote: "Do not get the idea that *The Restless Voyage* is a ponderous study of mental readjustment. Fact and fiction are adroitly interwoven by a writing style reminiscent of Robinson Crusoe."

A well-known Scottish writer declared:

> It is a very high achievement of the author to so steep himself in the mentality of Campbell, in the temper of the Lowland Scot of the early nineteenth century, that the narrative has the compelling power of simple, direct, vivid truth. For anyone reared on Ballantyne and Fenimore Cooper, for anyone who remembers *Treasure Island* with affection, this book is a 'must'. Let me warn off at once the reader who is a glutton for the intellectual, the subtle, the pretentious. This is not Bloomsbury meat.

Robert Millar, who wrote the foregoing comment, has, I must confess, diagnosed correctly my own simple literary rearing.

Naturally, I was pleased with any reference to my ability to put myself in the shoes of a Scottish seaman of nearly 150 years ago, speak his language, see things through his eyes, and make it sound convincing, but the damning facts remain that I am Irish-Australian rather than Scottish, a landsman, and a psychologist of sorts. Only the last consideration is in my favor. I would be a very poor psychologist of any kind if I lacked the ability to put myself in the other fellow's place and to some degree think as he does. I have had, however, some practice, not in putting myself in the shoes of sailors of a century or more ago, but in trying to understand the outlook of Australian aborigines who belonged in a stage of human history ten thousand years ago.

Besides acceptance of my imitations of how Scotsmen speak, there was also the tough problem of nautical language. As a landsman, I could make so many slips as to make the whole sea voyage sound ridiculous. A sailing ship's deck could provide such a very slithery stance that the novelist could very easily go overboard with his hero.

However, sailors themselves should be the best judges in this matter. Hence I was most reassured with the editorial verdict of *The Seafarer,* the quarterly journal of the Seafarers Education Service. It called the novel "a most fascinating book with the characterization excellent, and the whole effect living and vital. Altogether, this is a really unusually good book about sea life of the past, and Mr. Porteus is to be congratulated on a splendid imaginative job of reconstruction."

The above, together with Hewitt-Myring's judgment that the account of the shipwreck on the island of Sannack "deserves a place in any future anthology of sea literature," satisfied me completely that, nautically speaking, I had escaped being thrown on my beam ends.

Actually, while favorable reviews outweighed the unfavorable at least ten to one, those that were at all hostile mainly resulted, I believe, from a kind of backlash against one exceptionally enthusiastic appraisal by John Keir Cross, himself a well-known author and radio commentator. As I noted earlier, this review came over the Scottish B.B.C. I have never met nor have I corresponded with Mr. Cross, but again I suspect that he, too, has a literary upbringing somewhat similar to my own, which means, of course, that he is far past the freshness and enthusiasms of youth, yet can somehow revive something of the glow and fire of boyish experiences. As a psychologist, my diagnosis is that, quite happily for himself, he possesses a fourteen-year-old mind, with probably a mentality a year or two above my own.

Here is an immodest quotation from the Cross review:

> It is impossible not to dote on the undefeatable Archie—he is magnificent. And Mr. Porteus gives him, through it all, a profound humanity. He never loses his true modesty, never gives in to self-pity. It is a moving book, a splendidly tender book—how beautifully done, for example, are the portraits of Lualani, the Hawaiian girl, and

> Isabelle, the Paisley lass, who waited for the bold wanderer through thick and thin—what a woman is Isabelle, what a perfect companion for the restless voyager himself. It's an informative book, a philosophical book, an adventurous book, a religious book, a romantic book, a near-mystical book—and it has a whacking good story that's all true. In short, A BOOK.

This brings me to my final attempt to depart from the well-beaten and somewhat dusty tracks of professional writing. Largely as a result of the success of *The Restless Voyage* in England, my very open-minded publisher in London, Walter Harrap, encouraged me to make one more fictional effort, the material for which I gathered in 1949. It was a book about pioneering in southeast Australia, in the province now known as Gippsland. It was based in part on the experiences of my wife's great-grandfather's family, the first to come as a unit across the sea of mountains that stretched between New South Wales and Victoria. In my own rather unseasoned but biased judgment, it was the best book I had written, but I could not get the reviewers to agree with me to the extent of promoting its sales with enthusiasm. It sold out its first printing in Australia, and for some strange reason, possibly because they had their own colonizing history, the Holland firm of Uitgeverij Het Kompas bought the Dutch rights and republished it under the title of *Het Dorre Land*. The book took its original title, *Providence Ponds,* from a small stream and chain of waterholes in East Gippsland, near which the Scott family finally settled. Their adventures with blacks and their struggles against drought and bush fires were, of course, fictional, but conformed to the usual pattern of life in early Gippsland. The writing imposed but little strain on my imagination as I had a firm background of personal experience in this part of the country.

The book's publication gave my former admirer, John Keir Cross, a chance to offer a kind of apology for his former enthusiasm. He wrote:

> If I can't quite rave about *Providence Ponds* as I did about *The Voyage,* it is still a fine novel, full of true imagination, and I haven't the slightest hesitation at all in recommending it to those who just don't want love and more love—nor yet adventure and more adventure. And I do have this odd consolation in the light indeed of what I said earlier; that in being rather more reserved about this latest novel of his, I have possibly done Professor Porteus a greater public service than last time.

This was, of course, a nice review, but not the kind that would sell out a first printing in five weeks; but I would like to reassure Mr. Cross that his review really did me no harm nor himself either. He and Alistair Macrae, and a score of others who similarly over-praised *The Restless Voyage,* were merely returning quite happily to their pre-radio, pre-television, pre-crime-and-mystery youth, via Archibald Campbell and his restless voyages. Moreover, I believe they really enjoyed this regression as much as I did. We found ourselves in good company. As for myself, I truly appreciated the relaxation from the bondage of facts and theories of human behavior. My characters were my own creation; I did not need to predetermine their fate nor put their actions together tidily so as to fit in nicely with some causal hypothesis. I could make these personages what I willed, dispose of them as I wished, and thereby find a release of my own spirit. Neither Mr. Cross nor I need to apologize for such nostalgic trends even if they rise to the height of hyperbole. Our only regrets should be that we can never live through those joys again.

I do not want to leave the impression that writing *Providence Ponds* represented anything in the way of a let-down. I knew it was my last appearance in its field. I had other things to do, other projects to finish. In science, nothing can ever be finished, nothing can be more than half-said.

Naturally, I still enjoyed an extra bonus of appreciation for any results that accrued from my brief "walk about" out of real life into the cool mists of imagination. The following review pleased me greatly.

> This writing has much more than surety and deftness. It has deep feeling, high drama. It is both nostalgic and prophetic. . . . This story is one of heart-break—how the manifold forces of the wilderness brought disaster. . . . Readers will hardly be prepared for the depth of feeling or the stateliness of prose that marks much of this book.

A few brief excerpts from other reviews will serve to wind up this six-year record of what might well be called escape writing, undertaken with the additional purpose of testing the "metal" of a long-buried talent. They will also indicate the fact that old tasks and preferences in reading die hard. Quite possibly, after this present spate of quick entertainment and the demand for instant thrills have died down, people may revive some of their old affections and satisfactions. Judging by these reviews, there are still floating around a lot of old-fashioned ideas as to literary values. Listen to the old guard:

"A magnificent background to a very readable tale of courageous adventure" (*Northern Echo,* Darlington). "A workman-like affair" (*Sphere,* London). "This colorful strange account" (*Manchester Guardian Weekly*). "A gripping and entirely satisfying narrative" (*Irish Independent*). "A simplicity and truthfulness that are very convincing" (*Glasgow Herald*). "This story is as good and as gripping as any of the fictional stories of pioneering elsewhere" (*Daily Record,* Glasgow). "Those who read *Providence Ponds* will realize that the author is a master of description and narrative" (*Northern Chronicle,* Inverness). "A gripping story straightforwardly told. The whole novel has an authentic flavour of Australian life and standards subtly different from our standards here" (Edinburgh, Scotland). "A restless story, which at times becomes almost unbearably emotional, but it is well worth reading" (*Cape Times,* South Africa). "Ample evidence of the deeper insight that makes his work rather more than mere casual reading" (*Northern News,* Ndola, Africa). "This novel is well above the standard of most contemporary fiction" (*Times of India*). "The parallel between landseekers and pioneers in Canada and the southern continent makes exciting reading for Canadians . . . told with all the vividness and pathos of a sensitive spectator" (*Vancouver Daily Province*).

But one cannot please everybody, and John Hetherington, competent Australian newspaperman and author, supplied a very peppery comment, which deserves quotation. He found the book "a tangible demonstration that scholarship and ability to write clean English are not alone adequate qualification for a novelist, even when the author has a basically good story to tell." But he goes on to remark that I succeeded in "producing a book in the form of a novel, which is, at best, unexciting, and, at worst, plain tedious, because the reader does not care two hoots what happens to the persons of the story." Mr. Hetherington finally decided that "Professor Porteus would have been wiser to write it as historical fact and leave it at that."

Perhaps he was quite right, but at least the people of Gippsland, who are familiar with the story's background, seemed to enjoy the tale so much that the local booksellers could not keep it in stock. I certainly should have taken more time to write the book, but I knew it to be my farewell to fiction and there were other things that remained to be done. I knew I was pressed for time.

Perhaps I should devote one final paragraph in explanation of my preference for *Providence Ponds*. I think it was because, as a couple of the critics observed, it bore the imprint of truth. Pioneers are people, compounded, as we all are, of flesh and blood, the lusts of the flesh, of aspirations and bitter disappointments. They loved, they hated, they mourned and rejoiced. They even gambled with the earth, and some of them, like the Duncans lost.

Their story could be duplicated a hundred times over in a thousand localities. But from the author's point of view, nothing was unreal or contrived. The land I wrote about was my land, its people my people. In short, I liked *Providence Ponds* because in all its general outlines, it was true.

Undoubtedly the foregoing account of my excursion into "light" literature must constitute a break in the continuity of my main purpose of presenting a more or less oriented professional history. The chief extenuating circumstance was the fact that such a six-year divergence did occur in the main stream of my activities and therefore calls for attention. As previously mentioned, it was an experiment, and the only way I could assess its success or failure was through the verdicts of reviewers. To hold the balance even, I have taken particular care to include unfavorable opinions along with the more appreciative.

Generally speaking, the conclusion I reached was that if I had had uninterrupted time for writing, plus greater opportunity for re-writing and the development of new story material, I might have become a moderately successful professional writer. My chief handicaps were insufficient time and the lack of any apprenticement to the task of popular writing.

In support of such a conclusion, only two criteria seemed available; the first, financial, the other, opinions of reviewers. Both were affirmative. I earned more money, and in the second place, judgments of my popular writing were, on balance, much more approving than I expected. One's psychological critics tended to be more severe.

Several psychologists whom I have known have confessed to ambitions in the direction of fiction writing, and quite probably there already exist, hidden away, quite a number of unpublished manuscripts. Possibly members of a profession that concern themselves with problems of human adjustments are closely akin to novelists. My counsel would be to persevere in attempts to find a publisher.

One warning is necessary. Fiction writing is hardly a part-time job. The demands on the author's empathy are extraordinary. The author must steep himself in the history, activities, and personality of his characters. In one direction he should have no difficulty—in abstention from moral judgments. In my own case, the need to *feel* the environment of my primitive subjects was an imaginative one that undoubtedly came into play in fictional creation.

CHAPTER 17

The Long Day's Over

THE YEAR 1950 marked my return from Australia and also a turning back of my attention to psychological practice. Social problems in Hawaii were increasing, both in regard to the number of individuals affected and in the complexity of situations involved. Under pressure from my friends at the Juvenile Court, particularly the late Howard Simpson, Chief Probation Officer, I agreed for a while to view delinquency from a viewpoint that differed radically from research. In accepting the position of Court Referee, I would for the first time be assuming an authoritative position, holding in my hands the responsibility for practical disposition of cases. The psychologist's task was to throw what light he could on the motivation of the young offender, study his mental abilities and his personality, and offer the social worker or probation officer the best counsel he could. To these activities he was credited with bringing a type of insight superior to that available to the practical worker. It was usually assumed that either psychological or psychiatric training conferred that clearer understanding.

I am very doubtful as to the validity of that assumption. The psychology of the delinquent must be studied in the home, the playground, the school, the family, the streets, and the courtroom, more than in the university classroom, the hospital, or the clinic.

The one advantage that I believe is possessed by the more highly trained professional person resides in the fact that the counsellor is rarely responsible for the disposition of the case or patient. This is usually well understood by the subject of study or investigation, or if it is not apparent at first, it soon will be. The psychologist or psychiatrist does not exercise the strong arm of the law, enforce the teacher's discipline, nor reenforce parental or family disapproval. It is not his duty to assume the social worker's role of social advisor or adjuster. With the recognition of this voluntary relationship, the young offender can adopt a more relaxed attitude. The mere fact that his new questioner is addressed as "doctor" and disclaims all right to determine degree of punishment changes the situation radically. Many a lecture from the bench, many a homily from the pulpit, or parental criticism is preceded by an earnest profession of friendship or affection, but these make little real impression if the source of all this rather bland good-will ultimately holds the whip hand. It is not that the psychologist or psychiatrist has any more understanding than the social worker, probation officer, or parent; it is merely that the client or subject is ready to let down some of the veils of suspicion or fear, and to discount professions of respect or affection which every delinquent learns to recognize as forerunners either to an assault on his independence or to an invasion of his privacy.

I must confess that I did not particularly enjoy my change of roles, even though Judge Gerald Corbett, as head of the Juvenile Court, gave me a free hand, and the court clerks and probation officers proffered me their utmost in loyal support, friendship, and assistance. The judge and I collaborated in a legalistic-psychological report on court procedures in the United States having to do with the definition of mental defectives and statutory methods of commitment. With the approach of the retirement age (70), which applied to all state employees, I became uncomfortably conscious of the fact that there were several things left undone in my own special field, and that the shoemaker should get back to his psychological last. I had a feeling similar to that which overcame me in South Africa. I enjoyed exploring immensely, but that was not my business.

I do not think I made any great success as a Court Referee. The need to impress the delinquent with the dignity of the law imposed changes in my behavior that were foreign to my personality. So when the time came, I bade farewell to my friends at the Court and departed. I had made fewer friends among the juveniles as a Court Referee than I had as a clinician.

The first research job that awaited my return to university life was to produce practise-free forms of the Maze Test so that if it was to be applied a second or third time, practise effects could be counterbalanced, if not eliminated, in the scores. As previously noted, those practise gains concealed or diminished the effects of psychosurgery or any other treatment. What was entailed in this research was a careful examination of individual maze records, listing where mistakes were made and their frequency. The next step was to increase the test's difficulty by adding more traps to the labyrinth, lengthening the approach alleys to require greater caution from the subject and then to apply the modified designs to hundreds of new cases. The purpose of this labor was to augment the test's difficulty just enough to counteract the benefits of increased familiarity when the test was given twice to the same sample of cases.

Fortunately, I was able to work this out to the degree that 300 presumably normal adolescent girls and boys had scores almost identical with those they had gained on their original test application. I was extremely gratified with my success in achieving this equivalence, and results were published in 1955 under the title of *The Maze Test: Recent Advances.*

Four years later, the need for a third form having become apparent, I undertook a similar procedure and published this as *The Porteus Mazes. Supplement Series.*

In 1955 an invitation to give a paper at the International Conference of Applied Psychology in London came to hand, and was accepted. My wife and I then planned to extend our tour and through our friend, Dr. Hans Pettersson, F.R.S., the famous oceanographer, I was invited to visit Sweden and lecture at the University of Göteborg and later confer with psychological colleagues at the University of Stockholm. There I was anxious to meet with Dr. Gosta Rylander, one of the pioneers in the field of psychosurgery, with whom I had much in common, since we had both attempted to measure the mental effects of frontal lobe operations.

But before we reached Europe many other speaking engagements were pending. The school psychologists of California were holding their annual conference in a delightful location at Hoberg's Resort, and I was asked to give the main address. I chose to review the course of mental testing in relation to education. My criticism of scales of the Binet type and of IQ usage and standards was very well received, in spite of the identification of Terman's great reputation with California.

This is not the place to deal in any detail with academic relationships that determined my lecturing itinerary. In addition to conferences with the staffs at Stanford, U.C.L.A., and Berkeley, I spoke at the University of Missouri to an audience composed of its psychology staff and that of Washington University. The late Dr. Henry N. Peters, who had been my collaborator in Hawaii, was continuing then his research work at the local V.A. Hospital, using his circular maze, and this was naturally interesting to me.

At New Orleans I was anxious to meet Drs. King and Heath, both closely connected with psychosurgical work of various kinds. I spoke to the staff of Tulane University at the New Orleans Institute of Research. Here, too, we were most hospitably looked after by my close friend, Mr. George Lehleitner, with whom I shared many interests and viewpoints.

Then followed a four-day visit to the University of North Carolina, where I delivered lectures sponsored by Drs. Dashiell and Dorothea Adkins. The next stop was Washington, with visits to Catholic University, and again, meetings with the staff. Our stay in New York allowed of a reunion with such close friends as Professor Henry Garrett, Joseph Zubin, Carney Landis, Laurance Shaffer, and Joseph Shoben. The combined staffs of Columbia University and Barnard College provided me with an interested audience following a complimentary faculty dinner. I also spoke to an assemblage of Ph.D. candidates at Teachers' College, Columbia.

Europe offered a great variety of professional contacts as well as private entertainment. At Chapel Hill I had been lucky enough to meet Professor Thurstone, a former Scandinavian, who, when he learned that I would be visiting Göteborg, gave me some useful information as to the protocol attendant on any formal dinners.

As guests of honor, my wife and I would be formally welcomed by the host, who would also in his brief speech include mention of any other guests being entertained for the first time in his house. When our friends, Professor and Mrs. Pettersson, asked us to dinner in Göteborg, our host invited a number of people in psychology and allied disciplines to be present.

Thurstone had warned me that after being "skoaled" by a glass of schnapps by the host—which I was supposed to drain to the bottom—we would then be seated at table. When, however, dessert was to be served, I, as guest of honor, should attract the attention of the group, respond to the host's welcome and then, if I wished to make a really favorable impression, include in my thanks the names of all the other guests mentioned by the host. To this Thurstone added the warning: "Psychologists are supposed to have good memories you know, so keep those names in mind."

At the dinner in Göteborg, though I listened carefully to the long array of names, many of them foreign to my ears, and in addition absorbed the cumulative effects of numerous individual skoals, I found myself in a state of mental confusion. I had tried surreptitiously to note a few names on my table napkin, but had no chance to memorize them.

Fortunately, there came to my mind what the old Arunta in Central Australia told Bob Croll when he complained that I got by with all kinds of breaches of social regulations, whereas his much more venial errors met with derision; so I told the dinner group of the old men's comment as to my mental irresponsibility.

"So," I added, "if I am making all kinds of sins of omission and commission on this otherwise delightful social occasion, please excuse them on the grounds that I am weakminded." It seemed to me that the guests accepted the point rather too readily.

In Stockholm I met with another interesting situation at Dr. Ekman's home. I noticed that our hostess, in all the swirl of toasts, took only soft drinks. In reply to my comment, she said that she had no prejudices against the use of alcohol but that she and her husband took it in turns to abstain, and that it would be her turn to drive us home.

This brought forth the story of the American professor who had accepted the skoal procedure with such enthusiasm that when it was time to go home there was considerable doubt as to his driving ability. As everyone knows, the laws against manipulating a car while under the influence of liquor in Sweden are among the strictest in the world. You do not need to be actually driving—merely sitting in the car with the key turned in the ignition may mean arrest, and subsequent blood tests. Upon being notified that his departing guest was in police custody, the host telephoned the police surgeon, whom he knew very well.

"What was the result of Professor So-and-so's sobriety test?" he inquired.

"Well," said the surgeon, "I found just the slightest trace of *blood* in the sample!" So, to make sure nothing like that happened again, our host and his wife on social occasions alternated in drinking or driving their special guests home.

Our treatment after we left Norway was more than cordial. In

Italy, for example, we were met at the Swiss border by Dr. Abbele of the Organizzazioni Speciali in Florence, the leading test distributor in Italy, who made all arrangements for my trip. Owing to my wife having lost her voice after a cold, lectures at the Universities of Milan and Genoa had to be cancelled, but I was able to fulfill all engagements in Florence and Rome. In the latter University, I found the greatest interest in psychosurgical theories, since all the younger psychologists had their M.D. degrees. They told me that in Mussolini's day the only way to escape ordinary military service was to qualify in medicine. After the war there was a surplus of doctors, and they found that to earn a better living they should combine their medical practice with psychology.

In Paris I was almost overwhelmed with attention, being entertained at a cocktail party given at the famous Centre de Psychologie Appliquée. My presence in the receiving line and my limited conversational French caused me some embarrassment. After the line disbanded, I had a fine time talking with two Scandinavians, two Egyptians, and a West African, all psychologists with excellent command of English.

In considering the foregoing chapters, the reader might easily conclude that the record shows a hodge-podge of activities with only one constantly recurring theme, the Maze Tests. That may be largely true, but I should like to submit evidence that, aside from reporting my experiments and attempting to supply psychologists with a new measure of planning or foresight, I had done some thinking in allied fields.

As regards this corpus of achievement, the only appraisal that a man himself can offer is the verdict of his peers. Here again, as was the case with quotations of literary reviews, it is hard for the autobiographer to avoid a species of exhibitionism, a self-exposure that I hope falls short of flagrancy. This is particularly noticeable in the setting forth of awards of citations. These are prone to resemble obituary notices, which by common practice include all the nice things that can possibly be said or imagined about the departed. With this caveat in plain view, I shall quote the following from *Newsletter,* the official organ of the populous Division of Clinical Psychology, American Psychological Association, in its fall issue of 1962:

AWARDS AND CITATIONS

The fifth annual awards of the Division for DISTINGUISHED CONTRIBUTION TO THE SCIENCE AND PROFESSION OF CLINICAL PSYCHOLOGY were presented at the Annual Business Meeting on August 31, 1962. Starke R. Hathaway, Chairman of the Awards Committee, read the citations honoring Stanley D. Porteus and Carl R. Rogers.

"Dr. Stanley D. Porteus has written of himself that he had a single talent with which he became identified, which he buried several times only assiduously to dig it up again. His limited self appraisal conceded his contribution of the Porteus Mazes but was a classic example of understatement. The manifold validities of the Porteus Maze Tests as indicators of intelligence and its deterioration with senility, drugs, brain surgery, or other causes of cerebral deficiency have properly demonstrated a fundamental contribution of Stanley Porteus to clinical psychology. To these more objective validities of the Maze Tests, many psychologists would add their values as a projective technique.

"But a search for the published contributions of Stanley Porteus leads into areas as varied as are the validities of the Maze Tests. One must travel widely in the Dewey Classification system of the library stacks, psychology, anthropology, history, religion, and fiction.

"Few psychologists have a more solid recognition in the field of anthropology, and few contributions to that field have been as acceptable as those of Porteus in objectivity of reporting and balanced inferences from observation. Resistant to the cliches, he, for example, actually devised competitive tests to check the idea that the aborigine had tracking talent beyond that of civilized expedition members.

Stanley Porteus started out as an Australian and was trained in Australia. After becoming active in the anthropological study of the Australian aborigine, he became director of research at Vineland. This period prepared him for his work as leader of an expedition to central and northwest Australia from which emerged the significant *Psychology of a Primitive People*. His psychologically oriented anthropological studies were later continued in Africa. Already professor of clinical psychology in Hawaii, he recently (1932) completed his citizenship with the new state. Dr. Porteus officially (not really) retired in 1948. By then he was "Mr. Psychology" for Hawaii, but his contributions are known and studied by many experts in other specialties who gain added respect for our field from the unmistakable identification that Dr. Porteus expresses with clinical psychology.

Finally, a good case can be made for giving Dr. Porteus the credit for originating the modern connotation of the term clinical psychology.

This citation was signed by Starke R. Hathaway (Chairman), David Shakow, and David Wechsler, members of the selection committee, all men of exceptional eminence in this field.

As previously suggested, I have, from time to time, felt some stirrings of discomfort over the fact that recognition has come to me mainly through association with a single product, hence one reason for my satisfaction with the foregoing citation was that it did make mention of work done in wider fields. After all, the manufacturer of a brand of soap—provided it is a good one—may just as easily achieve world-wide notoriety. Personally, I did not aspire to being widely known only as a psychological gadgeteer.

I remember some such misgivings as I went up the steps of the University of London where the International Congress of Applied Psychology was to hold its July 1955 meeting, at which I was to deliver a paper. The thought suddenly struck me—what am I doing here? Did I really belong in such an assemblage or was I mentally still the headmaster of a little one-room bush school, 12 miles from Fernbank, East Gippsland, Victoria, Australia?

Then I had to assure myself that I was not merely the inventor of the Porteus Maze, useful as that might be as a small magnifying glass applicable to a segment of human behavior. I was a peddler of other new ideas. These had been the main topic of my European and American lectures, with only passing mention of the Maze Test. History had repeated itself. I felt as I had 42 years previously when I had walked into Mr. Gates' office in Melbourne with ideas to sell, in that case on the education of the mentally defective.

Now, thirteen years later, I feel that it is incumbent on me to complete this record on a more serious professional note, setting forth my stock-in-trade. These are what I like to term nuclear concepts, ideational cores or principles, about which my thought accretions have collected and revolved. Some of them have been verbalized recently, and must meet with the quite natural distrust that the cerebrations of any octogenarian are bound to excite. Scripture notes the fact that no man in his senses puts new wine into old wine-skins, for that means waste, but there does not seem to be any objection to putting old wine into new bottles, provided only that the vintner does the decanting with a sufficiently steady hand.

Because this recounting is addressed, in part I hope, to a wider audience than one of psychologists, readers must tolerate the use of some technical or anatomical terms, but that usage will be kept to a minimum. These discussions have been relegated to the back pages so that the non-professional reader can avoid them more easily if he so desires.

In spite of all appearances to the contrary, my main interests have centered about the story of the building of the brain. The initial guidepost to this thinking was a principle set forth by my eminent collaborator, Dr. Frederic Wood Jones. He called it "cytoclesis," and described it as "the call of cell to cell." It can be otherwise stated as the tendency of cells of like sensitivity and function to congregate as closely as possible, and thus, by forming sensory organs, to achieve a division or specialization of labor. This principle of cytoclesis was described in our book *The Matrix of the Mind,* and we took as an illustration the development of the eye. This process involved the collecting together into placodes of cells whose special birthright it is to be sensitive to light; this congregation or call of cell to cell culminated in the evolution of vision.

This specific sensitivity of eye cells is only part of a more general dual quality or function that belongs in every living cell. This is the capacity to be sensitive in varying degrees to relevant stimuli and to respond to them by contracting, the latter reaction being the proof of the sensitivity. The fact that cells do vary in sensitivity and responsiveness becomes the basis of the division of labor of which we have spoken. In my part of the book I enlarged upon this original contractibility of the living cell as a universal characteristic, and from this postulated a further principle—namely, that living cells profit by experience, and this is what I call cellular memory.

Taking the unicellular amoeba as my prime example, I instanced the fact that the amoeba, which lives by enfolding food particles within its protoplasm and then digesting them, can be "fooled" into capturing and ingesting carmine grains, which are unnutritious. But after long experience, the amoeba actually *learns* to reject the indigestible material, so this demonstrates the operation of what the psychologist calls memory. If, however, the carmine grains are withheld for a time and then again fed to the amoeba, they are once again ingested, but the process of rejection occurs much quicker. In short, the amoeba takes less time to relearn its lesson. What can this mean other than that some traces of its former experience have been retained? In other terms, the memory traces are cumulative. The amoeba is building on its past experiences, retaining something from its past responses. If we can assume that these findings are valid, then in discovering that even a unicellular organism exhibits the beginnings of memory, we are on our way to understanding the story of brain-building. The most sensitive and responsive cells, having been called together, form the

Dr. and Mrs. Porteus in photographs taken recently.

central nervous system. If the human brain is regarded as par excellence the organ of choice, the speed and effectiveness of response will depend on the ease and rapidity of communication between receptors and effectors, the cells that receive and the cells that act.

To Arien Kappers, a Dutch scientist, we owe a refinement of the principle of cytoclesis. Kappers showed that aggregations of cells of like functions will be placed as near each other in the brain as possible. He called this principle neurobiotaxis. As an example of neurobiotaxis we find that in the forebrain the sensory and motor areas are tucked in nicely side by side, in parallel strips of brain substance. This illustrates the need for ready communication. Thus when we suffer the sharp sensation of a pin prick in the big toe, the pain signal goes to the sensory center in the brain and right opposite and close to it is the motor center for the big toe, which at once triggers the mechanism of withdrawing, not only the toe, but possibly the whole foot or leg, away from the point of attack. As every comedian and schoolboy knows, the most ludicrously violent reaction is registered if a pin is unexpectedly applied to an area outside the victim's range of vision, such as the backside.

My own contribution to this story of brain-building represents a further extension or application of Kappers' neurobiotaxis. Again emphasizing the vital importance of neural communication, I have suggested another principle which I have called centroid neurobiotaxis. In the simplest terms I can achieve, I would lay down the proposition that speed of communication entails a favored position within the brain itself. Here I am compelled to bring in the Maze Test, since it involves decision-making. The brain operation known as topectomy[2] shows that the nearer the surgical injuries impinge on the most direct highway or neural path in the center of the nervous system, the greater the loss in the Maze-tested abilities of initiative, decisiveness, mental alertness and, therefore, planning. That direct pathway passes through brain areas 5 and 6, the sensory and motor tracts, which occupy the cerebral vertex or centroid position. On either side of this central position are in turn the areas numbered by neurologists 7, 8, 9, 10, 12, each marking an increasing distance from the vertical pathway. Injuries to 5 and 6 would make a man a vegetable, while operations on 7 and 8 entail almost complete inability to do a Maze Test, but damage to 9 and 10 has a lesser effect, while the removal of area 12 causes hardly any serious impairment in planning capacity.

[2] Surgical removal of selected areas of brain substance.

But if certain areas are situated in preferred position because they are related to mental alertness and survival, then any change in importance of a sense receptor may result in eviction from its position of advantage. To use a military analogy, putting the commissariat or even the reserves on a height commanding the battlefield would be suicidal. Obviously, such a height should be a center for observation connected most directly with intelligence. Information thus obtained might be essential to victory. Non-essential functions could be shifted elsewhere.

This is exactly what has happened to the brain areas that serve the sense of smell. To many wild animals smell is a vital warning receptor, but in man it is no longer as valuable for survival as hearing and sight. Fundamentally, touch is a vital receptor but it can only operate over an immediate range. It does not, therefore, except at an infantile level, serve as a main avenue of learning. Sight and hearing have superseded touch. Incidentally, this was the weak spot in the Montessori system, which tried to turn back the clock of evolution by wasting time in educating the tactile sense. Snails, having such inadequate mobility, are forced to rely on touch and smell, but humans are not similarly dependent, unless, of course, they lose their sight.

As for smell, organisms of the animal kingdom require space in the midbrain, which is the main informative highway through the brain, but in human evolution that vital position has been now preempted for more essential life-saving channels. The dethronement of the olfactory sense by hearing and sight has brought about a most important change in the ground plan of brain-building.

I have even suggested, somewhat to the horror of old-fashioned anatomists, that the fissuring of the surface of the brain came about for a purpose other than making more room in the skull for gray matter, the anatomy textbook explanation of the phenomenon. If the principle of centroid neurobiotaxis as assisting or determining ready communication is accepted, then it should be obvious that the interior of each convolution, and particularly the bottom of each fissure would be automatically brought closer to the central intelligence highway. I well remember the reaction of a highly respected senior anatomist when, in 1954, I first promulgated this audacious neural theory in a lecture series given at the University of Queensland, over which he presided. There is only one word adequate to describe his mental attitude. He was flabbergasted.

Another example of the operation of central communication and control is afforded by the functioning of what is called the reticular formation in the midbrain. This formation seems to be responsible for keeping us wide-awake. A tranquilizing drug, chlorpromazine, apparently dulls the individual's general sensitivity to his environment so that he becomes less anxious or disturbed. It does this through the reticular formation in the midbrain, which acts like the governor in an internal combustion engine, controlling the rhythm of activity. Long-continued medication with chlorpromazine brings about a mental slowing-down similar to that which follows lobotomy, and this brake on planning and initiative is reflected in lower Maze Test scores.

In the growing of sugar cane, plantation managers find that they do not always need to replant after cutting and harvesting, for there springs up in the fields what they call a rattoon crop, not as heavy as the previous season's growth, but certainly of considerable value when put through the mill. The phrase is frequently applied also to unexpected additions to human families occurring near the end of the childbearing period. It also fits the belated appearance of new ideas late in life, and I believe I have reaped a few rattoons. They probably represented the results of a too hurried previous gleaning that left ungarnered grain that managed to sow itself.

One example of this delayed intelligence occurred when I overlooked for many years some striking instances of inventiveness shown by primitive Australids. One of their original devices was the spear-thrower, which has at one end a short spur that fits snugly into a small hole drilled into the end of a spear shaft. When the spear is thrown, the propulsive force operates at the rear end of the missile. How does this differ from the principle of jet propulsion, so effective in aviation?

Another example of native ingenuity is provided by the boomerang, which is constructed and thrown so that the air-flow around the missile's edges gives it its distinctive flight and returns it to the feet of the thrower. It is probably the same principle that keeps the helicopter in flight and enables it to hover.

But most striking of all of the savage prototypes of modern inventions is one that I was just too stupid to recognize. When the aboriginal woman gathers grass or other seed for cooking her cake, she must get rid of the unnutritious husks. She first dehusks the material by putting it into a circular hollow in the rocks. She stands in the hole and by rotating her hips pushes her bare feet to and fro upon the seeds. Having separated or "thrashed" the seed, she then transfers the whole to a bark or wooden receptacle, which she calls a coolimon. This she rotates swiftly enough so that the seeds fall to the bottom, leaving the light detritus on top. Using the same technique as the skilled prospector employs when dish-washing gold, she partially rotates the coolimon and with deft flicks of the wrists the woman discards on the ground everything but the seeds. But the aboriginal was probably doing this five hundred centuries before the prospector was operating his dish. She was antedating still further the modern scientific use of the cyclotron, which has contributed so much to nuclear science.

How can anyone deny inventiveness to people who devised the prototypes and applied the principles of jet propulsion, the helicopter, and the cyclotron?

And speaking of cyclotrons, it seems to have escaped general notice that human-kind exists on the surface of a huge natural cyclotron, the earth. As far as I know, no one appears to have given adequate consideration to the idea that this might be a factor in human mental development and inventiveness. Certainly all the great technological devices seem to have been developed, not in the equatorial regions, where the speed of rotation is maximum, nor in the high latitudes where the rate is greatly retarded, but in the temperate zones where the medium rate of speed might possibly provide optimal conditions for inventiveness. If this condition should be a determinant, we may find out that when man reaches the moon, where there is no circular motion, he may find himself robbed of the fruits of human insight.

Essential to the study of cyclotronic effects would be the resources of animal psychology, foremost among which is the subhuman maze. But the trouble with ordinary labyrinths, such as the Hampton Court Maze, is that unless the chance to reconnoiter the terrain is afforded, solution can only be by trial and error. If I were not old (and tired), I would try an animal maze, circular in plan, but having raised levels from which the animal could survey the immediate terrain and plan his course. Perhaps someone may devise it and name it "The Reconnoitering Test."

But for myself, I feel it is time to put away the old bottle. There is no more wine.

PART II

Annotated List of Publications

PART II

Annotated List of Publications

IN THIS volume very little attention has been devoted to my educational preparation, for two reasons. In the first place it was unconventional in that it was self-selected, and under the circumstances of the time it was all that was attainable to fit my finances, ends, and purposes. (No Australian university then offered a Ph.D. program.) In the second place was the assurance that the work done in several related fields of social science would be accepted as proof of competency to do that work. Actually the adequacy of that training has not to my knowledge been publicly challenged. Education is commonly considered a preparation for intellectual labor. Like foot travel, arrival at any point along the way is sufficient evidence that the wayfarer had the strength, plus the good fortune to get there. How far I proceeded, or how worth-while was the effort is not for me to judge, for no matter how loud the self-recorded fanfare, or even a measured volume of applause, the reader will make his own appraisal. The only thing to do is to take the cash in hand and let the credit go, for I know of no method of reckoning the latter.

Since my education was so irregular and unconventional, I am at least partially absolved from making the ordinary acknowledgment to my teachers. I can, however, in all humility pay witness to many who either created opportunities or assisted me in taking advantage of those favorable chances when they occurred. First among these were the individuals who worked for and with me, setting me more or less free to do what was to my personal advantage. Marjorie E. Robertson (nee Babcock), Robert Bernreuter, Henry Peters, Chauncey Louttit were at some time or another my co-workers and collaborators. Professor John Smyth and Richard Berry, of the University of Melbourne, along with Education Director Frank Tate, Chief Inspector Gates, and Harvey Sutton, M.D., of the Victorian State School Department, gave me splendid encouragement in my earliest efforts to become established in my professional groove. My family, particularly my mother, thought I must carry a lucky charm; if so, one of the happiest things that befell me was meeting and working with Professor Frederic Wood Jones, who stooped, not to conquer, but to collaborate.

One of the inevitable results of longevity is the accumulation of creditors, and it is indeed felicitous when they also happen to be your friends. Any complete listing of these would needs be too lengthy, but among them I must mention my long-time secretary, Mrs. Lillie Mackenzie, who not only patiently deciphered my calligraphy but also put up with my squiggles of temperament and character. And of course I must call to attention one who through thick and thin bore with me, more or less patiently, for a small matter of sixty years. Her name will be found in this volume shortly after my own. Apparently I did not need Scripture to remind me of the urgent need for industry. The sub-title of this annotated list should be *The Day's Work,* and the day is very nearly ended.

For those who for any reason might wish to dig further into my personal kitchen midden, the title of this volume, *A Psychologist of Sorts,* seems apt.

During the first three years of the decade of 1911 to 1920 I did not publish anything, having been busily engaged in earning a living, teaching school in outback Australia, one hundred miles by four-horse coach from the nearest railway station. To avoid the weariness of instructing little children in the three *R*s, I had then embarked on a course of experimental education, the aim being frankly to encourage these infants to teach themselves, and save myself the trouble.

As previously set forth in the more truly autobiographic section, riding a bicycle for seventy miles along overgrown tracks to a disused road leading through the mountains, then walking another twenty on a bush bridle path, enabled me to catch a train that carried me another 160 miles to Melbourne, just in time to beat a deadline for application for the position of superintendent of special education of the mentally retarded in the State of Victoria. Apparently impressed with the physical and mental drive that sent me 300 miles on a mad dash by bicycle, foot, and train to his official doorstep, Mr. Gates, then Assistant Chief Inspector, decided to appoint me to the job, subject to final approval by Frank Tate, Director of Education for Victoria. The story is told earlier and more fully in this volume.[1] For those who are more interested in a professional account than a personal history, little more remains to be done than to present a summarized account in the form of the following annotated biography. Its inclusion herein demands a half-apologetic, but, it is hoped, acceptable introductory note.

The author is fully aware that the following text, both in title and treatment, is somewhat repetitious. The reason for this is that I chose, more than a half-century ago, to stake out for myself a corner of the psychological vineyard and proceeded to cultivate and recultivate the plot and harvest the grapes. As remarked elsewhere —the grapes may be sour, but the crop is my own. Very few of my fellow-workers in this field thought the prospects potentially fruitful enough to justify setting aside their own plans to gather an uncertain harvest. The laborers were few, and no doubt, had their own visions.

Furthermore, the work was not associated with any large or important center of learning. The writer did not stay long enough in the University of Melbourne to gain more than the inception of a reputation. There I was regarded by the administration as more of a phenomenon than an academic fixture, and for this gift of judicious negligence I am duly grateful. Otherwise, I might still be in Australia, possibly a schoolmaster, at best a country doctor. When I came to the University of Hawaii, joining the faculty in 1922, ours was indeed a small and undistinguished seat of learning, or as Scripture puts it, "a bed too short whereon a man may stretch himself." The Psychopathic and Psychological Clinic, which I came there to institute and direct, was rather grudgingly admitted to be a legitimate University function. There were no separate departments of psychology, education and psychology having but one academic chair, fortunately occupied by my life-time friend Professor T. M. Livesay, who, happily, was more psychologist than educationist.

[1] To be deposited in the Archives of the History of Psychology, University of Akron, Akron, Ohio, and Archives of the Pacific, Bishop Museum, Honolulu, Hawaii.

However, the Clinic—by the grace of God, the Board of Regents, and the local legislature—survived, ably supported by the University of Hawaii's President, Dr. A. L. Dean, who granted me a long-term lease on one of his aural appendages. His ear was always open. The legislative Senate was also on my side, mainly because I adopted a policy of giving the outer islands special attention rather then centering the Clinic's activities in Honolulu. Probably this note is extraneous—but our appropriations were based more on my ability to play a friendly game of golf, cribbage, or poker with influential senators than my research abilities.

But the fact remains that my productivity lacked the stimulus and encouragement of a large body of co-workers and students in a large institution. Professor Terman in California, for example, could both inspire and direct a large group of devoted disciples so that he did not need to carry on an almost single-handed effort. His shining example, plus the fact that the Stanford Revision of the Binet Scale was eagerly received throughout the world—too enthusiastically, I think—meant that a huge body of experimental data was accumulated and reported by many hands in many places. Duplication occurred, not once but scores of times, but from the point of individual authorship the fact naturally went unnoticed. How different was the situation in a tiny university where any special study had to be carried on with such aid as could be obtained locally, plus some rather adventitious support from the Rockefeller Foundation. This was apparently actuated by the charitable wish to encourage a small and inadequately staffed center, situated on a group of islands over 2,000 miles away from the nearest similar institution of higher learning. Thus the Porteus Maze had to struggle for recognition and survival only by blowing its own weak trumpet from the rooftops of a Polynesian hamlet almost awash in the great Pacific.

Surely, then, it is understandable that there should be repetition in reporting, none of which was, however, exactly needless. To get a wide audience, there had to be, and still requires, multiple presentation.

A very recent review of one of the books herein noted bore the headline "Amazing Utility." The claim still stands that the Porteus Maze adds materially to the credibility of the principles of the whole mental testing movement because it supplies a more significant psychological approach to human understanding. How long it will continue to do so only time can tell, but it is a hopeful augury that after fifty-five years it is still commanding increasing attention.

One other explanatory note should possibly be included. When the tale of the years is told, or nearly so, the reader may wonder at the number of titles relating to the Australian aborigines, or Australids. I do not think that this represents any illogical over-weighting, or attention to the problems of my native land. Supposing that there should appear, by some magical turning back of the pages of man's history, a living specimen of one of our earliest progenitors, equipped with his primitive tools, weapons and other artifacts, and his own philosophy in the form of legends, what a scientific sensation would ensue! What a rush there would be to examine all his technological skills and the purposes for which he applied them, what eager scrutiny there would be of his way of life, his religion, his art, to say nothing of minute recordings of the manner of man he was, his physiological and physical development. His mentality and sociological stratagems would surely be carefully analysed, his sexual and family life practices examined, and his ideas of social regulation noted in every detail. Undoubtedly the patience of this human survival from our forgotten past would be exhausted long before our scientific curiosity was allayed.

Yet such opportunities do exist today; the Australids represent a rather miraculously preserved primitive prototype, exemplifying a stage in our own evolutionary development. Hence, instead of a score or two of recorded investigations, there should have been hundreds. Undoubtedly anthropology—using the label in its widest, most logical sense as the study of man—has missed the bus. Whether or not it was the last vehicle on this educational highway is a matter of doubt and conjecture. It is like the question—what would have happened if Columbus had stayed home?

Items are grouped by decades and give (1) the decade, (2) the year of publication, (3) the serial number of publication, (4) the title of the book, monograph, or article, (5) the medium of publication, (6) the volume, (7) the month, (8) and the number of pages. An outline of study content follows, together with brief comments. On the theory that books are much more likely to be available to the student, less attention will be devoted to them and more to what might well be called fugitive articles, that are notoriously difficult to come up with. To analyse 7,000 pages of printed material and to achieve a tidy presentation is indeed difficult.

Finally, I must acknowledge with deepest gratitude the fact

that a scientist who continues his work and interest over an additional period of twenty years after formal retirement must have been lucky in two respects—the continuance of the necessary health and strength and financial support from friends who approve of his purposes.

Three local foundations have contributed generously, foremost among them being the Juliette Atherton Trust, the Castle Fund, and one other which prefers to keep its support anonymous. George Lehleitner, through his self-constituted Aloha Fund, has also been most encouraging. It so happens also, that Dr. Henry Garrett, distinguished psychologist, and I have found ourselves strongly allied to the validity of the principle of racial differences and had access to funds to back up my sympathetic studies of the Australian aborigines who for long were looked upon as being among the lowest peoples of earth. As Dr. Garrett knows, I have always insisted that the question was not one of racial superiorities but of racial differences. Those who have followed my work must unfailingly realize my belief that race differences go much further than skin deep and that I have admired to the full the Australids' courage and tenacity of purpose. Intelligence is the ability to adjust to environment—but which environment?

DECADE 1911–1920

1914

No. 1 Montessori Methods in Victorian Schools. *Victoria Education Gazette and Teachers' Aid,* 1914, Vol. 14, No. 10, October, 390–392. Pp. 3

This describes and illustrates a system for teaching writing based on an analysis of cursive script into its eight commonest elements. These are grooved into plywood forms, which the pupil traces with his finger until he has developed mental images of these forms and visuotactile-muscular memories of their reproduction. (See also No. 98.)

1915

No. 2 Motor-Intellectual Tests for Mental Defectives. *Journal of Experimental Pedagogy* (England), 1915, Vol. 2, June, 127–135. Pp. 9

This was the original study based on 92 individual mental defectives. The American article, which is listed next, was also published in June, 1915, and the description and discussions follow almost identical lines. The scale of test designs is the same in each article and agrees with sets mimeographed for the overseas meeting of the British Association for the Advancement of Science held at Melbourne University in August, 1914. The actual paper was listed by title only in the Proceedings and was wrongly attributed to another person, presumably a British Association member.

No. 3 Mental Tests for Feebleminded: A New Series. *Journal of Psycho-Asthenics,* 1915, Vol. 19, No. 4, June, 200–213. Pp. 14

This article also describes the reactions of mentally defective children (*N* 120) to the Porteus Maze Tests, as illustrated in the text. The author contends that a fairer appraisal of practical intelligence will be secured from these tests than is given by a Binet-Simon examination. Among the objections to the Binet were listed (1) the influence of previous schooling; (2) shyness of the child with a strange examiner; (3) verbal handicaps; (4) limited scope, since prudence, forethought, and sustained attention are insufficiently examined. These are described as special deficits of the feebleminded. The Maze is recommended as a necessary "supplement and partial corrective" to the Binet-Simon Scale.

Description of the three-, four- and five-year tests is then offered to indicate that prudence and planning enter into success, since the child even in following between guide lines of the design fails to anticipate changes in direction, frequently rounding the corners or cutting across lines. The higher tests in the Maze series examine more fully the child's ability to follow instructions about finding the right openings while his attention is focussed on keeping within the guide lines.

The rule with regard to stopping the test immediately *S* enters a blind alley and the principle of allowing a repeated trial are justified. Thus the amount of practise in the test itself is controlled. Many psychologists attempting to use the Maze as a group test misunderstand completely the reason for this "unsuccessful trials" procedure. Ways of increasing the difficulties of Maze-threading problems are pointed out. The new test is expected to yield slightly higher scores than the Binet, thus easing the diagnostic picture. In the scoring no provision was made for recording speed of performance, since the prime purpose was to gauge accuracy, not speed, the two types of scoring being assumed to be incompatible. Graphs of individual records showed that 15 per cent of cases tested within a year of their Binet levels. Out of 120 cases, 28, or about 23 per cent, tested more than a year higher in the Maze, thus lowering substantially the diagnostic standards and freeing more children from the stigma of feeblemindedness.

1917

No. 4 Mental Tests with Delinquent and Australian Aboriginal Children. *Psychological Review,* 1917, Vol. 24, No. 1, January, 32–42. Pp. 11

Reports the first application of the Porteus Maze Test to 22 delinquent boys in Australia. These were on the average two years below their chronological age when tested. A second group of reformatory inmates (*N* 20), actual age 15 years, scored in the Maze Test 9 years, 10 months. A number of cases were delinquent defectives.

With regard to ethnic group comparisons, 28 aboriginal children, mainly half-castes, were tested at Point McLeay Mission, South Australia. They were only slightly (5 months) below the level of white pupils in ordinary schools. Another section of this paper reported results of applying the tests to pupils of the school for deaf and dumb in Melbourne. Those adjudged mentally defective by the teachers tested just about 3 years below the level of the rest of the deaf children when examined by the Maze.

No. 5 Preliminary Account of Investigation into the Annual Rate of Growth of the Brain. (With Professor R. J. A. Berry) *Medical Journal of Australia,* 1917, June. Pp. 10

1918

No. 6 A Practical Method for the Early Recognition of Feeblemindedness and Other Forms of Social Inefficiency. (With R. J. A. Berry) *Medical Journal of Australia,* 1918, August. Pp. 12

In the two papers listed above, the present writer was the junior author. Dr. R. J. A. Berry was Professor of Anatomy at Melbourne University, and collaborated with me in determining the development of head size from infancy to college life. He was anxious to take into account extremes of head size and brain capacity as one approach to mental diagnosis. (See also No. 13)

No. 7 The Measurement of Intelligence: Six Hundred and Fifty-three Children Examined by the Binet and Porteus Tests. *Journal of Educational Psychology,* 1918, January, 10–31. Pp. 22

This was in the nature of a progress report as applied to *S*s dealt with in No. 13.

Before publication of this article there had been no adjustment of scores in those cases where *S*s had required more than one trial to deal successfully with any year design. It was here noted that a system of deductions should be instituted so that when two trials were required to pass any test below Year XII, the child lost a half-year of test age for each such second trial. Ordinarily three trials were allowed in the more difficult designs, with a deduction of another half-year for each unsuccessful trial. This system prevailed until the 1919 edition of the Maze was published, when four trials were allowed in the highest tests. The principle of altering the scoring of the tests rather than changing the tests themselves was discussed.

For the first time individual differences in the way of attacking the problem were noted, and these, 24 years later, became the basis of the Qualitative Score (*Q* score). These included observations on impulsivity, irresolution, mental confusion, over-confidence, heedlessness. The article also differentiated between the glib-tongued, quick-witted child with grave defects of temperament, whose intelligence is frequently over-rated. The resemblance between normal young children's performance and that of older mentally dull individuals was also noted. Binet and Maze reactions were discussed in detail.

For the first time, sex differences were reported, the girls scoring somewhat lower than boys. It was suggested that the puzzle interest of the tests appealed more to males, and impulsiveness seemed more common in females.

In 1915, Cunningham examined 100 children by the Maze, and Rolls re-examined 45 of them a year later. Results showed that gains tended to be larger and more irregular for the Maze than the Binet, indicating more variable practice effects. As expected, the ability to profit by experience is more adequately tested in the Maze.

Another experiment which was very interesting was the first attempt to show exactly where errors occurred in maze threading, data potentially useful in alterations of difficulty of the individual tests, if revision should be necessary.

Finally, results with delinquents and the deaf were reported. For the latter group, mental deficiency was suggested by markedly inferior test scores as compared with the general performance of deaf children.

1919

No. 8 Cephalometry of Feebleminded. *Research Publication, Training School Bulletin,* Vineland, N.J., 1919, June, 1–24.
Pp. 25

This was the first of a series of studies instituted by the author after his arrival in the United States from Melbourne to act as director of research at Vineland, following the resignation of Dr. Goddard. It discussed the deviations from normal brain capacities of fifty defectives, illustrating their abnormal standard deviations. Nineteen of these cases had brain capacities below the ten percentile of 9,000 normal cases, as compared with 7 individuals who were above the 90 percentile in brain size. The author concluded that "head capacity alone cannot be used as a measure of intelligence."

No. 9 Educational Treatment of Defectives. (With Alice M. Nash) *Research Publication No. 18, Training School,* Vineland, N.J., 1919, November, 1–19. Pp. 19

An educational essay dealing with the practical learning aptitudes of feebleminded. It criticises inadequate "special" or "opportunity" classes for mental defectives, since they provide nothing very special and little opportunity. It also points out that there is little basis for the idea that a child who is academically very retarded will compensate for this by capacity for manual training. The only reason for the shift of emphasis to practical education is that the retarded pupil may use this instruction to his future industrial advantage. Treatment in small classes is often beneficial, but the main advantage is that removing the backward individuals from ordinary classrooms gives the teacher a better opportunity to work with normals. Unfortunately, provision for after-care does not come within the educational province.

Nevertheless, though results are frequently discouraging, special class teachers are usually dedicated to their task, and in the hope that some ideas will be gathered that will be useful, this description of Vineland's experience was offered. In this work the selection of the trainable cases is essential, which necessitates the cooperation of psychologists. The Porteus Maze is here a better guide than the Binet, though the exclusion of very low-grade cases can be done easily by the latter. The program of manual and simple academic training of children selected on the basis of potentialities for progress is reviewed in detail.

No. 10 Porteus Tests—The Vineland Revision. *Research Publication No. 18, Training School,* Vineland, N.J., 1919, September, 1–43. Pp. 43

This was the first general account of the Porteus Maze Test published in the United States. It presented the test's earliest standardization on 1,000 normal children, showing that the scale was somewhat too easy at the younger age levels, too difficult at the upper. The results applied only to Australian children examined in 1915–16. A further standardization in 1918, with 1,255 cases, showed a similar disparity. This was not corrected since the author at that time believed that the Maze should be used with the Binet and that the latter was so difficult that it exaggerated the incidence and degree of mental deficiency. Arrays of correlations with other tests and independent estimates of intelligence appeared in this monograph, showing that except in educational status the Maze had somewhat higher coefficients than did the Binet with industrial and social adjustments, but that when the Binet and Porteus scores were combined, the correlations were distinctly higher than for each of these measures considered singly.

No. 11 A Standardized Information Record. *Research Publication, Training School Bulletin,* Vineland, N.J., 1919, October, 1–8. Pp. 8

This was an outline of information gathered at the time of admission of a defective child to the Vineland Training School. The object was to systematize record-keeping so that information relevant to the child's mental condition would be easily available.

1920

No. 12 Condensed Guide to the Binet Tests. (With Helen F. Hill) *Research Publication, Training School Bulletin,* Vineland, N.J., 1920, Vol. 19, March and April, 1–39. Pp. 39
(Part 1 by S. D. Porteus; Part 2 with Helen F. Hill)

In a footnote it was explained that this guide was based on the Stanford Revision of the Binet and therefore made no claims to originality. The author's deep indebtedness to Professor Terman and his Stanford co-workers was duly acknowledged.

The object of the monograph was to provide a form for special use with mentally defective children. Some minor changes in arrangement and procedure were offered.

No. 13 Intelligence and Social Valuation. (With R. J. A. Berry) Monograph. *Research Publication 20,* Training School, Vineland, N.J., 1920, May, 1–100. Pp. 100

This monograph dealt very largely with data gathered in Australia but published in Vineland after the present author came to America. It reprinted the tables of brain size and development based on measurements of three groups of cases: (1) 4,177 State School boys, (2) 2,104 private school and university students, and (3) 2,717 females. Thus the total of *S*s measured was 8,998. To these should be added special groups of 138 abnormal and subnormal cases, delinquents, deaf and dumb, Australian aborigines, etc., numbering in all over 10,000 cases.

This monograph also repeats some of the data previously appearing in publications Nos. 5, 6, and 8 above, and was later bound together (with 8 other reprints) under the title *Vineland Studies.*

The second part of the monograph is concerned wholly with psycho-physical and psychological measurements reported by the present writer. It contains, *inter alia,* results of the mental examination of 1,000 Australian children by the Binet and Porteus Maze Tests. The more than 11,000 cases reported in this monograph constituted for its time one of the largest groups of subjects ever examined in a single investigation. The Army testings carried out were far more numerous, but the work was carried on by a very large group of psychologists. *Vide* also No. 18.

No. 14 A New Definition of Feeblemindedness. *Training School Bulletin,* Vineland, N.J. Pp. 4

After discussion of a variety of proposed definitions, the author suggests the following:

"A feeble-minded person is one who by reason of mental defects other than sensory cannot attain to self-management and self-support to the degree of social sufficiency.

No. 15 A Plan for the Study of the Mental Defectives. *Proceedings, American Association for the Study of the Feeble-minded,* 1920, June, 1–12. Pp. 12

A schematic outline of various approaches to the study of defectives through physical, mental, industrial, and educational observations, and the recording of data in a form easily accessible for research.

No. 16 Sex Differences in Porteus Maze Test Performance. (With Dorothy M. Bassett) *Research Publication 22, Training School Bulletin,* Vineland, N.J., 1920, November, 1–16. Pp. 16

Apart from its summation of sex differences in the Maze, this paper is important in that it presents for the first time two adult tests to be added to the Vineland Revision of the Scale. Results are analysed as regards both speed and accuracy. Differences in attitude by the two sex groups are also discussed, males revealing a more casual approach, while females seemed more anxious about their performances. *S*s were attending New Jersey high schools.

No. 17 A Study of Personality of Defectives with a Social Ratings Scale. *Research Publication 23, Training School,* Vineland, N.J., 1920, December, 1–24. Pp. 24

This monograph presents a new and original approach to the problem of the external validation of mental tests. The criteria set up consisted of weighted ratings of seven traits or trait clusters, based on behavioral observations of Training School inmates. Correlations with a group of 38 males and 44 females showed equal coefficients of .6 for males with both the Maze and the Binet, but a much closer relationship in the case of females (Binet .69, Maze .75). When the two scores were pooled, the average Binet-Porteus correlation rose to .73 for males, .79 for females.

The process of setting up the scale consisted of securing ratings of the social behavior of a large number of Vineland Training School inmates by two judges who had known them intimately for at least two years. One of the raters was Mrs. C. E. Nash, who was responsible for the children's allotment to school classes, or in the case of older persons, to industrial training and service within the institution. The second was the director of the hospital and general supervisor of the cottages where the cases were housed. The first series of ratings was a "general social estimate" of the individuals' ability to get along in the community if they had to be discharged from the institution.

The second step was to correlate with this estimate the scores obtained by each *S* on the trait scale. The size of the correlations determined the weightings attached to each scale item. The general social estimate and the Social Rating Scale correlated .87 for the whole group of *S*s.

The traits were individually described and the basis of ratings given. It was thought that the list would constitute an external criterion for the validation of mental tests used with mental defectives. Unfortunately, though the validity of the Social Ratings Scale was never impugned, it was not used for the purpose proposed by the author, even though outside criteria, except for ordinary school progress, were nonexistent. Had the Scale been systematically applied, years of uncertainty as to the comparative validity of tests would have been unnecessary.

DECADE 1921–1930

1921

No. 18 *Vineland Studies.* Research Publications, Training School, Vineland, N.J., 1921, February.

This is a collection of five articles and four monographs bound together in a single volume. Pages are not included in this bibliography total. See also No. 13, which describes in detail one of these monographs.

No. 19 The Social Rating Scale. *Training School Bulletin,* Vineland, N.J., 1921, Vol. 18, No. 3, May, 33–39. Pp. 7

Criticises the "mental age" concept, mainly because it is usually determined on a too narrow or restricted sampling of individual abilities. Assessment of long-term social adjustment is necessary, and this the rating scale was intended to supply. (Abstract of No. 17 above.)

No. 20 Education of Truant, Backward, Dependent and Delinquent Children. *Proceedings 18th Annual National Conference,* Jacksonville, Florida, 1921, October, 60–68. Pp. 9

Discusses various types of socially maladjusted children, many of whom are trainable to an extent not indicated by the Binet tests. Consequently, grouping of mentally retarded by Binet mental age is not particularly useful. The Maze Test provides a much more practical approach, even though its scores are more difficult to interpret than a Binet IQ. But even more valuable would be an assessment of personality traits by a recent social rating scale. The scale, and its application in the State School at Rome, New York, is described. In comparison with success of girls in community life, the Binet correlated only .32; the Maze scores were not available for statistical analysis, but it was noted that the mental level in many cases "did not have a close relation to the degree of social maladjustment." Yet the correlation of the Social Ratings Scale with success on parole judged by the chief parole supervisor was .76. Nevertheless, this finding did not seem to make the Social Rating Scale more popular with institution staffs and psychologists.

No. 21 Personality in Relation to Social Mal-adjustment. *Training School Bulletin,* Vineland, N.J., Vol. 18, Nos. 6 & 7, October & November, 81–90. Pp. 10

Summarizes experience with Dr. Bernstein's Colony Plan in New York State in relation to ratings obtained with the Social Ratings Scale. This was a practical rather than a theoretical approach to the Scale's validation as an external criterion of mental test research. This article repeats for a larger audience the data given in the Florida Conference program. (See previous listing.)

1923

No. 22 *Studies in Mental Deviations.* Smith Printing House, Vineland, N.J., 1923, xi + 276. Pp. 287

The first full-length report of the author's researches at the Vineland Laboratory from 1919 to 1923. It reviews previous work done on brain growth and capacity. The largest section presents the relation of the Maze and Binet tests with the mentally retarded, divided on the basis of behavior into well-adjusted, delinquent, and psychopathic groups. These were again sub-divided according to IQ or test quotient levels. By mental classification this indicated that *the Vineland Training School contained a good proportion of children who should not have been termed feebleminded.* They were social problems rather than mental defectives. The "dull-normal but well-adjusted" group had relatively higher Maze scores than Binet, and still higher for the dull but delinquent cases. On the other hand, the psychopathic tended to score higher in the Binet. These findings indicated that the Maze was the better diagnostic instrument.

A thorough exploration of the relationship of the Maze Test to the Social Ratings Scale was reported by Dr. Marjorie Robertson (nee Babcock). Again, superiority of the Maze was demonstrated except that pooling the Binet and Maze scores gave distinctly higher coefficients. However, considerable space was devoted to proving that no mental test or series of tests told the whole story as regards individual achievement or potentialities. In other words, important sectors of human personality were still inadequately explored by existing tests, including the Porteus Maze.

This volume also presented an Education-Attainments Scale, and an Industrial Achievements Scale set forth an attempt at estimating practical attainments of defectives. It consisted of a job-training analysis of each occupation open to defectives. This provided ten steps in proficiency from the lowest level up to unsupervised or independent activity. In the author's opinion this Industrial Scale represented a very much neglected development, and anticipated Doll's Social Maturity Scale as applied to institutional environment.

1924

No. 23 *Guide to the Porteus Maze Tests.* Training School Publication, Vineland, N.J., 1924, March. Pp. 32

As this was superseded by later publications, little need for review exists. Two designs for Adult levels are illustrated and a time limit suggested. Reasons for not extending the scale still further are discussed, the main objection being that any marked increase in complexity of designs increased its puzzle character so that special abilities came into play.

1926

No. 24 *Temperament and Race.* (With Marjorie E. Babcock) Badger, Boston (Gorham Press), 1926, xiv + 364. Pp. 378

Summarizes researches among ethnic groups resident in Hawaii.

Studies involving mental tests and social ratings are reported, with particular reference to the community adjustment of the Japanese. Their part in the future of the Pacific and in Hawaii was predicted on the basis of inquiries into their mentality and personality traits. A classification by "psychosynergic" traits is attempted, and a new characterization of *antevert* and *retrovert* personalities is suggested. A series of mental test investigations into Binet and Maze levels of children belonging to different ethnic groups was reported in detail.

No. 25 Porteus Tests and Social Inadequacy. *Journal of Abnormal & Social Psychology*, 1926, 405–412. Pp. 8

This was written in the form of a reply to an article in this journal by Cornell and Lowden, which was critical of a statement by the present writer published several years earlier (1919). This claimed that the Maze could aid in evaluating certain temperamental qualities and does "detect the mentally unstable." This discussion occurred at a period before the purposes of the test were well defined, and the use of the term "mentally unstable" was too wide.

Cornell and Lowden give an excellent summary of the characteristics of that large group of *S*s whose inadequacy is not due to intellectual deficiency, but is exhibited in inert, passive, ambitionless behavior. "They show very little practical ability and they fail to develop any useful dominant interests." The authors admit the vagueness of such diagnostic labels as constitutional inferior or psychopathic inferior and they prefer the descriptive term "temperamentally inadequate." They note that such *S*s are not extremely dull but their tested intelligence is much higher than their social adjustment warrants.

Hence the article does not criticise particularly the usefulness of the Maze, but that of mental tests in general when applied to such cases. With this the present writer agrees, but points out that the Porteus Maze was not intended for the diagnosis of constitutional inferiors, dementia praecox cases, and the psychopathic. The inadequacy of the test for the understanding of some non-psychotic individuals, who, while not being feebleminded, find their way to institutions for defectives, has been fully acknowledged.

The writer in *Studies in Mental Deviations* (No. 22 of this list) had already discussed in similar terms delinquent and psychopathic institutionalized cases and had pointed out that both their Maze and Binet scores were often unrealistic, occasioning the comment that success in the Maze was not so important as failure.

1929

No. 26 The Social Psychology of the Australian Aboriginal. *Journal of Applied Psychology,* 1929, Vol. 13, No. 2, April, 131–144. Pp. 14

This marks the author's first intrusion into the field of social anthropology, his previous experience having been in physical anthropology. This must be considered a forerunner of field work undertaken in the next decade.

The author's analysis of Australid social customs and regulation was undertaken to show that "the most distinctive features of the Australian social organization have behind them an ingenuity of device and purpose which is surprising." This applies to "old-man government" instead of chieftainship, to a system of food taboos distributed selectively through the tribal totems, to exogamous intermarriage that diminishes the competition for women, and to initiatory practices which serve not only as "rites of passage" into manhood, but also as a means of an indelible impression on the initiates of the authority of the elders, and, over-all, the remarkable attuning of life to the grim demands of a comparatively hostile environment. Finally, the common view of the Australid as being stupid or degraded is vigorously combatted.

No. 27 A Protest. *American Journal of Psychology,* 1929, Vol. 7, April, 336–338. Pp. 3

This was a reply to a very critical review of the book *Temperament and Race* (No. 24) written by Joseph Peterson, which, together with Peterson's rejoinder, represented an excursion or descent into the muddy waters of controversy. This disagreement did not, however, prevent the critic's use of the Maze in his later study of Negroes in the South.

Joseph Peterson, a highly respected figure in American psychology, is unhappily long deceased, and now, 38 years later, this may well be the last of the present writer's dabbling in printer's ink. Though personal amends are impossible, I would still express regrets for any intemperance of tone apparent in this old encounter.

No. 28 *The Matrix of the Mind.* (With Frederic Wood Jones) 1st edition, University Press Association, Honolulu, January 1929. Pp. 457
2nd edition, Edward Arnold, London, 1929. Pp. 424

This book traces in detail the building up of the central nervous system from the beginnings of sensation and movement within the single-celled organism up to its highest development in the human cortex. The book is an attempt to bridge the gap between neurology and psychology. In the preface the co-authors denote the individual limits of responsibility in the division of labor as follows: "Whilst every portion of the book has been the subject of the fullest discussion between the authors, each is entirely responsible for his own part. Chapters I to XLIII, dealing more particularly with the developmental story of the brain, are the contribution of the author (F. Wood Jones), having the more special anatomical training; the remainder, treating of the evolution of human behavior, is the work of the co-author (S. D. Porteus), whose interests are mainly psychological." As the volume is still available for reference, no attempt will be made to summarize its contents.

Full-length reviews appeared in the *American Journal of Physical Anthropology, Eugenics Review, Medical Journal of Australia, Pacific Affairs, The Speculum, Journal of Applied Psychology, Brain, Quarterly Review of Biology, The Lancet, Eugenical News, Psychological Bulletin, Mental Hygiene, Journal of Abnormal & Social Psychology, Nature, Biological Abstracts, Journal Medical Association,* South Africa; *The Scotsman, British Journal of Psychology, British Medical Journal, The Australasian,* the London *Times Literary Supplement, The Medical Press, Archives of Neurology and Psychiatry, The Age* (Melbourne), etc.

The total of these reviews amounted to over 20,000 words. Though *The Matrix of the Mind* may have provided only a footbridge between neurology and psychology, for at least several years it was well travelled. That it occasioned such wide reviews appears to be proof of the interdependence of neurology and psychology. There is still urgent need for better mutual understanding in these related disciplines, but the trouble seems to be that psychologists rarely read neurology, and neurologists neglect to keep informed with regard to psychological findings.

1930

No. 29 Race and Social Differences in Performance Tests. (With Doris Dewey and Robert Bernreuter) *Genetic Psychology Monographs,* 1930, Vol. 8, No. 2, August, 93–208. Pp. 116

This was a comparative study by means of the Porteus Form and Assembling Test of a variety of ethnic groups of children resident in Hawaii. Apparently in 1928 the competition for attention among new performance tests was so keen that this measure, while it yielded very interesting results, soon dropped from sight. It is noteworthy that the Portuguese, who made inferior records in other tests, did very well in this test, probably because success depended largely on abilities underlying mechanical aptitude.

DECADE 1931–1940

1931

No. 30 *The Psychology of a Primitive People.* Edward Arnold, London, 1931; Longmans Green, New York, 1932, xvi + 438. Pp. 454

This book recounted fully the results of work done by the writer in Australia with aborigines in 1929 on behalf of the Australian National Research Council, with joint sponsorship by the University of Hawaii. It is noteworthy as being the first extended investigation into Australid mentality, using a variety of mental test and physical measurement approaches, but relying mainly on the Porteus Maze. Its primary aim was to establish the comparative status of the Australid in the scale of intelligence, where he was placed by common repute on the lowest rung of development. This study was the first objective appraisal that placed him much higher than he was, both popularly and scientifically, credited with being.

A modification of purpose that emerged during the investigation was concerned with throwing new light on the question of the effects of environmental conditions on ethnic group intelligence. The common sociological supposition that extremely unfavorable living conditions would result in depressed mental test performances was disproved. Natives living in the extremely arid, or drought-stricken regions of Central Australia proved, as far as Maze-tested abilities were concerned, to be superior to those who dwelt in the areas that lay within the belt of monsoonal rainfall, in which survival was comparatively easy.

From the standpoint of social psychology, tribal cohesion is cemented by many customs and regulations, which today apparently have no reason except tradition for their occurrence. In the course of ages the original useful purpose has been forgotten. The values of these social expedients are emphasized. Obviously, this volume is too lengthy for fuller annotation.

1932

No. 31 Human Studies in Hawaii. *Pacific Problems, Proceedings and Lectures, School of Oriental and Pacific Affairs,* University of Hawaii, 1932, July–August. Pp. 32

The object of this article was to report in brief outline the results of the anthropological and psychological studies undertaken during a five-year period ending December 1931, and carried out with funds allotted by the Rockefeller Foundation. This was a coordinated effort to provide an answer to the question—what is race? It summarized briefly Wood Jones' measurements from dioptographic drawings of Tasmanian, Australian, and Hawaiian skulls. It was followed by a presentation of psychological data accumulated by the present writer and Dr. C. M. Louttit in Hawaii.

Because of radical differences in approach to the question, sociological findings were reported separately by Dr. Romanzo Adams and his co-workers.

No. 32 The Psychology of a Primitive People. *Medical Journal of Australia,* 1932, October, 60–61. Pp. 2

This was written in reply to a review of the writer's book on the subject (see No. 30). The reviewer was somewhat incensed at the description of the investigation as a *pioneer* psychological study on the grounds that Baldwin Spencer, Howitt, Roth, etc. had already published psychological observations of Australids. This, however, was the first account of objective tests of mentality provided by a professional psychologist, together with discussion of the value of social customs and regulations with regard to tribal cohesion and survival.

1933

No. 33 Home in Hawaii. *Review of Reviews and World's View,* 1933, Vol. 58, No. 2, February, 60–63. Pp. 4

A short article which attempts to account for the home-feeling that spins itself like a cocoon of security around the resident here. Peace and quiet and a lazy procession of days do not necessarily spell somnolence. Hawaii's position midway between the seething vortices of East and West, and the consequent scientific, industrial, social, and commercial problems of adjustment put a premium on mental energy and the spirit of adventure. It is much more than a playground, and the prediction is hazarded that ours will remain an intelligent and well-informed community, developing its own distinctive points of view and policies. In the writer's present view, there is a tendency to over-orientalize the Hawaiian scene.

No. 34 *The Maze Test and Mental Differences.* Smith Printing House, Vineland, N.J., 1933. Pp. 225

Following the monograph "Porteus Tests—The Vineland Revision" (No. 10 of this bibliography) and the early guidebook, this volume was the first of a series of full-length books devoted to reporting and discussing results of extensive studies, together with instructions for application and test quotient tables. This was the authorized version displacing the Vineland Revision (so-called), published in 1919. It contained changes in the rules governing the tests' application and scoring. For example, since no adult tests were included in the "Vineland Revision," 14 years credit represented the ceiling score. The former five-year test was dropped and a new test for that level was added.

Since modification in scoring and procedures change the standardization, they also alter the character of the tests and constitute a new edition. For example, if only one trial were allowed for each test, its validity would be entirely altered. This form or edition of the test, therefore, could be covered, it was believed, by copyright until a new edition was authorized.

No. 35 Mentality of Australian Aborigines. *Oceania,* 1933, Vol. 4, No. 1, September, 30–36. Pp. 7

This was a follow-up investigation of aboriginal children's mentality by Ralph Piddington, who visited the same general area where I had worked in 1929. Piddington's results did not differ markedly from my own, and indicated very little difference from white children's norms. However, tests such as those of auditory rote memory showed decided inferiority. This deficiency may be partially accounted for on the basis of lack of motivation. Memorizing digits in order is to the native a meaningless activity, which demands only perfunctory performance. The Maze is in an entirely different category.

1936

No. 36 The Leiter Performance Scale. (Appendix by S. D. Porteus) *University of Hawaii Research Publication,* 1936, No. 13, May. Pp. 16

The writer's visit to South Africa in 1934 afforded opportunity to apply a modified form of the Leiter International Test. Though the Leiter Scale is independent of language, the situations depicted are to some extent affected by varying cultural factors. For example, in one test *S* is presented with photos of five Hottentot females arranged in order of age from infancy to old age, the problem being to arrange five photos of males in similar sequence. Two uncertainties arise—how well do really primitive people interpret still-life photographs, and secondly, how well could they judge age differences among utterly strange people? The very variety of the Leiter Scale provided its own greatest difficulty—that of interpretation.

1937

No. 37 *Primitive Intelligence and Environment.* Macmillan Company, New York, 1937. Pp. 325

This carried the investigation of the results of varying environments a long step forward. The Australian study contrasted the mentalities of groups of the same race living in varying environmental situations; this second study tried to compare two peoples of different races, both however living in desert conditions. The expectation that "deserts" present the same circumstances for survival was not fulfilled. The term "desert" connoted two very different ecologies in different continents, particularly as regards human habitats. This realization was only achieved in the field. The study, therefore, had to be revised on the spot so that it became a problem in comparative racial performances mainly in the Porteus Maze.

In comparison with Bushmen, Bantu tribes (such as Mchopi, Shangaans, Wakaranga, etc.), Ainu, Chinese illiterates, Senoi, Sakai Jeram, Bajou, Formosans, jungle peoples of India, the Australids occupied the upper middle ranges of Maze-tested abilities. The late Dr. Kilton Stewart collected the data for me in Southeast Asia, and these were reported by me.

1939

No. 38 Psychological Service in Hawaii. *University of Hawaii Bulletin,* 1939, Vol. 18, No. 5, March. Pp. 16

A survey of the relationship of a university psychological clinic with other agencies concerned with human adjustments. These included educational facilities, both urban, rural, and inter-island, ranging from elementary grades to high school and university, juvenile courts and other correctional institutions, the Prison Parole Board, Waimano Home for defectives, private schools, public health associations, social service agencies, Queen's Hospital Training School for Nurses, together with other activities such as university teaching, research, publications, scientific expeditions, etc.

Considering the date (1939), such close relationship with all types of community welfare was unique in America. It was, of course, largely dictated by special considerations, such as Hawaii's geographical situation as a group of islands located over 2,000 miles from the U.S. mainland.

No. 39 The Validity of the Porteus Maze Test. *Journal of Educational Psychology,* 1939, Vol. 30, No. 3, March, 172–178. Pp. 7

This paper was occasioned by an article published in the same journal by Moshe Brill. The subjects were 100 inmates of the State Colony for Feebleminded Males at New Lisbon, N.J. Brill reported that 50 socially well-adjusted boys scored lower in the Maze Tests than 50 "seriously maladjusted mentally deficient boys." The Binet averages of the two groups were about identical, namely 9 years, but their range of scores extended up to 15 years. Obviously, with mental ages varying, in about 50 per cent of cases, from 9 to 15 years, these boys were not "mentally deficient." To make comparisons between well-adjusted and maladjusted dull normals had no point. Louttit and Stackman's statement that "together the two tests [Binet and Maze] give a better picture of a child's performance ability than either by itself," would have been useful as a diagnostic guide.

No. 40 Racial Group Differences in Mentality. *Tabulae Biologicae,* Den Haag, Holland, 1939, Vol. 18, No. 1, 66–75. Pp. 10

The period 1926–1939 was marked by publication of five books. It also covered the provision of a Rockefeller grant, which enabled the University of Hawaii to employ for periods of research Drs.

Louttit, Bernreuter, Stewart, and Leiter as assistants, each for limited terms. Their work, carried out under my direction, was reported in *Tabulae Biologicae,* a Dutch publication. The article was noteworthy for the extremely large number of *S*s involved, in all over thirty thousand. Their range of habitat was large—Hawaii, Australia, U.S.A., Japan, China, Malaya, the Philippines, and Taiwan.

This work included comparative studies of auditory and visual memory, applications of the Knox Cube, the Goddard Form Board, the Porteus Form and Assembling Test, and the Leiter Performance Scale. Also summarized were Psychological Clinic examinations by the Binet Scales (Stanford Revision and Terman-Merrill), the McQuarrie Test, plus Maze Test performances of various primitive ethnic groups in Australia, Africa, and Southeast Asia. Altogether, 32 studies were outlined and reported.

Though separate articles on these topics were not numerous, the amount of experimental work made up a substantial corpus. The assistants mentioned above were at that time all young and inexperienced, but each of them later made significant contributions to psychology.

DECADE 1941–1950

1941

No. 41 *The Practice of Clinical Psychology.* American Book Company, New York, 1941 Pp. 579

Discusses role of the clinical psychologist as distinct from that of the psychiatrist, with special reference to use of tests and scales in diagnosing mental defectives. It presents an Educational Attainment Scale to measure scholastic status of feebleminded or of very young children. There are also chapters on delinquents, using a "self-indulgence scale," and on criminals. In connection with prison and parole history, a "time-line" was devised which sums up for the use of parole boards an individual record of offences and imprisonments. Other interesting but neglected approaches, such as a "Nurses Self-Rating Scale," are also given. It showed that girls with good nursing potentials could be differentiated from others on the basis of certain temperamental trends apparently not directly connected with specific skills of a professional nature. Almost complete national absorption by psychologists in World War II perhaps helped to account for the fact that this book was almost wholly disregarded. One potentially useful diagnostic aid was a Range of Local Information Scale that reflected common knowledge arrived at by the individual through a process of "social osmosis."

1942

No. 42 *Qualitative Performance in the Maze Test.* (Monograph reprinted in 1950.) Smith Printing House, Vineland, N.J., 1942. Pp. 47

A systematic attempt to score cumulatively infractions of instructions normally given in the application of the Maze, such as crossing lines and cutting corners, lifting the pencil in the course of maze threading, etc. It was thought that this special scoring would reflect temperamental tendencies in delinquents, who were so often unwilling to accept direction and control. Very significant differences were found between weighted scores of delinquent and non-delinquent cases. In ensuing years these differences were confirmed by Wright, Grajales, Docter and Winder, Fooks and Thomas, and other investigators. This approach was significant as a first attempt to take into account quality of Maze performance as well as mental age scores.

1944

No. 43 Mental Changes After Bilateral Prefrontal Lobotomy. (With Richard Kepner, M.D.) *Genetic Psychology Monographs,* 1944, Vol. 29, 3–115. Pp. 113

This, the senior author's first incursion into the field of psychosurgery, was made in conjunction with a psychiatrist and a neurosurgeon, Dr. Ralph Cloward. Subjects were 18 patients examined both pre- and post-operatively by a modified form of the Binet Scale specially adapted to local conditions. Thirty-nine per cent of patients improved their scores after operation, 39 per cent declined. By contrast, in the Maze, out of 17 operatees, only 6 per cent improved, while 76.5 per cent declined. Individual results were given and behavioral changes noted. This was the first indication of the greater sensitivity of the Maze to surgically controlled brain damage.

No. 44 Medical Applications of the Maze Test. *Medical Journal of Australia,* 1944, June 17, 558–560. Pp. 3

Reports previous results with lobotomy patients.

1945

No. 45 Q-scores Temperament and Delinquency. *Journal of Social Psychology*, 1945, Vol. 21, 81–103. Pp. 23

This was a follow-up study to No. 42, which introduced the qualitative scoring (*Q* score) to users of the Maze. It began with a review of previous attempts to validate tests in general, but in these efforts attention to temperamental factors in performance was conspicuously lacking. For this omission there was ample justification, namely, the difficulty of setting up adequate criteria for practical validity, a task just as onerous as devising and standardizing the mental measure itself. The Social Rating Scale represented a serious attempt to provide such an external criterion. Twenty years had elapsed since the author had first drawn attention to important differences between the Maze scores of individuals of similar mental ages.

The various steps taken to establish the scale were then outlined. The variety of samples unwittingly illustrated a process of validation long afterwards recommended by Dr. William Hunt as "wide standardization by application to different clinical and cultural groups and repeated demonstrations of reliability and validity." Following this plan, results of application of the Social Ratings Scale were given for high school students in Hawaii, delinquent boys and girls, part-Hawaiian groups, cannery workers, Filipino plantation workers, criminals, and students whose scholastic progress was considered by teachers to be unsatisfactory in relation to their mentality.

Later on, the Qualitative Score was extended, with some modifications, to Australian aborigines.

No. 46 Porteus Maze Tests: Applications in Medical and Allied Fields. *British Journal of Medical Psychology*, 1945, Vol. 20, Part 3. Pp. 4

A brief summary of various applications of the tests over a period of thirty years to Australids, Alorese, Southeast Asiatics, African Bushmen, and among Caucasians in the fields of delinquency, leucotomy, mental deficiency, vitamin deficiency, and other abnormal conditions.

No. 47 *Calabashes and Kings*. Pacific Books, Palo Alto, Calif. (1st printing), 1945, *et seq.* Pp. 261

This was the first of five printings and two editions of this book. It bore as a subtitle "An Introduction to Hawaii," and was thus primarily addressed to the visitor or new resident, but was intended to be more than a guidebook even though it describes the four main inhabited islands in turn.

Since this is a professionally slanted bibliography, the inclusion of a "popular" book may call for justification. It should be remembered that the projection of two scientific books, one with an Australian, the other with a South African setting, called for environmental pictures to help in the interpretation of the scientific results. It may well be that the author's fascination with words, apparently stimulated by his father, carried over to the Hawaiian scene, issuing in a strong desire to observe, appreciate, and describe. It was still the psychologist speaking, but not psychologizing. The book (see also Nos. 53, 54, and 57) may be considered an exercise in "sensitivity training."

1946

No. 48 Lobotomy. Contributed to *Encyclopedia of Psychology.* (Edited by Philip L. Harriman), Philosophical Library, New York, 1946, 363–369. Pp. 7

Briefly describes the recently introduced brain operation and reports degrees of improvement following psychosurgery on patients. Studies cited include those by Moniz, Freeman and Watts, Lyerly, Kisker, Schrader and Robinson, Porteus and Kepner. A brief discussion of the psychological changes effected followed.

No. 49 Porteus Maze Tests. Contributed to *Encyclopedia of Psychology.* (Edited by Philip L. Harriman), Philosophical Library, New York, 1946, 537–544. Pp. 8

Sets forth a brief history of the setting up of an (unofficial) mental clinic at Bell Street, Fitzroy in Melbourne, the first in Australia. It also relates the circumstances of the devising and application of the Porteus Maze Tests in the work of diagnosing mental defectives and their segregation in a special school.

Series of correlations of the Maze with various samples of subjects were then briefly reported, thus emphasizing its width of sensitivity. The coefficients covered industrial and social ratings of defectives, industrial training with British manual training groups, and the performance of Negro cases. Peterson and Telford, for example, found that children on the island of St. Helena, off the

South Carolina coast, yielded higher inter-test correlations for the Maze than any other performance test used. This catholic relationship of the test is explained on the grounds that planning and prehearsal enter into success in every form of mental activity. Scores of more or less primitive ethnic groups are compared.

No. 50 Primitive Mentality. Contributed to *Encyclopedia of Psychology*. (Edited by Philip L. Harriman), Philosophical Library, New York, 1946, 570–583. Pp. 14

This is a discussion of the meaning of race and its physical characteristics, with a brief review of the landmarks of evolution in human brain development, particularly of the frontal lobes. The Australid does not readily fit in with any other type; he is dark-skinned and dolichocephalic like the Negro, wavy-haired like the Caucasian and with similar blood groupings, taller than the average oriental, with marked transorbital ridges similar to those of Neanderthal man, with sufficient anatomical features to warrant Hrdlicka's statement that he probably represents "a derivative of the late glacial man of Western Asia, a remnant of an ancient stock." However, the warning is given that the term "primitive" as applied to him must not be interpreted narrowly.

Attention is also paid to Australid denial of relationship between sexual intercourse and conception, often advanced as proof of low intelligence, and the position is taken that this denial results from a conflict between common observation and the aboriginal philosophy of life, a contradiction just as obvious as some Christian beliefs, such as in the virgin birth of Christ. That common-sense values lie at the back of many Australid social regulations can be easily demonstrated. The primitive Australid is very far from being an impulsive, whim-driven individual, but on the contrary is a well-disciplined member of his own society.

1947

No. 51 Psychosurgery and Test Validity. (With H. N. Peters) *Journal of Abnormal and Social Psychology*, 1947, Vol. 42, No. 4, October. Pp. 3

Sets forth the threefold problem that confronts test devisers—what does a test measure, how well does it measure it, and what is the social significance of the traits measured? It then reviews findings of recent psychosurgical research with regard to the Maze, and discusses the temporal factor in deficits following operation, the test responses of patients classified by degree of social improvement, and specific errors such as repeated errors in the Maze.

No. 52 Maze Test Validation and Psychosurgery. (With H. N. Peters) *Genetic Psychology Monographs,* 1947, Vol. 36, 3–86. Pp. 84

This monograph reported a follow-up study to No. 43 on this same subject. Reviews briefly the validation problem as it affected the Porteus Maze and cites the inadequacy of the procedure of making this depend on correlation with the Binet.

The plan of research was to examine 55 patients who had suffered pre-frontal lobotomy and compare their pre-operative and post-operative Maze Test performances. To serve as a practise control group, we selected 55 inmates of Oahu Prison who had not been operated upon, but for whom repeated Maze applications had been recorded.

The first question was the sensitivity of the Maze to brain damage. About 80 per cent of operatees tested below their pre-operative level in at least one post-operative testing. But no clear relationship was discoverable as to predictive value. As regards ultimate improvement or recovery, actually a √ or "check-shaped" pattern of recorded level of response was characteristic of the much improved. The same individual profile was also noted by King and Landis in the Columbia-Greystone project reports, and they called it the "drop-rise" pattern. This consisted in an immediate deficit after operation, followed by a steady rise in succeeding Maze applications. Their conclusion that Maze deficits were transient was finally refuted by an eight-year follow-up study by Dr. Aaron Smith.

No. 53 *And Blow Not the Trumpet.* Pacific Books, Palo Alto, Calif., 1947. Pp. 315

This volume is an on-the-spot account of the Pearl Harbor attack, and was published to refute statements made by high Army officers before congressional committees of investigation to explain why the assault was so effective. They alleged that Hawaiian sugar plantation officials refused the Army permission to carry out maneuvers on their properties, or to set up mobile batteries to defend the fleet. The book demonstrated also the great paradox of civilian preparedness on every island compared with military unreadiness, and the psychological attitudes which brought about a relaxation of vigilance at the most crucial moment.

1948

No. 54 *The Restless Voyage.* Prentice-Hall, New York, 1948. Pp. 263
As was noted with regard to No. 47 of this bibliography, this book, though classified as fiction, may still be regarded as an exercise in sensitivity, or as some modern psychologists term it "sensitivity training," otherwise called Basic Encounter Groups, which are subject to minimum structuring and meet to discuss and criticize each other's opinions, actions which naturally engender emotional reactions.

Fundamentally, this does not differ from the role of the novelist who exercises all the empathy that he can offer in the understanding and analysis of his fictional characters. It is a sampling of human behavior in specific situations.

This book is based on a personal account of the true-life adventures of Archibald Campbell during his voyage around the world from 1806 to 1812, in the course of which he was impressed into the British Navy, deserted in China, went to Alaska, was shipwrecked there, lost his feet through freezing, stayed ten months in Hawaii, and returned to Scotland.

Campbell's own account, published in 1816, served as the framework of the book, but the rest depended on the novelist's ability to enter into the adventurer's life and mind and thus interpret his actions, an exercise in empathy and sensitivity.

The above is by way of explanation for including these items in a professional biography.

1949

No. 55 *The Restless Voyage.* (2nd edition) Reprinted 1950. Harrap & Co., London. Pp. 280

1950

No. 56 Thirty-five Years' Experience with the Porteus Maze. *Journal of Abnormal & Social Psychology,* 1950, Vol. 45, No. 2. Pp. 6

This was the context of an address given in 1949 at the University of Melbourne, where the Porteus Maze Test was originally devised and standardized. Presentation began on a note of self-gratulation that the test's author was still alive and able to assess its progress. Now, eighteen years later, the longevity of both the instrument and its maker is still satisfactory from the long-term viewpoint. Something of value must be inherent in a tool that has retained its edge for so long.

The rest of the address reviewed what was then an entirely new approach to test validation, namely, sensitivity to surgical damage to the prefrontal lobes. Such a basic consideration must be faced in relation to the validity of any measure of intelligence or aspect of intelligence, since brain damage or inadequacy is a determining factor in competent, everyday functioning.

No. 57 *The Porteus Maze Test and Intelligence.* Pacific Books, Palo Alto, Calif., 1950. Pp. 203

This volume should be classed as an extension and a new edition of *The Maze Test and Mental Differences,* 1933.

Changes in methods of application, the addition of the qualitative score, tables of test quotients, and citation of new studies had changed the character of the Maze so much that the book describing its uses became in effect a new edition, displacing the Vineland Revision in substance, if not in complete form.

DECADE 1951–1960

1951

No. 58 *Providence Ponds.* Harrap & Co., London, 1951. Pp. 272

Presenting in the form of a novel an environmental picture and a psychological study of its impress on the character, personality, and life of pioneers during their overland journey to and later establishment in the unsettled country of southeast Australia. The psychological effect of human isolation is the book's main theme.

No. 59 Recent Research on the Porteus Maze Test and Psychosurgery. *British Journal of Medical Psychology,* 1951, Vol. 24, Part 2, 132–140. Pp. 9

This is an extension and elaboration of an earlier article in the same journal (No. 46 above), setting forth medical applications of the Maze. This material is briefly reviewed, with particular reference to studies of delinquents, using the Qualitative Scoring (*Q* score). In addition, earlier works on the effects of psychosurgery are outlined.

This summary (in journal form) also presents the results of the

Columbia-Greystone projects reported from New York (Selective Partial Ablation of the Frontal Cortex, 1949, Psychosurgical Problems, etc.). The Porteus Maze was selected for these studies because of its "fundamental difference of approach." The reports of observers agree that the deficits immediately following lobotomy (leucotomy) and topectomy amount to what Freeman and Watts call "surgically induced childhood." In brief, the two Columbia-Greystone projects and the supplementary New York Brain Study support the claim of the almost unique sensitivity of the Maze to various types of frontal brain damage. The only major difference between these results and those attained earlier by me and my co-workers is that the deficits were considered transient by the Columbia-Greystone Associates, and permanent by us. My conclusion was that deficits were masked by practise effects due to the repeated application of the same Maze designs.

1952

No. 60 Revue des Etudes sur le Test des Labyrinthes de Porteus. *Revue de Psychologie Appliqueé,* 1952, Tome 2, No. 1, Paris, Janvier, 59–74. Pp. 16

A French review of recent Maze Test findings.

No. 61 *Manuel du Test des Labyrinthes de Porteus.* Centre de Psychologie Appliqueé, 1952, Paris. Pp. 60

No. 62 A Survey of Recent Results Obtained with the Porteus Maze Test. *British Journal of Educational Psychology,* 1952, Vol. 22, Part 3, November, 180–188. Pp. 9

This article was published in reply to "The Porteus Maze Test and Intelligence: A Critical Survey," J. Tizard, *British Journal of Educational Psychology,* 1951, Vol. 21, No. 3. The aim of the survey was to discuss the test's advantages and disadvantages, its reliability and validity, and the new qualitative scoring. The usefulness of the Maze, both in America and Britain, was acknowledged and its adoption by both Burt and Arthur was noted, as was also a modification of procedure by Vernon.

The chief objection advanced against the test was its low test-retest reliability. The present writer has pointed out that this coefficient is merely a measure of uniformity or consistency of scores and that it does not apply to a test which purports to measure the opposite tendency, namely, capacity to improve with experience, or to make adjustments of response within the framework of the test itself. Absolute identity of performance in successive applications would destroy its value as a measure of on-going adaptability. To provide such an index was the reason for the provision of a limited number of repeated trials in the designs where errors were made. This criticism has appeared again and again since 1929 when Mackie in Australia first reported a low test-retest "reliability." It was unfortunate that these critics mistook the nature and purposes of the Maze. A perfect reliability (so-called) of a test-retest of 1.00 would destroy its value completely. The fact that changes always appeared in the same direction and thus indicated a practise effect (improvement) was overlooked entirely.

Criticism of the validity of the test as demonstrated by psychosurgical studies was voiced on the grounds that reports by other investigators were not wholly consistent with American results. Quoting Crown, Tizard cites Strom-Olsen et al., who found only insignificant changes after brain operations (they appeared to have only 11 subjects), and also by Jones when the latter's sample had an initial average at or about the floor of the test, so that any changes in score could only be upward. To term these studies "among the most important investigations" was extraordinary.

Nevertheless, Tizard winds up his article by saying, "In spite of these criticisms the writer is impressed with the figures given by Porteus showing the test's validity as a measure of intelligence and of qualities of behavior."

In concluding his reply to Tizard, the author declared, "I have never thought the Maze could stand alone in the evaluation of intelligence. In other words, it is a supplement, but a necessary supplement, to other mental measurements."

No. 63 *The Porteus Maze Test Manual.* Harrap & Co., London, 1952. Pp. 64

A brief guidebook for British users of the Maze.

No. 64 *Het Dorre Land.* Uitgeverij Het Kompan N.V., Antwerp, 1952. Pp. 320

A Dutch translation of No. 58 above. The fact that the Dutch had been for centuries one of the great colonizing nations may help to account for their interest.

1953

No. 65 Statutory Definitions of Feeblemindedness in U.S.A. (With Judge Gerald R. Corbett) *Journal of Psychology,* 1953, Vol. 35, 81–105. Pp. 25

Reviews accepted definitions of mental defectives back to the time of Edward I, the feebleminded person being then described as "a born fool," the psychotic (lunatick) as one who "at birth hath had understanding, but by disease, grief or other accident hath lost the use of his reason."

After setting forth the background of legal interest in the subject and the confusion of ideas notable in different American states, the authors suggest as a legal definition, "Feebleminded persons are those who by reason of permanently retarded or arrested mental development existing from an early age are incapable of independent self-management and self-support."

This, it will be noted, is an industrial, social, and mental definition combined. Suggestions are made for methods of diagnosis, commitment, expert examining, certification, and discharge.

1954

No. 66 Maze Test Qualitative Aspects. *British Journal of Medical Psychology,* 1954, Vol. 27, Parts 1 & 2, 72–79. Pp. 8

This reported ten years' experience with the Maze *Q* scores, based on poor quality of performance, first described in 1942 and applied to delinquent and non-delinquent groups, and prison inmates. Scores ranged from 22 to 25 points of error scores in non-delinquents to 57 points in the adult criminal group.

Reviews of the work of Catherine Wright in California, Grajales in New York, Docter and Winder (a repetition of Wright's California study), Jensen at Lackland Air Force Base in Texas, Porteus in Hawaii, and Fooks and Thomas in Connecticut brought to light a quite remarkable agreement of *Q* scores among delinquent groups, ranging from 40 to 49 error points.

The article also reports a modification of the qualitative scoring as applied by Foulds to types of psychoneurotic patients. Psychopaths and hysterics exhibited characteristic performances as distinct from those with anxiety states, reactive depression, and obsessionals. These findings indicate that quite apart from overt delinquency, qualitative scores should be interpreted as indices of socio-industrial trainability of patients.

No. 67 *P oceedings of Third Research Conference on Psychosurgery*. U.S. Department of Health, Education, and Welfare, Government Printing Office, Washington, D.C., 1954, 106–109. Pp. 4

This assemblage, mainly of medical experts and psychologists, discussed post-operative results of lobotomy and topectomy. The present writer in his paper on "Psychological Testing and the Definition of Intelligence" upheld the view that practise effects masked mental deficits when the same test was repeated. The aspects or components of intelligence measured by the Maze underlie planning, in which mental prehearsal is an essential process. Psychosurgery provides evidence for test validity, which has hitherto not been available to psychologists. Dr. Carney Landis followed with a statement that the Columbia-Greystone Projects "confirmed his (Porteus') finding that a brain operation on the frontal lobes gives rise to an immediate post-operative loss in mental age of 1 to 2 years in some 80 per cent of psychosurgery patients." He went on to say that none of the other tests of intelligence or of intellectual function gave any systematic evidence of interference with performance, with the exception of the Porteus Maze Test.

1955

No. 68 *The Maze Test: Recent Advances.* Pacific Books, Palo Alto, Calif., 1955. Pp. 72

The necessity, for research purposes, of the repeated application of the Maze to psychosurgical cases suggested the provision of a new form of the test, standardized and controlled as regards practise so as to yield scores equivalent to the original or Vineland form. Using in part a mirror reproduction of the designs and adding to the length of pathways, the writer put forth a new series, which was called the "Porteus Maze Extension."

Using as *S*s tenth-grade high school students in three Honolulu high schools, the Extension series was applied to 300 students. There was only .02 of a year difference in test age between the original and Extension series. As regards qualitative scores, the two forms or series of the Maze yielded almost identical results.

Thus it was evident that the Extension series was made just difficult enough to balance any practise effects, so that it would be possible therefore to use the Extension series whenever a practise-controlled testing, involving a repetition of the Maze, was desirable.

1955

No. 69 *Il Test dei Labirinti: Recenti Progressi*. Organizzazioni Speciali, Firenze, Italy, 1955. Pp. 81

Italian translation of No. 68 by Dr. F. Ferracuti.

No. 70 Give Them the Tools. (Reprint of series of articles.) *Honolulu Advertiser,* January, February, 1955. Pp. 27

A series of five articles dealing with Honolulu's responsibilities for the mentally retarded, the delinquent, the criminal, and the psychotic. At that time the care of all of these and the institutions which housed and trained them were vested in the Department of Institutions. The legislature then divided these responsibilities and regrouped this authority, probably a backward step for a small community. These articles showed the advantages of a unified attack on these social problems.

No. 71 Some Commonsense Implications of Psychosurgery. *British Journal of Medical Psychology,* 1955, Vol. 28, Parts 2 & 3, 167–176. Pp. 10

This article attempted to reconcile differences in neurological theories, which resulted from new information that has accrued as a result of psychosurgical approaches. Foremost among these changes is the clarification of the role of the frontal lobes, which had been challenged by workers such as Lashley and Franz, whose findings with sub-human species supported the notion of equipotentiality of all parts of the cortex. On the other hand, experiments by Fulton and Jacobsen with chimpanzees, and with humans by Freeman and Watts indicated that planning capacity was mediated by the frontal lobes. However, Carney Landis and his associates, King, Zubin, etc., on the basis of the Columbia-Greystone projects, disputed the traditional pre-eminence of the fore-brain. Yet the whole story of development of the frontal regions seemed to demonstrate orderly progression of mental ability correlated with frontal brain growth.

The evidence as to frontal lobe functioning is then reviewed by citing the mental test changes observable after operation. Maze test declines are apparent after lobotomy, topectomy, venous ligation, thermo-coagulation of area 9, and thalamotomy, with, on the whole, much more marked defects of superior as against inferior cortical ablations. Transient versus permanent changes are discussed.

Maze performance in operatees is often marked by good performance in the easier designs but rather sudden loss of efficiency when the more complex designs are introduced, a phenomenon called "shattering" by Brundage. A tendency to repeat the same errors is also noted. This led to the theoretical formulation of multi-local coordinated functioning, though not amounting to equipotentiality. For example, simpler spatial discrimination involved in Maze performance appears to be centered in the temporo-parietal region, but with a shift in the mediating centers to the frontal lobes when more complex choices in planning have to be made.

Also, the nearer the brain injury comes to the precentral cortex and its pathways, the more serious the mental disability becomes. This observation led to the formulation of a principle of "centroid neurobiotaxis." The dethronement of the sense of smell as a dominant distant receptor led to displacement of the olfactory centers from their centrally situated position. This moves the temporo-parietal cortex into close relationship with the human learning processes.

There followed an exposition of the idea that brain fissuring brought the depths of each sulcus nearer the centroid pathways of body-brain communication. The suggestion that fissuring of the gray matter had little to do with enlarging the space for nerve cells was a novel theorization. The whole subject was then briefly reviewed.

More space has been allotted to this discussion on the grounds that, in general, psychologists are not concerned as much with medical psychology as they should be.

No. 72 Los desenvolvimientos del Test de Laberintos de Porteus. *Revista de Psicología General y Aplicada,* 1955, Vol. 11, No. 37. Pp. 16

Spanish review of Maze Test uses.

No. 73 Recent Advances in the Porteus Maze Test. *Proceedings, International Association of Applied Psychology,* London, July 1955, 130. P. 1

This paper briefly summarized major changes that have taken place, mainly in the direction of the addition of the qualitative scoring for application to delinquents. Studies by Wright, Grajales, Docter and Jensen were cited as confirming the usefulness of this approach.

The latest addition was the Extension Series, which controlled practice effects when a second application of the scale was advisable.

Also noted were demonstrations by Porteus and Kepner, Porteus and Peters, Columbia-Greystone Associates' Projects 1 and 2, and the New York Brain Study, which all confirmed the finding that "the only test which showed a uniform or almost uniform loss was the Porteus Maze" (Carney Landis).

1956

No. 74 Porteus Maze Test Developments. *Perceptual and Motor Skills,* 1956, Vol. 6, 135–142. Pp. 8

This article repeated the substance of the paper delivered at the University of London, the abstract of which is given in No. 73 above. The topic of prehearsal or anticipatory reactions as part of the planning process was expanded. It was stated that muscular prehearsal took place with appropriate innervation when any physical activity, such as looking at the ceiling, was contemplated. Thus the role of prehearsal in all anticipatory reactions was apparent.

The validity of the Maze as a test of planning has been shown by extensive examinations of mental defectives at Vineland, but these proofs were naturally indirect since deficits in test performance were only assumed to be due to inferior mental development. The more recent work in psychosurgery has indicated a "before-and-after" causal relationship between brain damage and Maze Test responses. These findings were reviewed in detail.

The work done by Milton Jensen at Lackland Air Force Base showed that the approach to practical intelligence and its measurement was necessary for selection of candidates for Air Force training. A follow-up of trainees showed that many men who had normal scores in the Maze Test but failed the 6½-hour Qualifying Test succeeded in completing the basic training course. Seventy-two per cent of these retested cases were rated satisfactory as against 83 per cent who passed the Qualifying examination. The Extension Series was also described and recommended for use to control practice effects. Jensen's work was important as showing the relation of Maze scores to industrial efficiency among normal males.

No. 75 Variations Specifiques du Comportement sous L'Effet de la Chlorpromazine. *Revue de Psychologie Appliqueé,* Paris, 1956, Vol. 6, No. 3, Juillet, 187–202. Pp. 16

This paper, first published in France in 1956, represented the writer's incursion into the field of drug administration. Medication amounting to 300 mg. chlorpromazine was administered daily for six weeks to chronic psychotic patients located in two wards of the state mental hospital in Kaneohe, Oahu, 16 miles from the University of Hawaii. In order to measure the effects of the drug, a simple ward behavior scale was arranged for application by psychiatric aides trained in its use. The eleven behavior traits to be rated were: aggressiveness, negativism, speech disorders, untidiness, restlessness, hallucinations, delusions, over-emotionalism, mental confusion, asocialization, and impulsiveness. Patients were rated graphically along 6-inch lines, ranging from non-appearance to excessive or extremely exaggerated behavior. Patients on one ward received chlorpromazine, the others placebos under a double-blind procedure.

In all eleven traits, modification of the degree of appearance was observable among the experimental group. The exception was the negative trait of "asocialization," which improved. The most striking changes were effected in hallucinations and delusional behavior, the common pattern being marked by erratic changes during the first six weeks and a sudden continued drop in severity to extinction in the next 6 to 12 weeks in many cases after medication. Apparently 6 weeks is the critical period for improved or changed behavior. Besides group averages, graphs of individual changes were also presented.

1957

No. 76 Maze Test Reactions After Chlorpromazine. *Journal of Consulting Psychology,* 1957, Vol. 21, No. 1, 15–21. Pp. 7

During the study No. 75 reported above, unexpected changes in Maze Test performances appeared among the experimental group of patients. Because its members were classified as chronic patients, many of whom had been resident for many years in two "closed" wards, only 13 of 50 inmates were susceptible to meaningful testing. Later the group was augmented to include 22 cases. Though many of these had derived therapeutic benefits from chlorpromazine treatment, there was a mean loss of 2.08 years in Maze performances. Sixty-eight per cent of the drug patients declined in scores. To some degree, therefore, chlorpromazine has effects which resemble those that follow lobotomy.

It was noted also that some investigators have found evidence that the site of action of chlorpromazine is in either the reticular system of the brain stem or the hypothalamus. Also, one initial effect of the drug is drowsiness and dulling of emotional sensitivity, psychological changes also apparent after lobotomy. Suggestions for further exploration of social adjustment after chlorpromazine treatment are indicated.

No. 77 Specific Behavior Changes Following Chlorpromazine. *Journal of Consulting Psychology,* 1957, Vol. 21, No. 3, 257–263. Pp. 7

This is a follow-up presentation of results reported in the French journal (No. 75 above). The general conclusion was that the control group, who had taken only placebos during a four-month period, 5.5 per cent changed for the worse while 11.3 per cent improved. Of the chlorpromazine treated group, 4 per cent were worse, 60 per cent showed significant improvement. Improved social adjustment, either post-operative or post-drug, associated with Maze Test deficits after treatment suggested a paradox, foreshadowing analysis of the test problem at a later date.

No. 78 A Further Note on Chlorpromazine: Maze Reactions. (With John E. Barclay) *Journal of Consulting Psychology,* 1957, Vol. 21, No. 4, 297–299. Pp. 3

This very brief article contains some important information as to the effect of a commonly used tranquilizing drug on Maze Test performance when medication was extended up to a six-months' period. As before, the post-medication testing was by means of the Extension Series so as to avoid practise effects. The availability of a control group also offered an opportunity to compare Original and Extension Series scores to ensure that any drop in the Maze was not due to the greater difficulty of the Extension Series.

In addition, two groups of subjects, paired on the basis of having identical Maze Test ages prior to the experiment, were compared. The mean score of the experimental group (*N* 20) was 11.85 on the original Maze premedication testing, falling to 9.65 years after chlorpromazine, a loss of 2.10 years when the Extension Series was applied. However, the control group (*N* 20) rose only from 11.85 years to 12.05 years, or a practice gain of 0.2 years. Thus when no drug was administered, improvement to a negligible extent, or near-equivalence, was shown by the control group against a marked decline for the drug cases.

Whether the deficits were transitory or permanent could not be determined.

1958

No. 79 What do the Maze Tests Measure? *Australian Journal of Psychology,* 1958, Vol. 10, No. 3, 245–256. Pp. 12

This was the content of a paper delivered in September, 1957, at a symposium on the Porteus Maze Test at the American Psychological Association meetings, with Richard F. Docter, chairman, S. D. Porteus, Milton B. Jensen, and Henry N. Peters, participants; Carney Landis and J. P. Guilford were discussants.

The data presented constitute a review of the most relevant studies undertaken in the twenty years prior to 1958. It includes those that seemed to indicate most clearly what the Maze Test measures. It then discusses the information accumulated through various approaches, such as frontal lobe damage, vitamin B deficiency, ataractic drugs, studies of delinquent personalities, relationship to planning capacity among primitive peoples, temporal lobe surgery, etc.

The important question as to what kind of active social adaptation is measured by the Maze is also considered, with the conclusion that it is not only "imperturbable good nature with rather blunted sensitivities that enables an individual to get along with people," but something much more dynamic and initiatory in nature. The lobotomized or the tranquilized, the vitamin deficient or the non-competitive passive personality may exhibit tolerant, non-aggressive behavior along with a very moderate or low Maze Test level.

Intelligence is defined as capacity to make planned responses to a wide range of relevant stimuli, with the proviso that the determination of relevancy is an individual matter with which the psychologist is not primarily concerned. These matters belong with religion, ethics, and morality rather than with psychology.

The writer suggests that the paper reflects his own philosophy.

1959

No. 80 *The Maze Test and Clinical Psychology.* Pacific Books, Palo Alto, Calif., 1959. Pp. 205

The 1950 volume entitled *The Porteus Maze Test and Intelligence* was intended to fill the seventeen-year time gap from 1933. But so much developmental and critical experimentation followed in the succeeding decade that it seemed advisable to bring research findings up to date. An important feature of the earlier presentation had been the demonstration of the extraordinary catholicity of relationship that existed between the Maze and a great variety of other measures. This evidence had been presented by a considerable number of investigators and was put forward by the present writer as indirect proof of the test's validity. This was a reversal of the principle of guilt by association, which can be expressed as validation (or respectability) by width of relationship with other tests.

The catholic nature of this association was shown by many published studies, none of which was carried out by the author of the test. The extraordinary range of coefficients can be judged by the following findings: Maze with Stanford-Binet .75 (Worthington, 1926); .54 (males), .68 (females) (Louttit and Stackman, 1936); .59 (Weisenberg, Roe, and McBride, 1936); .47 (Earle, 1931); .54 (Morgenthau, 1922); .52 (Gaw, 1925); Maze with Healy Picture Completion .70 (Morgenthau, 1922); with Spearman *g* .57; with Printed Analogies .62 (Weisenberg, et al., 1936). Even more extraordinary were the coefficients found with extremely dissimilar measures, such as Alpha Reading .70 and Healy Picture Completion .70 (Morgenthau), Goodenough Drawing .53 and Digit Symbol .51 (Peterson and Telford, 1928), Gates Spelling .41 (Weisenberg, et al., 1936).

Besides listing such strange connections, these arrays of correlations clearly demonstrated that as McGeoch has described it, the correlation technique is indeed "slippery," the size of the coefficient being largely affected by the nature of the experimental sampling. Hence the evidence of validity must be supplemented, and this was presented in the 1959 volume.

In 1950 the evidence was not all in, since the Columbia-Greystone findings were not complete at that time, nor indeed was the practice-free or practice-controlled form of the Maze available until 1955, while Smith's eight-year follow-up investigation of the New York Brain Study was not reported until 1959.

The new volume also presented a peculiar phenomenon that could be the basis for a new usage of the test, namely, as a projective-expressive measure. This discovery announced the fact that in about 90 per cent of cases an individual's record, if the test were repeated within a brief period of time, could be recognized without any identifying data, such as his name. The two performances could be correctly paired by an analysis of his distinctive patterns of response, such as point of beginning and ending the test and the type of turns he made in drawing through the Maze design. The extent to which a subject is stimulus-bound and response-limited, or on the other hand is extremely variable in his reactions, can be determined.

This discovery that each person's style of doing a job, in this case threading a maze design, was just as overloaded with distinctive responses as is his conversation with gestures, or that his signature is recognizable as peculiarly his own, I called a projective phenomenon, mainly because the subject is completely unaware that he had betrayed his authorship almost as clearly as does an artist when he adds his signature to his painting. But whether this almost unbreakable mental set, this self-limitation of variability was a species of self-betrayal that might provide a key to his character or personality was not clearly apparent. The interesting point to a psychologist was not merely that the great majority of people are "compulsive" in this way, but rather that a small minority *are not so*. These deviates should be worth intensive study. The writer was so impressed with the need for extensive research into the relation of Conformity-Flexibility (C-F) scores that he labelled this account "unfinished business." The effects of intelligence, age, sex, race, crime, delinquency, etc. have not yet been studied.

No. 81 Research with Feebleminded. (With Edward T. Ching, M.D.) *Hawaii Medical Record,* 1959, Vol. 18, May–June, 491–493. Pp. 3

This brief paper signalized the closing of an episode—the writer's interest in the behavioral effects of tranquilizing drugs, particularly chlorpromazine. Up to this point his research had concerned only psychotic patients as outlined in Nos. 75, 76, 77, and 78 of this bibliography.

Reports by other investigators revealed that ataractic drugs when used with mental defectives brought about a ten-point rise in IQ scores if the measurement of ability was made by verbal tests of general intelligence (so-called). The investigators reported that the usual side-effects of drowsiness and decreased mental alertness were evident.

In this experiment the authors tested 20 defectives before and after six weeks' medication with thorazine in daily doses of 100 mg. Little change in general behavior was apparent, though drowsiness and inertia were reported in certain individuals noted for aggressiveness; a decided improvement as regards belligerence and resistance to authority was also observable. As one very pugnacious boy put it, "I lose fight."

As was the case with adult psychotic patients, there was a decrease in mental alertness, vigilance, initiative, and planning, as shown by decline in Maze scores. Social relaxation in institution relationships was, however, furthered, but whether this would extend to community adjustments should these boys be paroled was a matter of doubt. The social improvement was due to loss of tension and greater passivity or indifference to the activities of others.

No. 82 Recent Maze Test Studies. *British Journal of Medical Psychology,* 1959, Vol. 32, Part 1, 38–43. Pp. 6

The closer orientation of clinical psychology in regard to medical theory and practice was reflected in published articles at this time. The follow-up study by Smith (1958) of patients still available for examination eight years after they had suffered topectomy of various frontal areas provided an opportunity to judge whether or not the brain deficits were transitory or permanent. The project concerned was the New York Brain Study, which was the last of the Columbia-Greystone Projects. Smith's important paper was entitled "Changes in Porteus Maze Scores of Brain-Operated Schizophrenics After an Eight-Year Interval." Smith stated that all three of these projects showed definite deficits—1.21 years in the first, 1.5 years in the second, and 2.21 years in the third—while control groups all showed practice gains. In the second project the more caudal the site of the topectomy, the greater the Maze deficits. Superior cortical ablations brought a loss of 2.88 years as against 1.43 years when an inferior or more orbital site was selected for operation.

There were no comparable deficits in any other tests, although four Wechsler-Bellevue subtests indicated a lessened ability to improve with practice, but there were no significant declines, thus demonstrating a unique sensitivity to brain damage evinced by the Porteus Maze.

At the time of Smith's study 27 of the original patients and 33 controls were still available. Sixteen out of seventeen patients (94 per cent) then showed declines, with a mean Maze deficit of 3.88 years or 28 points of test quotient. Smith summarized these results by commenting: "The unique nature of the Porteus Maze Test and its greater sensitivity in discriminating the operatees . . . is shown by comparison with the 11 subtests of the Wechsler-Bellevue, the Capps Homograph and Weigl Sorting test." Smith also demonstrated that the deficits after operation, which were formerly considered temporary, are actually permanent and increase with age.

This article also emphasizes the effects of other than frontal operations. It cites a study by Brown, French, Ogle, and Jahnson, which showed a decrease of 24 Maze test quotient points after temporal lobe ablations, and further states that neither pre- nor post-operatively did these patients consistently give other test evidence of the kinds of intellectual deficit traditionally associated with organic brain damage. Such insensitivity is extraordinary in view of the claims commonly made that the conventional tests, which like the W.A.I.S. are part of the clinical psychologist's repertoire, reflect brain damage. This point is underlined here on account of the failure of clinical psychologists to keep up with medical or surgical findings. The results of chlorpromazine are also briefly reviewed, together with indications that the reticular formation of the mid-brain mediates the kind of vigilance measured in part by the Maze.

The new procedure for observing the self-consistency of Maze performance on repeated applications is also described, and the possibility of quantifying items of similarity or identity for use in the study of personality is discussed.

No. 83 The Porteus Maze: Supplement Series. Psychological Corporation, New York, 1959. Pp. 12

The advisability of providing three forms of the Maze—the Original, the Extension and now the Supplement—was recognized, although the necessity of using the tests in repeated applications has diminished with the almost complete discontinuance of psychosurgery in America. Nevertheless, a second practise-controlled series would still be useful in longitudinal studies of individuals.

In this booklet the history of the development of the three forms is briefly recounted. In this most recent study, 508 *S*s, all of whom were tenth-grade students at an intermediate high school in Honolulu, were examined by the Extension and the Supplement. The mean Extension score of all cases was 15.599 years, the Supplement mean being 15.6, a difference of only .001 of a year. Thus in cases re-examined after prior application of the Extension series, identical mean scores by the Supplement are obtainable. When *S*s were divided by sex, males, as is usually the case, had a slight advantage in mean scores in both the Extension and the Supplement series.

As regards qualitative error scores, this advantage was reversed in favor of females, the average for females being 28.94 Q-score points as against 31.1 points for males. (In the case of Q scores, the lower the error score, the better the performance.)

Though the *S*s were all supposed to be non-delinquent, questioning by the examiner brought many admissions of having had troubles with the police, the complaints being mainly minor bicycle traffic offences. These 48 self-admitted mild delinquents had an average Q score of 43.6. If these cases are omitted, the mean score of the remainder fell 15.5 points to 28.1 error points, close to the normal non-delinquent average. Designs of the Supplement series were then illustrated.

1960

No. 84 Measurement of Subconscious Memory. (With J. E. Barclay, H. S. Culver, and J. P. Kleman) *Perceptual and Motor Skills, Monograph Supplement,* 1960, 2, V10, 215–229. Pp. 15

The foregoing represents a complete departure from the ordinary usage of the Porteus Maze and hence does not belong in the field of mental testing but rather among projective devices (see also No. 80). The process of identification of a repeated performance of the XI-year test has already been described, and as this lies outside the range of rules or regulations governing execution, there is no correct or incorrect achievement. Hence, it is not a test at all but could be termed the scoring of a subconscious tendency based on comparison of two performances of the same design with an intervening interval of time. To the extent that similarities or consistencies can be quantified after a temporal gap, the score may be termed a measurement of subconscious repetition or memory. It has also been called a Conformity-Flexibility (C-F) score. *S* is so engrossed in the task of finding his way through the Maze that he is quite oblivious to the fact that he is demonstrating his characteristic style of attacking a motor-intellectual problem.

At first the major portions of the individual's repeated performances were compared in the endeavor to match and identify each double performance or pair of efforts. Then it was discovered that this extensive comparison was unnecessary. In all but 10 per cent of cases, correct pairing could be achieved on the basis of examination of the beginnings and endings exhibited in a single XI-year maze design. Generally speaking, the tracing or rather the threading of the maze was more easily paired if *S* employed careful right-angled turns throughout the design. Quite probably this type of response is characteristic of the readily conforming, almost compulsive individual. But it must be remembered that regardless of specific instructions, the type of performance exhibited is imposed from within. These individuals tend to set up self-standards of excellence of performance. Conscientious secretaries, careful housewives, meticulous or systematic performers in many fields probably fall into this category.

The method of assigning scores on the basis of similarities or consistencies of patterns of response is described and illustrated in this article, but the senior author has been concerned only with demonstrating the phenomenon rather than in elucidating its meaning in social terms. No attempt has been made to assign values to various types of performance other than to place individuals into the most grossly determined categories, such as over-consistent (meticulous), as compared with haphazard, or non-conforming performances.

Interpretation was left up in the air, so to speak, because of the realization that this new approach might easily open up years of research, obviously impossible to the senior author, so senior in fact that no more than the vaguest suggestions for further research are forthcoming. However, the suggestion made elsewhere was repeated—namely, that intensive study of those who deviate from the usual patterns of behavior might bring the most interesting reactions.

No. 85 Memoria Sub-conscia e sua Mesurazione. *Bollettino di Psicologia Applicata*. Firenze, Italy, February, 1960. Pp. 10

Italian translation of No. 84 above.

No. 86 La Memoire Subconsciente et sa Mesure. *Revue de Psychologie Appliqueè,* 1960, Vol. 10, 3, Paris. Pp. 12

French translation of No. 84 above.

No. 87 Mental Changes in Psychopharmacology. Chapter 21 in Uhr and Miller, *Drugs and Behavior,* John Wiley & Sons, N.Y., 1960. Pp. 3

Describes briefly the experimental work with drugs as previously listed in Nos. 75, 76, 77, and 78 of this bibliography. It was stated on the basis of this experience that the setting up of control groups within a mental hospital setting is inadequate unless the two groups can be equated on the basis of suggestibility. At present the means for doing this are not available. Sudden fluctuations in behavior occur and change ratings of ward behavior. It is also most important to train psychiatric personnel in the giving of behavior ratings. If at all possible, special research wards should be set up; otherwise it is difficult to ensure conformity of treatment, proper medication, continued supervision and control. Knowledge of research methods is usually lacking in psychiatric personnel. The double-blind procedure is rarely effective, especially when the treatment involves easily observable side effects, and thus distinguishes the experimental group.

No. 88 A New Anthropometric Approach. (With J. P. Kleman) *The Mankind Quarterly* (Edinburgh), 1960, Vol. 1, No. 1, 23–30. Pp. 8

The use and possible value of Conformity-Flexibility (C-F) scores are discussed as new approaches to the study of personality. Since the method is largely unaffected by education, economic status, is completely non-verbal, and as far as the subject's unawareness that he is exhibiting his characteristic style of response is concerned, the process is subconscious. Apparently differences in performance by race and sex are real, though what their significance is has not yet been determined. Racial differences, with Australian aboriginals as *S*s, are shortly to be studied. The C-F scoring system is described and illustrated.

DECADE 1961–1970

1961

No. 89 Ethnic Group Differences. *The Mankind Quarterly* (Edinburgh), 1961, Vol. 1, No. 3, 187–200. Pp. 14

This article sets forth the situation with regard to science and scientists and the study of racial differences. The Hitlerian aftermath brought about such a contrary reaction that for a time the climate for investigation of racial differences was most unfavorable, nor was this situation helped by the fact that many of the tests employed to measure individual differences were culturally overloaded. This was true not only of language tests, but also of performance tests, so-called. Because of these and other factors, the opportunity offered to psychologists to examine the mentality of primitive peoples was grossly neglected. With regard to Australids, it was almost too late. In Australia and Africa the difficulties in the way of obtaining adequate samples of Australian aboriginals or Bushmen are tremendous.

As a compensating circumstance, the Maze Test was accepted eagerly by both ethnic groups after contact was established. Obtaining adequate samples of these populations remained a problem, but its difficulty was at least not compounded by disinterest or outright rejection of the psychological measures. Australid acceptance was perhaps assisted by their habit of incising patterns on various objects which were in principle not unlike the Maze designs. As for other primitive groups, such as Bushmen in the Kalahari, jungle tribes of India, forest people in Malaysia, etc., they looked upon maze-threading as an absorbing game, which provided a worth-while challenge to their ability.

Once the examiners realized the necessity of a degree of fore-practise, these *S*s in many cases attained a very remarkable level and spread of scores. The individual range of performance overlaps completely with that of whites, a rather striking proof of test validity. To offset the handicap of unfamiliarity with the type of endeavor there could be placed the fact that no less than three Maze series, yielding equivalent scores, were now available, thus ensuring a more adequate index of individual ability.

The racial psychologist, now being freed from the objectionable label of *racist*, could also add to his Maze Test repertoire the new qualitative scoring, still applicable, even if more difficult of interpretation because of *S*s's inexperience with paper and pencil. Any aboriginal workman in his own culture may differ from his fellows in neatness, fidelity to self-standards of excellence, carefulness to be exercised in the constant matching of form in relation to function. The savage artisan could not be more meticulous in fashioning spear, spear thrower, or boomerang, since any marked deviation from his plan would make the tool or weapon ineffective.

The recent provision of measures of conformity or flexibility may serve to emphasize differences in personality as well as in mental traits, though this approach must await further research in order to make meaningful judgment-values possible.

The paper ends with tables of Q scores, test ages, and C-F scores for Japanese, Chinese, and part-Hawaiian ethnic groups.

1961

No. 90 Measurement of Psychomotor Perserverative Tendencies. (With A. L. Diamond) *Nature* (England), 1961, Vol. 189, No. 4765, 691–692. Pp. 2

The new Conformity-Flexibility scores obtained from repeated XI-year maze design performances are discussed and a method of scoring deviations is suggested, using IBM marked-sense cards. If this approach is feasible, then the comparison of individuals and groups will be possible.

1962

No. 91 The Will to Live. *The Mankind Quarterly* (Edinburgh), 1962, Vol. 3, No. 1. Pp. 16

This publication represents a revival or continuance of interest on the part of the writer in the subject of Australid mentality, after a gap of 33 years. While associated with the University of Adelaide in 1962 he was able to revisit Central Australia and arrange for Dr. James A. Gregor to carry on further investigations among natives of the Wailbri, Pintubi, and Arunta (Aranda) tribes.

As an introduction to this research, the writer attempted to summarize briefly previous work of this nature and at the same time to present a verbal picture of the Central Australian environment in order to acquaint the reader with the difficulties of survival that are imposed on the inhabitants who are to be the subjects of study.

Dr. Gregor's research involved the application of the three series of Maze Tests, the Original, the Extension, and the Supplement, amounting in some cases to a three-hour intensive examination. The following description illustrates the isolated situation of these primitive *S*s.

On the journey north from Adelaide and Port Augusta, the railroad passes through almost a thousand miles of extremely arid country, which for the most part is featureless except for bare brown hills and dry streambeds, their courses outlined with thinly spaced eucalypts. On either side of Alice Springs the desert surface is broken by weird mountain ranges strangely sculptured by wind and water, the vegetation consisting of mulga bushes, desert oaks, and "ghost gums," wherever there is underground moisture.

Under such circumstances the Australids have carried on for

thousands of years a grim struggle for existence, making use of every possible item of food that the near-desert affords. Nomadism is a way of life imposed on these people, and their social regulations, including old man domination and marriage restrictions, are geared to an environment that is one of the harshest on earth. An environmental comparison with the Bushmen of the Kalahari favored the latter.

Incisions in the bark of eucalyptus trees making up patterns of parallel lines are shown side by side with one of the simple maze designs, indicating that the test is not in principle completely unfamiliar to the Australids.

A qualitative scoring (Q score) is also usable with Australid *S*s, but it is emphasized that the Test Age is derived in a completely different manner from the Q score, the one being an index of caution and foresight to be exercised within the structure of the test itself, whereas the latter is an error score based on quite the reverse attributes of disregard for instructions, carelessness, or disorderliness in approach to a task. The one trait that brings about both a low mental age and a high Q score is impulsivity. A further distinction is drawn between what may be termed proximate and distant foresight, the first being more immediately perceptual in operation, the second when decisions are deferred and thus are more conceptual in operation. This latter approach allows for temporal intervention, when choice is delayed until all factors can be duly considered. With primitive people, everyday foresight is mainly immediate. Whether to stay or move on, to hunt or rest, to explore this or that locality in the daily harvesting of food are decisions dependent on the present situation and rarely reflect conditions a month or a year ahead. With civilization comes the extension of foresight, involving moral purposes intended to advance social as well as individual welfare.

No. 92 Maze Test Reports. *Perceptual and Motor Skills,* 1962, Vol. 14, No. 58. Pp. 1

A study of an experimental and a control group (*N* 24) of mental defectives involving the repetition of the Maze design for Year XI and a comparison of their Conformity-Flexibility (C-F) scores was undertaken. The interval of time between the first and second applications was two months, during which period *S*s in the experimental group had been given daily dosages of 150 mg. chlorpromazine.

The controls had a mean loss of 3.75 C-F points, indicating increased variability due to the fading of subconscious memory of responses to the earlier application. With the drug cases, however, there was a reverse tendency, shown by a gain of 1.36 points in the direction of increased conformity. Apparently the drug strengthens the set patterns of behavior. This may be interpreted as a trend toward fuller acceptance and adoption of social standards.

In contrast to defectives, Chinese female high school students had higher conformity scores than males. On the other hand, part-Hawaiian females were less rigid as regards (social) conformity standards than were males.

This study also notes that Loranger and Misiak (1960) found that in 50 selected women between 74 and 80 years of age, resident in retirement home conditions, the Maze Test indicated greater resistance to age impairments than any other tests used, 16 per cent of *S*s reaching the 15-year level. Moreover, the Maze discriminated female performance much better than did any of the other standard tests applied.

1962

No. 93 Porteus Maze Changes After Psychosurgery. (With A. L. Diamond) *Journal of Mental Science* (England), 1962, Vol. 108, No. 452, 53–58. Pp. 6

The almost complete displacement by tranquilizing drugs of psychosurgery as a therapeutic measure made it advisable to summarize its results before those results were forgotten.

The indifference shown by psychologists to psychosurgical findings has been frequently noted and is understandable since therapy with regard to psychotic patterns is the prime concern of psychiatrists, not psychologists. But psychological measures are being used and may continue to be employed so long as there is any need to classify individuals on the basis of mental or personality levels. This article suggests that Aaron Smith's 1960 investigation of the effects of topectomy might very well be the last word on the subject.

Smith's study showed that statistically significant changes occurred after frontal lobe operations in the Porteus Mazes and seven other measures and that these deficiencies were permanent. After reviewing the Columbia-Greystone findings as well as the New York Brain Study, Smith segregated patients according to age, a younger group with a mean of 42 years and an older group aged

59 years. According to him, the Porteus Maze scores were "unexpectedly definitive." Of four aggregate scales and fourteen individual tests applied to patients still available, the Maze "was the most sensitive indicator of early and long term post-operative change." He also divided his cases according to the site of operation, superior or orbital.

Between the last pre-operative and the latest post-operative Maze averages there was a deficit of 4.74 years, but the loss *was greater for the younger than the older subjects,* indicating that the deficiency was not to be ascribed to age impairment. The orbital operations caused a lesser deficit, with 3 of the older patients showing the most marked decline.

The factor of advancing age and its effects on test results was investigated, as previously mentioned, by Loranger and Misiak, their subjects being 50 women selected from 140 in eight different homes for the aged, where the atmosphere of isolation from the general community "was virtually non-existent." They found that practically "no elderly person performs as well as the average adolescent and young adult, except on the Porteus Maze." The other measures used were the Wisconsin Card Sorting, Raven Progressive Matrices, the Digit-Symbol, and the P.M.A. Reasoning Test. The writers suggest that resistance to age impairment is dependent largely on the exercise of the function and remark that business, social, family, and personal decisions must be frequently made by the aged. (See also No. 92 above.)

The article concludes by emphasizing the fundamental differences between test age and Q-score findings, and points out several instances in which research workers have been confused between the two approaches.

No. 94 A Century of Social Thinking in Hawaii. Pacific Books, Palo Alto, Calif., 1962. Pp. 376

This represented a special excursion into the field of Hawaiian history, and hence is related to No. 53 of this bibliography.

The material dealt with was selected from the Proceedings of a rather exceptional society which was established in 1882 in Honolulu under the name of the Honolulu Social Science Association. Members were limited in number to 30, though latterly extended to 40, and were supposed to represent a broad spectrum from the occupational fields that were most concerned with the development of this island community. They included government, law, medicine, education, science, the press, business, and industry. Though clergymen, such as C. M. Hyde, initiated the idea of the Association, two topics were officially banned from discussion—religion and politics. Actually, in many of the proceedings both were discussed but in a non-controversial context.

Monthly meetings were held at members' houses, and papers were given by each in turn. As these men numbered among them many who had exerted a great influence on the history of Hawaii, as for example Sanford Dole, president of the Republic prior to annexation by the United States, the Association's proceedings did actually cover a century.

As the story of the Islands during this period included government by kings, a provisional interregnum, a republic, United States territorial status, together with participation in two world wars and finally statehood, it was a varied and interesting picture. Points of view were presented within the confines of a private club, and the debates and discussions could be carried on without fear of publicity or misrepresentation.

However, in 1962, the then existing membership decided that historical insight would be greatly furthered if the self-imposed ban on publicity were lifted, and the present writer was commissioned to select the most revealing papers, summarize and analyse them and cement the whole by means of an editorial commentary. In this way a community's thinking at a high executive level could be followed, with possibly some degree of predictive guidance. This was carried out from the viewpoint of a psychological observer.

1963

No. 95 Studies in Intercultural Testing. (With A. James Gregor) *Perceptual and Motor Skills,* 1963, Vol. 16, 705–724. Monograph Supplement 7–V16. Pp. 20

Work carried out by the senior author in 1929 on Australid mentality had languished, with only brief and sporadic attention during the three following decades. Fry and Pulleine, Piddington, and Meadows (in an unpublished report) seem to have been the only persons interested. For this neglect of an important field of enquiry, the psychologists themselves were to blame, since for many years expeditions to the Yuendumu area had been carried on by scientific personnel from the University of Adelaide including men of such calibre as Professors Abbie, T. D. Campbell, Sir John Cleland,

N. D. Tindale, etc., while excellent photographic records were collected by Mountfort and moving pictures directed by Campbell and Barrett. Over the same period of time Professor Elkin, his students, and colleagues carried out excellent anthropological surveys so that complex systems of marriage among the natives became much more clearly understood. But apparently in the long list of distinguished contributors to the understanding of the Australian aborigines, beginning with Roth, Howitt, Spencer and Gillen, and continued by Basedow, Horne and Aiston, the names of psychologists do not figure. The senior author's experience, as recorded in No. 30 of this bibliography, was affected by the necessity of trying out various tests and measurements without any knowledge of how suited or otherwise they might be to Australid interests and capabilities.

Taking advantage of a visit to Central Australia in 1962 and the availability of Dr. Gregor, I made arrangements to carry out more extensive work with the test, which over the years had proved completely acceptable to primitive ethnic groups throughout the world. Thus it was possible to reactivate psychological interest in a contemporary stone age people before either assimilation or extinction put a full stop to scientific racial investigation.

As previously noted, a particularly advantageous center for this type of investigation was Yuendumu, about 200 miles northwest of Alice Springs. This aboriginal settlement had been for about 15 years a base of operations for University of Adelaide research, so that the natives in the area were quite accustomed to examinations undertaken from the standpoints of physiology, anatomy, nutrition, dental science, and anthropology. Only the idea of mental testing was new to these primitive people. If contact with less acculturated aborigines was desired, the newly formed settlement of Papunya, situated about 100 miles to the south, was available. The two main tribes represented were Wailbri and Pintubi.

How they would react to Maze Test examinations was, of course, unknown, but Dr. Gregor, who had been trained in the use of the test by the senior author, soon discovered that interest in what the natives called "the American game" was far greater than he expected. Gregor was particularly impressed by his *S*s' complete absorption in the task of finding their way out of the Maze. He reported that they "neither looked up for passing planes, trucks or fighting dogs," occurrences in the settlement that normally drew unfailing attention. Even taking flashlight photos of a man at work on the test failed to divert him from the task of careful examination of the designs. Gregor was applying the three series—Original, Extension, and Supplement. One man took over 25 minutes to solve one single test design, and some of them worked three hours continuously. "Not a single recorded performance was perfunctory;" Gregor reported. "In some cases the three series took three hours to complete. . . . In the majority of cases the *S*s did not show signs of fatigue and in many gave evidence of wanting to continue" (from field notes).

The Wailbri average score in the Original series was 10.4 years, while the northwest Kimberley natives was 10.39 years, as examined by Porteus 34 years previously, with the Adult test omitted in both studies. Gregor, using the complete scale, arrived at a mean of 11 years in the Original series, 11.68 for the Extension, and 11.52 for the Supplement. Thus the protracted application showed improvement rather than fatigue, undoubted proof of sustained interest. A rather highly selected group (*N* 25), which included all available full-blood males at Hermannsburg, reached the extraordinary level of 14.3 years in the Original series, rising to 14.9 in the Extension, and 14.6 years in the Supplement. Again, there were no visible fatigue symptoms. However, this sample could hardly be considered representative as it contained six aboriginal water-color artists and others trained and employed in industrial work at the Mission. Their mean was at about the same level as that of ninth-grade students in a Honolulu intermediate high school, and about a year higher than delinquent and non-delinquent cases examined in Honolulu.

Of special interest was a comparative table giving results obtained by anthropologists (Ray, Chowdhury, and De, 1953) working with jungle tribes in India. They ranged from 7.44 years (rural Bhil) to 9.63 years in Adi Pasi in Upper Assam. Thus the Australids enjoyed a considerable advantage in scores. Possible reasons for this comparatively excellent showing by Australids were briefly discussed. Apparently a test of finding one's way through fairly complicated designs appealed particularly to Australids, the appearance of the Mazes seeming to fit in well with ornamental designs cut by them on tree trunks, sacred ceremonial or totemic patterns incised on wooden or stone tjuringi (churinga).

No. 96 Namatjira: Famous Australian Artist. *Perceptual and Motor Skills,* 1963, Vol. 17, 13–14. Pp. 2

Much more important than the work of psychologists in improving the popular image of the Australid in his native continent was the success in water-color painting achieved by Albert Namatjira, a full-blood aboriginal who lived for most of his life in Hermannsburg, Central Australia. His story was briefly recounted.

While attached as camel boy to a painting expedition undertaken by two well-known white artists (Battarbee and Gardner), Namatjira observed with great interest the painting techniques; then he asked Battarbee for the use of brush, paint, and paper to try what he could do. Surprised at Namatjira's interest, Battarbee then gave him a couple of lessons on picture composition, color mixing, and techniques, and was so impressed with Albert's drawing skill and color sense that he encouraged the latter to continue with his efforts.

Namatjira's success was phenomenal. Within the space of a few years tourists were travelling up to Alice Springs to buy the canvases off the easel, until finally the pupil was outselling the master. In a little while the possession of one or more Namatjiras became almost a status symbol for Australians. The artist was overcome with popular attention, and visited the capital cities of the Commonwealth with increasing acclaim.

Unfortunately, Albert began to drink heavily, and when he was accorded full citizenship it became legal for him to purchase liquor for his own use, though the law did not permit him to assist his fellow tribesmen in obtaining alcohol in any form. This at once set up a conflict between his obligations as an aboriginal and as a citizen. Under aboriginal rules tribal relatives expected to share equally in all his possessions. Convicted of supplying a fellow artist with drink, Namatjira was sentenced to a mild form of imprisonment, a kind of aboriginal-reserve arrest, and this disgrace undoubtedly hastened his death. His sons and other relatives continued to paint, but none of them has attained equal fame, though several find a ready sale for their work. This case illustrates the difficulties in the way of an Australid attempting to adjust to two conflicting social and industrial systems, even when high attainment in the alien culture was assured.

1964

No. 97 Australid 'Assimilation.' *The Mankind Quarterly* (Edinburgh), 1964, Vol. 4, No. 4. Pp. 12

The tendency among anthropologists and other scientists interested in the intelligence of very primitive peoples is to write off anthropometric results as insignificant. With regard to Maze performance, the tests were at one time dismissed as baby plays or kindergarten puzzles, their scores considered to be irrelevant as an index of these subjects' status as intelligent human beings. Sitting in a native camp watching an Australid tracing his way through a more or less complicated design seemed to be what the Scotch call a "feckless" activity, in comparison with the serious business of an anthropologist talking by the hour with an aboriginal informant and recording his verbal accounts of tribal organization, customs, and beliefs. This, unfortunately, could also prove to be an unreliable business.

On the face of it, to some scientists Maze threading appeared to be a rather futile proceeding, especially when the task was assumed to lie quite outside the savages' range of interest. Two general findings, however, quite upset this indifferent, not to say contemptuous attitude. The first development was concerned with a quite unexpected sensitivity of this particular mental test. Simple as the task appeared, the evidence, accumulated over the years, showed that psychosurgery could affect test performance to a large degree of consistency. Surgical *insults* to frontal or temporo-parietal brain areas, administration of ataractic drugs over a long period, induced vitamin-B deficiency, the onset of debilitating diseases, all brought about a significant degree of Maze test impairment. These "baby plays" were under the aforementioned circumstances strangely revealing, and thus they became quite respectable, almost essential tools of research.

The approach was, of course, experimental, but declines below average or normal performance were found to be associated with various kinds of subnormal or abnormal development. The mentally retarded, especially those who were industrially incompetent, together with many of the emotionally disturbed had consistently low scores. On the other hand, many who would be classed as defective if examined by ordinary standard mental scales were shown to be capable of self-management and self-support. In short, the Maze, if consistently used in diagnosis, removed from such cases the stigma of inherent inefficiency.

Moreover, another scoring of the test revealed traits of personality that could, under unfavorable social conditions, result in delinquent behavior. Though inferior status was indicated for many culturally retarded ethnic groups, at the same time a normal range of distribution of scores was frequently demonstrable.

A change of attitude toward the culturally deprived or the environmentally handicapped became apparent. In line with modern thinking, it was felt that the burden of inequalities should, wherever possible, be lightened, but this policy if successful must be discriminatory, giving the advantages of education and opportunities for social assimilation to those most capable of helping themselves in the problem of bettering their status. Here, again, the mental test approach could be of great value, since improvement can rarely be achieved en masse but is usually selective.

The article presently being annotated reviews this whole subject of aboriginal assimilation from the standpoint of one who has done what he could toward making the Australid people more clearly and sympathetically understood. My respect and admiration for the original inhabitants of my own native land are, I hope, not tinged with any sense of racial superiority, pride, or arrogance. Because of almost forty years' absence from contact with the Central Australian scene, I would also disclaim any special knowledge and insight, and for this reason I have chosen to rely largely on the presentation of the case for the aborigines on the writings of a man who was born and brought up at Hermannsburg with the Arunta and who became a scholar of high repute. This is Mr. T. G. H. Strehlow, M.A., Reader in Anthropology at the University of Adelaide. In his *Nomads of No Man's Land,* he contributes a most sympathetic analysis of the problems of assimilation with many reservations about its ultimate success. His summary sets forth its main perplexity.

> We should remember at all times that no matter how much assistance is given to any human being, only that human being can take the final steps necessary for his own rehabilitation. All that other men can do is to help his efforts by example, by precept and by financial assistance. But the use made of this help depends on the response of the individual to whom it is given.

This applies as much to governmental as to individual efforts to improve the status of minorities in the general population.

1965

No. 98 *Streamlined Elementary Education.* Pacific Books, Palo Alto, Calif., 1965. Pp. 32

This monograph is unusual in that it turns back the leaves of the writer's experience about 57 years to a period when his main interests were educational, concerned mainly with the schooling of elementary-grade children and the development of teaching aids and methods that led on to the diagnosis and training of mental defectives, now more euphemistically, but probably less accurately termed "mentally retarded." The former is a more definite classification with emphasis both on social and on educational incapacity.

The stimulus that triggered this backward view was the rather sudden interest of teachers, parents, and investigators in teaching methods applied to the very young learner, and the consequent realization that those methods had not changed materially for at least one hundred years. For various reasons, principally the supposed incapacity of pupils of tender age to master properly presented rudiments of reading, spelling, and arithmetic, it had become accepted that the beginning age for conventional schooling was six years. True, in modern society it was realized that a great unfilled gap occurred in the child's learning experience between his third and sixth birthdays, and the void was hastily filled with kindergartens, nursery schools, and what was strangely termed "preschool education." Suddenly we began to hear of *reading readiness*, the inference being that if a child were taught to read before some vague probationary period, he would suffer some mysterious harm or handicap. From what shrine of normal school remembrance this extraordinary theorem issued the writer has never been informed. Boiled down to the bare facts, the failure of young children to read, spell, and do simple arithmetic is based on the incapacity of the teacher, not of the child.

Sixty years ago (see No. 1 of this bibliography), the writer became so bored with the painful process of teaching multiplication and division of numbers that he realized that mutual suffering would be eliminated if a new system of factor-product notation could be devised. If, for example, the prime factors of 2, 3, 5, 7 were allotted respectively the colors red, blue, yellow, and black and these were combined factorially as color bars (e.g., a blue and red bar would be read as 6, 2 blue bars and a red as 12), then as soon as the notations were visually memorized the pupil could mentally read off the required number facts, and this would obviate the painful necessity of learning multiplication tables. In a little while the pupils became quicker at this exercise than the teacher. As for addition and subtraction, all that was necessary was to give the child a gold-buyer's scales and cardboard boxes graduated by weight and he could teach himself all the facts he needed for simple arithmetic.

Other experiments with "flash cards" soon showed that if the teacher conveniently forgot phonetics, it was possible for the child to recognize words by their visual form. Had the reading teacher thought about the evolution of the senses, he would have known that the eye is a much more reliable and quicker informant for most human beings than the ear. But unfortunately the inventors of the English language made it only partially phonetic so that the learning process had two very diverse methods which made trouble for the learner. If a machine could be constructed that would give the child the opportunity to learn by doing in the easiest possible stages, a machine that would appeal to extremely youthful interests and in which the learner could make no errors, the dual problems of reading and spelling might be solved. About sixty years ago Montessori relied upon another sense receptor, "learning by touching," but this went so far back into the early stages of brain evolution that it was almost as much out of date as "to learn by smelling." Some uninformed people are at present trying to revive the system, but the Montessori method should be left to rest in peace.

In the writer's efforts to measure and compare civilized and primitive rates of learning, it seemed utterly unfair to use as testing material items from an environment unfamiliar to primitive peoples. After I had experimented with a machine, the keys of which bore photos of dingoes, snakes, kangaroos, etc., Dr. A. L. Diamond devised a teaching machine, cards for which fell into slots for each letter by gravity. Fifty cards in the Arunta language were provided, the task being to press through windows the letters of the object's name in the correct spelling order so that the word appeared alongside the item's picture. If the letters were pressed in the wrong order, the machine would not work. Experimental work carried out in Central Australia showed that children learned to spell and read these 50 Arunta words almost as quickly as did white pupils.

Advantages of this learning machine were: (1) Interest of subjects; (2) Continuance of effort based on successful manipulation; (3) Lack of frustration since failure cannot occur; (4) Self-correction; (5) Adaptability to any language in which words can be pictorialized; (6) Verbalization of instructions unnecessary; (7) Self-measurement of progress by pupils; (8) Cards are slotted at their base so that they drop into correct position by gravity instead of electric power; (9) Compactness (weight about 3 lbs.); (10) Cheapness of manufacture (about $10).

These points were illustrated in the monograph.

No. 99 Educational Wastage. *Perceptual and Motor Skills*, 1965, Vol. 20, February, 51–58. Pp. 8

This article was intended as a follow-up to No. 98 of this bibliography, but was addressed to a joint audience of educational psychologists and primary school teachers. The present system of withholding formal school training from children below six years of age was strongly condemned and the ease with which writing and arithmetic could be mastered by the use of new teaching aids was described. By analysing cursive writing into its commonest elements and allowing the child to practise them by running his finger along these shapes when grooved deeply in plywood, it was shown that writing could be taught in a very few learning sessions. Moreover, by the use of the Porteus-Diamond Learning Machine, Japanese pre-school children from 3 to 5 years of age were taught to spell and read without error as many as 15 three-letter words in eleven practice sessions of three minutes each.

The most noteworthy advance in the techniques of reading and spelling had been attained through Dr. Diamond's use of gravity as the motive force in the machine, instead of complicated machinery, thus bringing the device within the reach of the most isolated schools and pupils. After the machine was successfully used for six months with Australian aboriginal children in Central Australia, it was rejected by a committee of Sydney teachers on the grounds that "it did not fit in with their current methods of teaching elementary school children." How it could possibly fit into a system that had not produced a single new idea in generations of elementary education was beyond imagination. It was like prohibiting the use of automobiles unless drawn by horses!

The reason why the devices described are not commonly in use is the difficulty in making any suitable arrangements for production and distribution of the learning machine and the other supplementary apparatus.

Finally, the necessity of the child gaining educational experience on a broad front rather than in single or limited directions was emphasized. Attention can easily be confined to teaching reading or arithmetic whereas the elementary school pupil is expected by teachers and parents to keep up with a wide variety of demands extending to skills in spelling and writing as well. There is no better stimulus or reinforcement than success, and the child makes such self-evident progress under this new system that he is fascinated with his own achievements.

No. 100 Problems of Aboriginal Mentality. *The Mankind Quarterly* (Edinburgh), 1965, Vol. 5, 3, January–March. Pp. 10

Actuated by modern concern with the underprivileged, whether as individual or groups, the writer, even at the risk of some tiresome repetition, continued with his endeavors to stimulate scientific interest in the Australid people. It is becoming very evident that for a long time important segments of mankind must be assisted in the setting up of movements or schemes for their own development. This is one result of what Alan Moorehead has called the "fatal impact" of civilization on comparatively untutored aborigines.

From an attitude of general contempt based on a belief that the "blackfellow" belonged among the most mentally backward, practically ineducable races, on earth today, the pendulum of popular opinion now tends to swing too far in the opposite direction. Many Australians apparently believe that the aboriginal's social progress and acceptance depend wholly on giving him citizenship. At the back of this unwarranted optimism undoubtedly lies the superliberal assurance that all men are born equal, an empty faith presented by the American framers of the preamble to their Constitution. Many of these men were themselves slave-holders. What they wanted to affirm was a belief that all *white* men with respectable social inheritance were born equal! The author here re-emphasizes the self-evident fact that men are born mentally and temperamentally unequal or different. Anyone who has seen a feebleminded child needs no further instances to illustrate that fact. One way in which this inequality is evidenced is through the different resistance that individuals display toward geriatric decline and fall, particularly as affecting both the initiation and receptivity of new ideas.

Apparently there is an optimal period of development during which adaptivity essential to successful living and progress is easiest of achievement. Apparently, according to a study by Milton Jensen of inmates of Veterans' Hospitals, there is a decline after 45 years of age in verbal intelligence but a much slower impairment in tests of initiative and planning as measured by the Maze. In general (verbal) ability, the impairment amounted to 8 IQ points after age 45, with level of education having little influence. With the Maze the case stood differently.

Cases with less than eighth-grade schooling showed the same general decrease, but those with better education among the older cases maintained the better Maze Test levels, prompting Jensen to state that "cerebral cortical functioning is little or very late affected by senescence."

The present writer suggests in explanation that longevity is itself related to foresight and prudence, and that this planfulness is associated with the longer continued and more successful attempts to secure a better education. The article then quotes Loranger's and Misiak's study of elderly women. This showed that Maze-tested abilities held up longer than those measured by other tests, so that 16 per cent of women 70 to 80 years of age scored 15 years or above in the Maze.

Considering the wide variation of Australid Maze scores, this might easily mean that the outlook for further development through practical education is brighter than was expected, but that selection of cases for further opportunities should be on the basis of their test scores, particularly in the Porteus Maze.

Actually, the system of old man government could have acted as a discouragement of intellectual initiative and inventiveness among the younger men. Another approach to educational selection could be through the use of the Porteus-Diamond Learning Machine, which is here described. It was urgently recommended that more Australian psychologists turn their attention to studies of the Australid population since the problems of their assimilation are so plainly evident. However, the difficulties in the way of research on *Ss* living in such physical and cultural isolation are undoubtedly great.

No. 101 *Porteus Maze Tests: Fifty Years Application.* Pacific Books, Palo Alto, Calif., 1965. Pp. 320

Measured in terms of individual experience, a century or fractions thereof have little significance. Except in very rare cases, one hundred years is not an end to be reached nor is fifty years a half-way point. Actually, decades are not significant milestones in individual experience nor do twenty years delimit even legal responsibility. The "three score years and ten" of the Psalmist is, of course, merely a convenient approximation; nevertheless, anniversaries are commonly remembered in divisions of a century and thus it seemed appropriate to use fifty years in this bibliographic accounting, even though the list now extends to fifty-five, since that was the time at which my occupational planning began.

Since this volume is so recent as to be easily available, and being bound in hard covers ensures at least a modicum of permanency, it will not be necessary to provide here a complete summary of published findings, merely a brief mention of what seem to the writer to be its more salient features.

A late lamented colleague, Dr. Henry N. Peters, in reviewing an earlier book, wrote: "Porteus is primarily concerned with practical conclusions and is impatient with a cautious assessment of data. The remarkable thing is how consistently his conclusions have withstood the test of time."

In relation to this accounting, a whole chapter is devoted to demonstrating the unreliability of one of the most highly cherished approaches to the interpretation of statistical data, namely, the Fisher *t* test as applied in this instance to sex differences in Maze scores. Out of 105 experimental studies, an almost consistent, if slight, superiority is apparent in 97 of these experiments. Quite obviously this masculine superiority is real, but the *t* test, which takes no account of consistency, but emphasizes the size of disparities, would declare the difference to be insignificant. Another stand-by of the statistically inclined psychologist is the correlational technique. Under ideal conditions this approach is sound and unassailable, but this book shows over and over again that representative samples are rarely attainable, with the consequence that coefficients are of the most bewildering size and variety. Even among a recognizable group, the mentally defective, an extraordinary range of correlations has been found, dependent upon how cases are segregated, whether by age, industrial training, length of observation, sex of subjects, type of external criteria, physiological status, therapy involved, length of institution experience, and perhaps a score of other considerations or conditions. In any case, psychologists in general pay far less attention to these findings than I do myself. For example, study after study confirms the fact that as a practical expedient pooling and averaging a Binet scale score with Maze-level results is a far better diagnostic measure than relying on either test quotient separately. But who shows concern about this theoretically dubious but practically useful procedure?

Taken as a whole, this book attempts to follow the principle of selection of tests set forth by Dr. William A. Hunt, namely that of "wide standardization over all sorts of clinical and cultural groups and the repeated demonstration of reliability and validity throughout this standardization." This I have called "range of sensitivity," but the term "reliability" should be interpreted most cautiously with relation to the nature of the test. Obviously, in a test such as the Maze, which sets out to measure individual ability to profit by experience within the framework of the test itself, a mere test-retest coefficient does not apply. This has been pointed out several times but the fact that this reliability bogey still crops up seems to make repetition necessary.

Otherwise Maze experiments are reported in relation to delinquent responses, psychosurgery, tranquilizing drugs, mental abnormality, sex differences, practical or industrial competency, trainability of the educationally retarded, ethnic group differences, and projective uses of the scale.

One other feature of this work is its lack of concern with purely artificial standards of mental-level determination as evinced by reporting by psychologists of units of test performance in five-point intervals only, and the refusal to regard very high IQ levels as being of any very specific significance. There is also my strong recommendation that the term IQ be dropped altogether from usage on the grounds that it is not an intelligence ratio at all, but merely a test quotient, descriptively qualified as the Binet, Wechsler-Bellevue, Kohs Design, or Porteus Maze Test, etc. performance.

1966

No. 102 Mental Capacity. Chapter 5 in *Aboriginal Man in South and Central Australia.* (Edited by B. C. Cotton of the Board for Anthropological Research, University of Adelaide, South Australia), 1966, 47–57. Pp. 11

The popular practice of allotting Australids the lowest rung on the human evolutionary ladder was rarely approved by anthropological field workers, who had occasion to make close contact with these interesting people. Missionaries, whose aim was to convert them to Christianity, could hardly be expected to approve of their unregenerate beliefs, ideas, and practices. The failure of many of their charges to adopt alien moral standards and adapt themselves to ordinary educational methods could very readily be ascribed to low mental capacity. On the contrary Professor Elkin wrote a book entitled, *Aboriginal Men of High Degree,* implying that such individuals were by no means uncommon. It is fair to say that many white students such as Baldwin Spencer and Gillen, who had most to do with them, regarded them very highly. However, it is rather strange that explorers, who were very dependent on their assistance or guidance, seldom came to their defence.

The writer of this chapter stated that the material culture of these aborigines has not been ranked highly enough. Ingenuity in the making of the returning boomerang has been acknowledged but insufficient credit has been given to the inventiveness that lay behind the fashioning and usefulness of the woomera or throwing stick, which added so much to the efficiency of the spear. But its value as a tool or weapon was tremendously augmented by attaching a sharp flake of stone to one end of the implement, which thus became an adze, most helpful in the fashioning of other wooden artifacts, to say nothing of its uses in fire-making by friction, in clearing a camping space, digging a cooking oven, or for many another casual purpose. Should we not, therefore, pay tribute to the ingenuity and economical foresight of men who, by some variation of design and an industrial addition of the adze to its manufacture combined in this one easily transportable implement so many essential usages? What single implement of steel-age man could be of such value to a nomadic people whose lot was cast for centuries in a huge country entirely devoid of animals suitable for burden and transport?

This naturally raises the question as to how these people respond to tests, which have been devised by people of a superior culture, and which reflect foresight and practical intelligence. It was pointed out that the Maze as a measure of these abilities by three series was no longer to be considered a "thin" test; that the experience of many field workers has confirmed its acceptance by primitives; also, that its sensitivity to brain damage has been amply demonstrated; and, finally, the general approval of psychologists is being rapidly attained.

Such being the case, the time was certainly ripe for comparing the responses of Australids with those of other ethnic groups of similarly unsophisticated status. In Gregor's experience (see No. 95), he records that as long as three hours of steady, uninterrupted work was sometimes involved in working through the three Maze series, and that attention was so closely required that ordinary distractions had no effect on performance. Gregor notes that his *S*s "neither looked up for passing planes, trucks or fighting dogs"—usually matters of great interest to aborigines.

The results of experimental investigations of 35 groups are given in the text, showing that no Australid group appeared among the list of very low performers, three were listed as scoring in the middle range (Keidja, Karadjeri, Wailbri), while two groups of Arunta were found among those with high average scores. Thus there is available adequate evidence that Australid practical inventiveness is indeed reflected by their psychological test performance. This should finally dispose of the imputation that these people are "among the lowest on earth." Australid Maze performance can also be compared with results obtained in a very recent study ("The Porteus Test and Various Measures of Intelligence with Southern Negro Adolescents," by Cooper, York, Daston, and Adams).[1] Their *S*s consisted of 58 institutional cases individually divided into two equal groups consisting of adolescents, who in the judgment of teachers, nurses, social workers, and attendants "were functioning socially and vocationally at levels far above those to be expected of persons mentally retarded," and another group "who were grossly deficient in effective and adaptive social behavior." I have calculated the average test quotient of the whole group as being 11.25 years (TQ 92), whereas the mean of 18 Australid adolescents examined by Gregor at the Finke River Mission was 11.5 years.

Incidentally the authors of the journal paper found the mean of the socially inadequate group to be 62.6, of the behaviorally satisfactory 121.7 TQ points. They remark that "the Porteus results permitted a perfect discrimination between behaviorally retarded and behaviorally non-retarded subjects." Obviously, the Maze provides a far fairer measure of the social competency of subcultural ethnic groups than any other available test. The Wechsler-Bellevue, for example, failed completely to discriminate between the two behavioral groups. These results put Australid performance in a very favorable comparative light.

No. 103 Australid Mental Development and Geriatric Decline. (With Kenneth David) *Perceptual and Motor Skills,* 1966, Vol. 23, 75–87. Pp. 13

In this contribution a most important question is raised, namely, what are the facts as regards the time of onset and course of age

[1] *American Journal of Mental Deficiency,* March, 1967, 789–792.

impairment among Australids of Central Australia, and what is their significance? The answer to the second of these questions depends on an easily observed hypothetical basis, and this briefly is that originality or inventiveness has temporal bounds set by senescence.

In discussions of this subject with the late Dr. Kenneth Mees, formerly director of research for the Eastman Kodak Co., he steadfastly maintained the thesis that practically all the great innovations were formulated by men under thirty years of age, with the next twenty or thirty years being devoted to developing these ideas or devices. From my point of view, undoubtedly influenced by the fact that I was and hoped to be still productive with at least glimmers of insight occurring even though I had passed three score years and ten, I was inclined to place the optimal period somewhat later. With regard to my one essay into creativity, the Maze Test was devised at age thirty, but it was very much later that entirely novel usages and applications of the measure came to mind. If my inventive spark first appeared in my third decade of life, then there was quite a long temporal lapse of time when originality slumbered. I may be mistaken, but some of these later flashes of insight were just as important as the initial discovery.

Unfortunately, innovators are too few and their biographies too uncertain for us to determine just what is the most fertile period of mentation, but I must admit that the weight of evidence seemed to support Mees' contention. I was, for obvious reasons, an insignificant instance to the contrary.

In the article presently undergoing annotation, I presented the theory that if there were a blossoming period for invention, any constriction of that season either by social or natural causes would be likely to hinder very seriously the industrial progress and status of a people. Among the Australids our data indicated that there was no early decline of Maze-tested abilities but impairment first became apparent between 41 and 50 years. Gregor's results indicated that his adolescent subjects (*N* 17) averaged 11.18 years, those in the 21 to 30 years scored 11.32 (*N* 22), while those in the 31 to 40 decade averaged 11.15 years (*N* 11). Subjects in the 41 to 50 group reached a mean of only 9.05 years. This represented a marked decline. The study presently under review showed that older men (70 years plus) scored only 7.04 years (*N* 23). Working with a more highly acculturated group at Palm Island, 11 cases between the ages of 41 and 60 scored 10.14 years, not far removed from Gregor's older subjects.

Other factors, of course, affect Maze scores. Impairment of eyesight among the aged is certainly important, while general health conditions, such as hepatitis, tuberculosis, hookworm, leprosy, and venereal diseases, were quite prevalent. At least one of these complaints (hookworm), has been shown to affect Maze performances unfavorably. On the other hand, there seems to be among whites a relation between longevity and higher Maze scores, since survival may depend largely on cautious and prudent mental alertness. Jensen has also shown a relationship between previous educational level and the retention of Maze-tested abilities. In other words, the disposition to make sacrifices to obtain a higher degree of education may be evidence of long-range foresight, resulting in delay of gratification to ensure larger ultimate awards.

These results are touched on to show the complexities of research in this field. Prevention of eye diseases is an obvious remedial measure that only the government could implement.

No. 104 Australid Environment: External and Internal. *Perceptual and Motor Skills,* 1966, Vol. 23, 223–231. Pp. 9

The absence of any constant circuitory ocean currents bringing the Australian coasts into easier contact with other parts of the Pacific area is suggested as a main reason for the cultural lag of the Australid people. The very unfavorable reports of early British, Dutch, and French navigators of the continent's north-western coasts held out no prospects of successful colonization. In the other compass direction, the comparatively empty stretches of the Coral and Tasman Seas and the central Pacific put a ban on human intercourse. Thus, left to their own resources for possibly thousands of years, Australia's aborigines were left with their own meagre resources to maintain survival in a terrifyingly repressive environment. Success was only attainable if their inner resources included courage, hardihood, mechanical ingenuity, acuity of vision, superlative skills in hunting and collecting foods, plus the social foresight that can set up psychic defences against loneliness, one of the greatest possible threats to mental health or sanity.

Just one fact may be cited to emphasize the material poverty of the Australid physical environment and that is the circumstance that the discovery and exploitation of the continent has added only one foodstuff to the world's larder—the Queensland nut or macadamia, now transplanted to Hawaii and California. As far as inventiveness is concerned, what has the Australid contributed to the solution of his own peculiar problems?

As previously noted, one technological device, the woomera or throwing stick constitutes the "blackfellow's" chief tool-weapon, and this has claims to be considered as the product of his own ingenuity. The present writer at least knows no other instance in which a primitive artificer has combined into one easily handled implement of wood and stone such a widely purposeful device. Other peoples have made and used spear-throwers, but to suddenly extend its usefulness so radically by fastening at one end a stone adze was apparently the Australid variant of converting, not a sword into a ploughshare, but a fighting weapon into a tool of multiple usage. How much more effective the spear became by the addition of this rear-propulsion principle has to be seen to be appreciated, but to have in hand a tool with a dozen other utilities showed very remarkable originality of invention or planning.

The writer then proceeds to criticise the undue significance attached to the term "stone age" as if indicating that this marked a new and important stage or high point in human technological history. From this point of view it is doubtful whether there ever was a "stone age." There was without doubt a combined stone-and-wood age. The use of shaped and sharpened stones was mainly to develop far more effective wooden implements or weapons. Unfortunately, archaeologists, who seem to be responsible for this mistaken emphasis, never saw the *ligneous* products of many stone tools, since they had long ago mouldered into dust. Fortunately, the survival of the Australids gives anthropologists the opportunity not only to observe the techniques of a stone culture but also to understand what those techniques developed in the way of wooden implements.

We can, for example, observe what the Australid nomad carries with him on the march. Because nomadism is enforced by the nature of his habitat, his ligneous possessions outweigh and outnumber those of stone. No aboriginal on the march could travel without a wooden spear and spear-thrower, possibly also a shield, and a boomerang, while the women carry a wooden container, a digging stick, and at times a fighting club. Stone possessions are limited to a spear point or two, and the stone adze, the value of which is immensely increased by its attachment to a two-foot-six-inch wooden handle.

If the aboriginal is lucky enough to own a stone axe, it is probably hidden away near one of his frequently used camping sites near permanent water. Stone churinga, which are made to endure, will be hidden away in a cave or rockhole, and rarely if ever carried on the march. The point is made that museum collections naturally treasure the *liths* since those are all that are left.

Fortunately, the photographic work of Campbell and Barrett is providing, for scientific study, excellent colored moving-pictures, showing the manufacture of aboriginal implements, their uses in development of further products. These make up a record of what "stone age" men produced in wood and what they do with these ligneous tools and weapons. Our own age is also more than an age of steel and cement. Wood still holds its extremely essential place in our lives.

The paper ends with a plea for continued study of what appeals to the writer to be earth's most interesting people.[1]

[1] The fact that more space and further discussion has been accorded to studies devoted to Australids perhaps calls for a word of explanation. The writer confesses to a sense of urgency in presenting these topics, as already government efforts to assimilate these people into communities under white supervision have changed very materially their way of life. It may already be too late to set up adequate studies of their distinctive culture.